Suzi Mirgani
Target Markets – International Terrorism Meets Global Capitalism
in the Mall

For Barb

Suzi Mirgani is Manager and Editor for Publications at the Center for International and Regional Studies, Georgetown University in Qatar.

Suzi Mirgani
Target Markets – International Terrorism Meets Global Capitalism in the Mall

جامعة جورجتاون قطر
GEORGETOWN UNIVERSITY QATAR
Center *for* International *and* Regional Studies

[transcript]

Published in Collaboration with the Center for International and Regional Studies (CIRS), Georgetown University in Qatar.

 An electronic version of this book is freely available, thanks to the support of libraries working with Knowledge Unlatched. KU is a collaborative initiative designed to make high quality books Open Access for the public good. The Open Access ISBN for this book is 978-3-8394-3355-3.

This work is licensed under the
Creative Commons Attribution-NonCommercial-NoDerivs 3.0 (BY-NC-ND).
which means that the text may be used for non-commercial purposes, provided credit is given to the author. For details go to
http://creativecommons.org/licenses/by-nc-nd/3.0/.

Bibliographic information published by the Deutsche Nationalbibliothek
The Deutsche Nationalbibliothek lists this publication in the Deutsche Nationalbibliografie; detailed bibliographic data are available in the Internet at http://dnb.d-nb.de

All rights reserved. No part of this book may be reprinted or reproduced or utilized in any form or by any electronic, mechanical, or other means, now known or hereafter invented, including photocopying and recording, or in any information storage or retrieval system, without permission in writing from the publisher.

© 2017 transcript Verlag, Bielefeld
Cover layout: Kordula Röckenhaus, Bielefeld
Cover illustration: © Gamut / Fotolia.com
Typeset by Justine Haida, Bielefeld
Printed in Germany
Print-ISBN 978-3-8376-3352-8
PDF-ISBN 978-3-8394-3352-2

Table of Contents

Acknowledgements | 7

1. **Introduction: International Terrorism Meets Global Capitalism in the Mall** | 9
   Terrorism at the Mall | 12
   The Politics of Shopping | 16
   The Ideological Complexities of Terrorism and Capitalism | 21

2. **Developing the Shopping Mall** | 27
   The Making of a Middle Class | 28
   The Globalization of Consumption and Contestation | 30
   Standardization of Consumption | 32
   Neoliberalism and the City | 34
   Make Way for the Mall | 36
   Transnational Networks of Capitalism, Terrorism, and Poverty | 39

3. **Designing the Shopping Mall** | 45
   A Brief History of the Shopping Mall | 47
      Exhibitions and Fairs | 48
      Arcades | 49
      Department Stores | 51
      The Shopping Center | 55
      The Contemporary Shopping Mall | 57
   Architectonics of Entrapment | 61
   Atmospherics of Enchantment | 65
   The Spectacle of Consumption:
   A Carnival of Contested Identities | 69

4. Securing the Shopping Mall | 75
  The Architecture of Security | 79
  The Panopticon of Shopping: Discipline and Purchase | 81
  Marketing Violence | 87
  Surveillance for Terrorism | 89
  Shaping Employee Behavior | 90

5. Spectacles of the Shopping Mall | 95
  Digital Media and the Globalization of Terror | 98
  Social Media and Personal Narratives | 102
  Commodification of Terror and Media Productions | 106

6. Conclusion: Specters of the Shopping Mall | 115
  Privatizing Public Space | 117
  Social Contract vs. Commercial Contract | 119
  Escape from the Mall | 121
  Chimeras of Consumption | 125

Endnotes | 129

Bibliography | 173

Acknowledgements

This book would not have been possible without the support of the Center for International and Regional Studies (CIRS), Georgetown University in Qatar. I am especially grateful to the director of CIRS, Mehran Kamrava, for his infectious work ethic, and to my colleagues Zahra Babar, Barb Gillis, Nerida Child Dimasi, Elizabeth Wanucha, and Islam Hassan. I am deeply indebted to Rodney X Sharkey for innumerable things, but, for the purposes of this book, his delicate balance of encouragement and critique. My family, Mirghani, Olga, Nadia, Tatyana, and Julietta I thank for their continuous support, and Kathryn King deserves much gratitude for selflessly offering her opinion on my half-formed thoughts as the manuscript progressed. I am thankful for the assistance of the amazing interns at CIRS who all contributed in one way or another to the realization of this book: Salman Ahad Khan for his brainstorming skills and incomparable eye for design, and Arwa Elsanosi, Badr Rahima, and Hazim Ali for their research prowess. I also thank Elizabeth Graham for her help with digging through social media archives, Nicholas Kulish for taking the time to respond to my inquisitive emails, and Jakob Horstmann without whose encouragement this book would never have materialized. Finally, grateful acknowledgment goes to the Qatar Foundation for its support of research and scholarly endeavors.

1. Introduction: International Terrorism Meets Global Capitalism in the Mall

Headline after recent headline has been broadcasting the increase in terrorist attacks being launched in urban areas all over the world. Many of these attacks have targeted centrally-located businesses and commercial entities in metropolitan spaces, whether the Westgate Mall in Nairobi,[1] the public transport systems of London and Madrid,[2] hotels in Mumbai, Tunis, and Ouagadougou,[3] restaurants and cafés in Kampala, Copenhagen, and Sydney,[4] or, more recently, the Charlie Hebdo offices,[5] the Hyper Cacher supermarket,[6] and the Bataclan concert hall in Paris.[7] Urban terrain and populated central city spaces comprised of shopping centers, hotels, transport hubs, concert halls, cafes, theaters, and restaurants have become, in effect, "the battlegrounds of the future. And the urban siege, with its commando-style tactics and guerrilla infiltration of a big city's ebb and flow, is increasingly the tactic of choice for a wide range of adversaries."[8]

Terrorist attacks against urban commercial enterprises have become worryingly frequent, seemingly arbitrary, and increasingly international. With widespread availability and access to information and communication technologies, these incidences have become highly publicized through corporate news media networks and personal social media platforms, affecting people with a heightened fear of public spaces. As extremists engage in open urban warfare, official responses are complementary in their combative stances with an enhancement of the security apparatus and an entrenchment of surveillance structures. With the escalation of urban atrocities, there is a concomitant and intensified infiltration of the military-industrial complex into everyday public spaces and increasing representation of violence in the media and on both sides of the ideological divide. The standoff between terrorist crime and policing progressively imbues global cities, and places of business, with increasingly visible hallmarks of war, including a perceptible surge in weapons, patrols, barricades, and city streets filled with masked gunmen on both the terror and anti-terror fronts—to say nothing of the many reactionary policies and incremental erosions of civil liberties that heighten the sense of urban conflict, fear, and fortressing. In many urban commercial spaces, capitalism and terrorism as the most powerful discursive forces of contemporary culture—the most mainstream and the most extreme—meet in increasingly militarized urban space.

During times of political and economic unrest, shopping centers and other retail businesses are often targeted as private spaces for the public enactment of political dissent and violence, such as when the suffragettes "protested against their lack of the vote by smashing shop windows" in Newcastle,[9] or when a variety of retail businesses became the targets of the 1948 Accra riots,[10] the 2007 Kenya riots,[11] and the 2011 England riots,[12] to name but a few occurrences. Shopping centers, malls, and retail spaces are common targets for all kinds of opponents, including spontaneous civil disobedience protests as well as more extreme premeditated attacks against people and property. Terrorist attacks against shopping malls, especially, have become an increasingly common occurrence. In the period between 1998 and 2006, there were over 60 shopping mall attacks in 21 countries,[13] and there are further warnings of increased threats in which shopping malls "are likely to feature in the attack plans of terrorist organisations in the future," since these spaces "afford the potential for mass fatalities and casualties."[14] Attacks against shopping malls have been motivated by a variety of ethnic, religious, political, and economic ideologies and perpetrated by a number of disparate actors all over the world, including Basque Fatherland and Freedom (ETA) attacks in Spain, Kurdish Workers' Party (PKK) attacks in Turkey, Union of Revolutionary Writer attacks in Russia, People Against Gangsterism and Drugs attacks in South Africa, Maoist rebel attacks in Nepal, Revolutionary Armed Forces of Colombia (FARC) attacks in Colombia, and al-Shabaab attacks in Kenya.[15]

Specifically, for the purposes of this study, al-Shabaab's 2013 Westgate Mall attack is used as a contextual case study that allows for an interactive reading of the relationship between capitalism, globalization, and terrorism, and how these grand narratives relate to people's lives within everyday space. Since it is difficult to examine each of these disparate disciplines exhaustively, this study examines their intersections at a particular meeting point: the shopping mall. From this vantage point, spatial, socioeconomic, and political implications of the mall's existence can be read against the history of urban commodity forms, both local to the Kenyan context, as well as globally. Because of the complexity involved in studying a commercial venue that is subject to so many interpretive paradigms, I do not purport to examine these issues uniformly, or progressively, nor entirely within the strict confines of their disciplines. Rather, through the lens of the shopping mall, unifying theoretical threads can be highlighted within the broad methodological understandings of cultural studies as underpinning contemporary everyday experience.[16]

Studying the shopping mall as a center of the contemporary urban experience is a truly multidisciplinary project. The concept and construct of the mall speaks to, and is spoken by, a variety of different academic disciplines, including marketing research, studies in psychology, cultural studies, media studies, architectural scholarship, and security studies, among other targeted disciplines such as demography, political geography, and urban planning. The analysis of a shopping mall is as multifaceted as the shopping mall itself, and, by turn, examines various elements related to the historical evolution of the mall, its relationship to society and consumption patterns, and its alignment with media and market research. The shopping mall, regardless of one's position on matters of consumption, is a key center of contemporary social life in many countries of the world, and has been successfully designed to attract attention—not always positive—to itself. Thus, the shopping mall locates key social and political tensions that oscillate between the quotidian and mundane and the spectacular and violent. The shopping mall, thus, becomes not only a site of cooperative consumption, but equally a site for the production of contestation.

A shopping mall's simultaneous role as an agent of global corporate capitalism, and yet as a place of everyday encounter, serves to localize many international tensions. The US Army, for example, uses al-Shabaab's Westgate Mall attack to make direct—yet global—connections to mitigate against similar hostilities should they occur in the United States, arguing that "although the Westgate Mall attack was a long way from the U.S. homeland, the methods on display during that attack provide lessons that can guide preparatory efforts and information collection to help prevent or respond to a similar event involving the Army community worldwide."[17] The concept of the shopping mall can be used as a constant reminder of broader dynamics of global exchange, even as Westgate Mall is anchored to a specific locale. As such, this study is not solely about Westgate Mall and al-Shabaab's attack against it. The Westgate Mall story provides a conduit for examining key contemporary global concerns within a local setting, including the complex relationships between corporate capitalism, socioeconomic inequalities, and the menace of terrorism. In this sense, the shopping mall becomes a site *for* and a site *of* communication and contestation.

Terrorism at the Mall

On September 21, 2013, a news headline read: "Gunmen Kill Dozens in Terror Attack at Kenyan Mall."[18] On what was incidentally, and ironically, the United Nations' declared International Day of Peace, four members of the Somali extremist group, Harakat al-Shabaab al-Mujahideen (HSM), or al-Shabaab meaning "the youth" in Arabic, staged an armed attack on the Westgate Mall in Nairobi. To inflict maximum damage, and to garner worldwide publicity, the attacks took place on a Saturday at lunchtime—a day and time when the mall was guaranteed to attract thousands of visitors, including a large number of children and their families attending a cooking competition.[19] The attack has been labeled a "swarm attack" that "featured two teams of two (or more) assailants who attacked from two different points and then linked in the mall supermarket."[20]

For a variety of reasons that remain largely unexplained, the attack turned into a four-day, or 80-hour,[21] siege, ending with "65 civilians, six soldiers and police officers, and four terrorists among the dead. Hundreds more were injured and 27 people were listed as missing by the Kenyan Red Cross."[22] True to the globalization tenets of the shopping mall, the victims were citizens of Kenya, the United Kingdom, India, Canada, France, Australia, China, Ghana, the Netherlands, Peru, South Africa, South Korea, and Trinidad and Tobago.[23] Similarly, the attack exhibited international characteristics in which it was reported to have been "conceived in Somalia, planned from a United Nations refugee camp and executed from Eastleigh in Nairobi" by a group of al-Shabaab terrorists—one of whom was raised as a refugee in Norway.[24]

Westgate Mall, which opened in 2007, consisted of five levels, eighty shops, a cinema, two banks, and a casino.[25] As the al-Shabaab terrorists stalked the mall's corridors and shops for the first three and a half hours of the attack, government forces attempted to organize themselves, with many departments, such as the Kenya Police and the Kenya Military, wrangling over who was in charge.[26] While the government departments squabbled, armed civilians, off-duty police officers, and Kenya Red Cross medics formed ad hoc tactical teams, rescuing hundreds of people from the mall.[27] Because there were so many different armed responders, plainclothes law enforcement officers, as well as armed civilians stealthily roaming the mall corridors with little communication between them, there was a great deal of confusion as to who was a terrorist, who was a victim, and who represented an authority. Witness testimonies of the attacks vary wildly, with many disagreeing on what they saw.[28]

The contemporary regularity of such urban terror attacks, and the ubiquity of surveillance systems in commercial settings, increases the chances that these atrocities are recorded, disseminated, and consumed through a variety of media. Through an extraordinary diversity of camera angles and feeds, the Westgate Mall siege was a made-for-television event from the beginning. What is understood to have transpired is what can be gathered from investigating the visual evidence recorded by "more than 100 security cameras inside the mall, video from television crews and modest cellphones, as well as still photographs."[29] Additionally, information about the attacks was delivered by the perpetrators themselves, with al-Shabaab live-tweeting their actions, marking Westgate as "the first major terrorist attack in history in which the group that mounted the operation used Twitter to announce to the world it was responsible."[30] Using social media, al-Shabaab "confirmed it was behind what it described as the 'Westgate spectacle,'"[31] tweeting "258 times between September 21 and September 25."[32]

Much of what we know about the Westgate Mall attack is what was reported by the media and screened on news networks, including how violently, and arbitrarily, victims were interrogated and killed, and how long and silently survivors hid in, behind, and under desks, storerooms, refrigerators, air vents, and anything that could conceivably conceal a human body. With all the elements of a reality show drama, the footage also shows how some government units "looted shops, broke open safes, and emptied tills."[33] A number of false reports emanating from government officials, witnesses, terrorists, and the media only added to the salaciousness and longevity of the "live event."

This wealth of visual evidence, however, was suddenly disrupted when "a rocket fired by the Kenyan army collapsed the back of the mall, dropping the rooftop car park into the basement,"[34] turning the area into a volatile war zone, burying the bodies of the injured and the dead, and destroying much of the forensic evidence.[35] To this day, it still cannot be definitively confirmed if the four attackers were killed, how they were killed, and, indeed, if there were only four perpetrators. At the time of writing, more than two years after the events, the Kenyan government, working in conjunction with the US Federal Bureau of Investigation (FBI) and British and Israeli intelligence, has yet to deliver conclusive answers on the sequence of events over the four days.[36] In the aftermath of the attacks, "President Uhuru Kenyatta announced his intention to appoint a commission of inquiry into Westgate 'lapses and how we can avoid them in the future,' but no such report had been released."[37] In the current confrontational climate, buoyed by the divisive discourse of the war on terror, the official media-infused stance appeals to the "state of exception,"[38] where no justifications are deemed necessary for how investigations are conducted, how accusations are accumulated, and how punishments for terrorists are concluded.

The formulation of the modern terror discourse necessitates the perpetuation of entrenched and oppositional ideological positions by reducing complex conflicts to simple binaries. However, despite the many ideological oppositions between the terror and the anti-terror narratives, the two discourses are surprisingly similar in their basic assumptions. In the latest incarnation of the meaning of modern terror, both the terror and anti-terror discourses are in agreement when emphasizing the religious underpinnings of the majority of contemporary attacks. The dominant media narrative frames atrocities as an exercise in militant Islam, as do the terrorists themselves whose language is saturated with religious ideology as they set about killing victims. Even though al-Shabaab announced that they had come to "save" Muslims, suggesting that Muslims were being held, against their will, in the corporate capitalist structure of the shopping mall,[39] they fired indiscriminately into the crowd. Although al-Shabaab claimed to be avenging Muslims, and at times spared mall visitors if they could correctly answer questions on Islam, the gunmen launched grenades, and shot people at random, killing many Muslims in the process.[40]

As this study shows, there is a much more complex story underlying the Westgate Mall tragedy, and conducting an analysis of the attacks requires examining more than the singularity of the religious approach. During the Westgate Mall attack, al-Shabaab used a multitude of communication platforms, especially Twitter, to deliver an extraordinary volume of online public communications in which they announced a series of other justifications for the atrocities: that they were, in turn, revenge for *political* injustices and *military* incursions into Somalia; a response to *economic* inequalities; a retaliation against Western government and corporate *exploitation* and *injustice;* as well as vengeance in the form of jihad, or *religious* holy war.[41] Many of these myriad grievances can be identified in al-Shabaab's statements claiming that the attack was "retribution against the Western states that supported the Kenyan invasion and are spilling the blood of innocent Muslims in order to pave the way for their mineral companies,"[42] and in retaliation to "the persistent theft of their land's resources which the Kenyan leaders and Western companies have conspired to plunder,"[43] and to foil "the clandestine schemes of the Zionist Jews in Kenya."[44]

The official media and government narratives, as well as those of al-Shabaab, gave precedence to the militant jihadist angle of the story, despite the many complex grievances articulated over the course of the four days. Although the modern terror discourse has been embedded in religious ideology, with a particular focus on holy war, much can be understood about extremist groups by examining the real or perceived political and economic grievances directed at powerful globalizing forces, with an emphasis on the "West." Extremist networks often take on the self-ordained duty of destroying global symbols of modernity and conspicuous consumption. With its ubiquitous products offered by powerful global capitalist distribution networks, it is in the shopping mall that Nairobi most resembles New York. An attack on one can be read as an attack on the other.

Since the kaleidoscopic declarations given by al-Shabaab regarding the attacks cannot be studied in their entirety, it is important to concentrate on the *intersections* of many of these issues as they encountered each other in Westgate Mall, and as they became reflected through the prism of the shopping center over the four days. In this way, the shopping mall becomes contextualized as a primary signifier of global consumer culture, and as a site for the juncture of longstanding socioeconomic and political tensions. By using Westgate Mall as a contextual case study, I analyze the overlap between two of the most prominent issues defining the contemporary era, namely, the relationship between the twin forces of international terrorism and global capitalism. The victims of the Westgate tragedy experienced first hand, and in a situation of extreme violence, the tensions arising from being caught in between these supposedly opposite ideologies.

The tragic story of Westgate Mall shines a light on many international concerns that, while pertinent to the Kenyan context, are symptomatic of broader global challenges related to socioeconomic and political inequalities. The shopping mall becomes exemplary of the contemporary invisible divide between what can be considered a normal and everyday urban space for those who can afford to partake in it, and an alien and discordant one for those who cannot. The shopping mall, in this formulation, represents a coalface of contemporary culture—a space where hostilities are ignited through the increased friction of local and globalizing forces. The Westgate Mall case study unearths the many competing socioeconomic and political tensions that have troubled this particular shopping center since its conception, having occupied an affluent area of the Westlands neighborhood directly bordering a sprawling Nairobi slum.[45] In a city where half of the population "lives in slums or informal settlements,"[46] Westgate Mall had been the subject of contestation long before al-Shabaab's attacks. Similarly, malls in urban spaces around the world are embedded in such socioeconomic matrices of access, prohibition, and global exchange.

Despite these many brewing hostilities, witness testimonies and news reports on the Westgate attack are unified in their expression of disbelief regarding the sudden intrusion of violence into such an everyday setting. Permeating the entire edifice is shock at the incompatibility of shopping and violence, and an incomprehension of how mass murder can occur in a mall. Terrorism is articulated as being so out of place in the typical bright, colorful, and cheerfully designed setting of a shopping center. Violence and shopping simply do not go together. Or so it seems.

The Politics of Shopping

Shopping malls provide more than just the benign, upbeat shopping centers typically characterized in everyday narratives and popular culture—in many ways, they represent an essential extension of the military-industrial complex. There is an underlying history of militarism that permeates the concept and architecture of shopping malls as contemporary commercial bunkers. These complexes are shelters custom-built to safeguard contemporary corporate culture, and represent the architectural epitome of globalized capitalism. Fortified by a panoptic security apparatus, malls guard against undesirable and disruptive elements of modern society in order to protect the continuous circulation of money within the mall and, ultimately, around the world in a network of global flows. As commercial powerhouses, these giants of the retail industry are of such value that "yearly sales at Wal-Mart," for example, "exceed the GNP of three-quarters of countries in the world."[47] In the United States alone, retail sales numbers for 2013 "registered nearly $2.5 trillion in sales," and "shopping center-related employment accounted for almost than 12.5 million jobs."[48] In order to protect these ideal spaces of corporate capitalist practice and the massive revenues they generate, shopping malls become subject to an intense underlying militarism in terms of how they operate as well as how they are secured against external threats.

With increased threats of terrorist activity and the concomitant intensification of security measures, enclosed urban developments, including shopping malls, are being advertised as "safe places" where "you can leave your troubles behind."[49] Especially in the urban contexts of many developing countries defined by sharp socioeconomic divides, these corporate enclosures are being built with security in mind from their conceptual stages, and are erected with visible signs of outward aggression and hostility in their design, as exemplified by the height of the walls, the thickness of the barbed wire, the sharpness of the spikes, and the programed paranoia of the all-pervasive security systems. For the foreseeable future of the security industry, fighting terrorist activity "is limited by neither time nor space nor target. From a military perspective, these sprawling and amorphous traits make the War on Terror an unwinnable proposition. But from an economic perspective, they make it an unbeatable one: not a flash-in-the-pan war that could potentially be won but a new and permanent fixture in the global economic architecture."[50]

Even as these fortifications and "gated communities" are being built for security, they have other economic implications, driving up property values, and making these walled-off sections of the city the most expensive as well as the most sought after areas—for good or ill. Increasingly, the rising costs of installing and operating a private and pervasive security apparatus is transferred onto the public in the form of higher commodity prices, steeper transactions, and increased government service fees.[51] Thus, ultimately, ordinary people—whether defined as citizens or consumers—are the ones who bear the combined brunt of terrorism and anti-terrorism measures, and become the target markets for both. As terrorists engage in open battles against shopping malls and places of leisure, the response of governments and urban developers is declared in the language of real and symbolic violence, and in the barricading, privatizing, and securitizing of urban areas in a kind of "low-intensity warfare."[52]

Especially since September 11, 2001, both terror and the war on terror have been progressively extending into everyday commercial spaces. The Mall of America has its own private counterterrorism unit made up of hundreds of security guards,[53] and Westgate Mall "had precautions similar to an airport; cars are checked with mirrors for bombs and pedestrians are frisked"[54]—although many admit that security checks were performed in a "perfunctory manner."[55] Shopping malls have become embroiled in the war on terror as an everyday extension of the military-industrial complex and advocate for merging of shopping with notions of patriotism. In the United States, for example, "the security services industry is an ideal career for transitioning military,"[56] with many war veterans working as private security guards. US companies providing security services for shopping malls regularly employ veterans as part of the "Hire our Heroes" program, cementing a circular relationship between the military, private security, terrorists, and shopping malls. Private businesses have increasingly become directly involved in anti-terrorism measures with active attempts at politicizing the act of shopping. In the aftermath of al-Qaeda's attack on the World Trade Center—a locus of global capitalist power—the Bush administration's immediate response was to tell Americans: "We cannot let the terrorists achieve the objective of frightening our nation to the point where we don't—where we don't conduct business, where people don't shop."[57] Within the war on terror narrative, stimulating the economy by spending has been framed as a patriotic duty and as a way for citizens to "stick their thumb in the eye of the terrorists"—an act of retaliatory aggression through increased commerce.[58]

Mass consumption is promoted as an engine of the economy with citizens billed as being directly responsible for the state of the nation's economic success. Within this consumption-oriented rhetoric, the citizen-consumer is located as "a critical part of a prosperity producing cycle of expanded consumer demand fueling greater production, thereby creating more well-paying jobs and in turn more affluent consumers capable of stoking the economy with their purchases."[59] When an economy is framed as being dependent on individual spending habits, "the best measure of social consciousness is now the *Index of Consumer Sentiment*, which charts optimism about the state of the world in terms of willingness to spend."[60] Within this frame, shopping malls become a central locus around which other forms of social life orbit. This conceptualization, although part of a normalized contemporary discourse, has been in the making for some time. In the immediate aftermath of World War II, "business leaders, labor unions, government agencies, the mass media, advertisers, and many other purveyors of the postwar order conveyed the message that mass consumption was not a personal indulgence. Rather, it was a civic responsibility."[61] Conspicuous consumption has been historically tied to perceptions of patriotism and, by spending to strengthen the economy, it is imbued with a notion of altruism.

Creating a continuity between state politics and shopping malls, and forging a direct link between patriotism and consumerism is unabashedly and undisguisedly presented in the likes of the Mall of America, where the shopping mall purports to represent the interests and ideology of the nation, and is saturated in US symbolism, colors, and flags.[62] Countries all over the world have followed suit, and have directly linked politics and commerce by establishing "national" malls, including the Dubai Mall, the Mall of India, the Mall of Mauritius, the Mall of Mozambique, the Mall of Gambia, and the Mall of Zimbabwe, to name a few.[63] By being actively promoted as national symbols of patriotism, however, malls also become national targets of contestation, with one survivor of the Westgate Mall attack, Raheem Biviji, noting that it "looked like there was a war inside the mall."[64] And there was.

In this sense, the al-Shabaab terrorists entered Westgate Mall as though it was a mutual battlefield. Since consumption is politicized as a patriotic pastime by investors, developers, and governments all over the world, the al-Shabaab terrorists responded to this politicization by attacking it as a suitable target. Westgate Mall was an attractive target for al-Shabaab's high profile attack with its high-end stores catering to wealthy shoppers so out of sync with the rest of the poverty-stricken Kenyan—and Somali—landscapes. A tweet sent by al-Shabaab during the attacks directly addressed this: "If #Westgate was Kenya's symbol of prosperity, it is now a symbol of their vulnerability."[65] Al-Shabaab did not necessarily perceive of mall visitors as helpless victims caught in the crossfire, but as the privileged partakers of a prejudiced capitalist system, noting that

Westgate "was frequented by 'the one percent of the one percent'. Most victims indeed came from Kenya's business and political elite, as well as the expatriate and diplomatic community."[66]

The "reopening" ceremony of Westgate Mall on July 18, 2015,[67] just shy of two years since the attacks, was attended by President Kenyatta Uhuru, along with a large number of high-ranking government officials and business elites, as well as a mob of local and international media networks.[68] The terror attacks were used to promote and publicize the reconstruction of a "new and improved" Westgate Mall, highlighting how "the disruption to business, although not insignificant, is temporary."[69] Although Westgate Mall was destroyed, both physically and as a symbol of a safe space to enact a modern lifestyle, the new Westgate is now billed as bigger, better, and safer than before. A number of US brands including KFC, Subway, Domino's, Cold Stone Creamery, and Converse, that could not be persuaded to set up shop in the old Westgate are now being introduced to the Kenyan market with great fanfare.[70] There is a strategic ideological alignment drawn between these US brands and how international capitalism can play a role in conquering international terror. That the mall has been rebuilt to exceed its former self is evidence that the corporate capitalist paradigm considers itself ultimately victorious.[71] The reopening ceremony was used as an opportunity to encourage more people in Kenya, and elsewhere, to think of shopping as a civic duty, thereby constructing consumerism as the direct opposite of terrorism, even though one is in a binary interdependence with the other.

Ironically, even as al-Shabaab claimed it was attacking the mall as a symbol of consumerism, the terrorist group was attracted by, and responded to, the "call of the mall,"[72] as any other "consumer." Even though terrorism and consumerism are conceived as antithetical practices in their respective literatures, Westgate Mall provided a ground zero for these supposedly oppositional ends of the spectrum to meet on common ground—a space where daily consumption is increasingly militarized and where terrorism and security are increasingly commercialized. Within the space of the contemporary shopping mall, capitalism and terrorism are both products imported through the same networks of global exchange, and are engaged in an act of brutal reciprocity. Thus, terrorists attack symbols of consumerism as a political act and the anti-terror discourse similarly highlights shopping as an act of political resistance against terrorism. Politicized shopping has been consistent for both capitalists as well as those who most vehemently oppose them. The discourse of consumption and the discourse of terror have been in synthesis for some time, with one relying on the other for increased publicity on both sides of the ideological divide.

The Ideological Complexities of Terrorism and Capitalism

In an inescapable twist, in order to compete against a predominantly Western capitalist system, al-Shabaab militants must first appeal to it, and engage with the very ideology they are supposedly opposing. Despite anti-capitalist pronouncements on the part of al-Shabaab and other terrorist networks, they must necessarily operate within an enveloping capitalist and neoliberal framework. As one of the most voracious global forces, the corporate capitalist model is adept at infiltrating economic systems and subverting many forms of resistance, turning opposition into begrudging collaboration. The contemporary model of neoliberalism has "become hegemonic as a mode of discourse and has pervasive effects on ways of thought and political-economic practices to the point where it has become incorporated into the commonsense way we interpret, live in, and understand the world."[73] Terror groups like al-Shabaab have been vehemently anti-capitalist in their public pronouncements and in the targets of their attacks, even as they themselves engage in capitalist enterprise, and as they utilize the latest digital communication technologies as integral to their operations.[74]

Despite widespread opposition to the corporate model, many incarnations of modern international terrorism, in the form of loosely affiliated, ideological networks, are stealthily following the trails blazed by networks of international commerce. Al-Shabaab "has shifted from one illegal business to another, drawing money from East Africa's underworld to finance attacks like the recent deadly siege at a Nairobi shopping mall."[75] In order to fund its activities, al-Shabaab has engaged in a number of profit-making business ventures, including illicit international trade in ivory and charcoal.[76] Thus, the neoliberal model, despite its formal discursive distancing from illegal activities, has been of direct benefit to the formation of international crime syndicates and terrorist networks. The differences between markets and black markets, and terrorists and entrepreneurs, are not always easy to define and often become subject to prevailing discourses.

Even as terrorist acts disrupt businesses locally and internationally, delay operations, and cause financial losses, especially for enterprises related to tourism, aviation, and hospitality, these disturbances are reflective of only one side of the story. Conversely, there are many legitimate businesses that find their genesis in terrorist activity. Especially since September 11, 2001, governments and private enterprises all over the world increased spending on security industries and emergency responses in their funding of the "war on terror."[77] The security industry has grown exponentially in operation and profits, and has had a great impact on the strengthening of the military-industrial complex in order to both secure and stimulate the economy. The war on terror quickly became a "for-profit venture, a booming new industry that has breathed new life into the faltering U.S. economy,"[78] with many traditional government functions regarding the safety and security of citizens outsourced to private companies.

In modern metropolitan settings such as Westgate Mall, corporate capitalism, terrorism, and the military-industrial complex meet head on. Despite it being under siege and paralyzed by the attack, the mall still played a part in the global circulation of capital and performed its market role, albeit under a different guise. While the activity of shopping was halted during, and in the aftermath of, al-Shabaab's attacks, the wider capitalist apparatus was still in motion, and the circulation of capital was transposed to other areas of operation, including the corporate media frenzy that surrounded the Westgate Mall attacks, and that prolonged their salience, and the immediate investment in a more robust security apparatus. Even as the cash registers ceased their ringing in the mall, they worked overtime in the surrounding security industries and media networks.

The pervasiveness of mobile technology, social media connectivity, and corporate media network competition means that most of these tragic events are inevitably turned into global media spectacles that happen for home audiences in real time to the twin delight of extremists, whose message is reverberated internationally, and the media, which is provided audience share and advertising revenues.[79] The mainstream of capitalism and the extreme of terrorism do not always inhibit each other, but often align symbiotically to produce new markets and new networks. Westgate Mall became an archetypal site for the production, consumption, and commodification of terror, where corporate news media, terrorist networks, and government authorities all took part in the events, and competed for control of the emerging narrative.

Even as the al-Shabaab terrorists entered Westgate to wreak havoc on the corruption of an unjust capitalist system, and to battle against the ideals of consumerism, their oppositional actions became as commodified as many of the other items on sale in the mall. The Westgate attacks have now passed through the hands of many corporate systems, and the violence of these events have been packaged, circulated, sold, and consumed as news stories, documentaries, DVDs, books, internet content, and social media materials supported by online advertisements.[80] Continuities between terrorism and capitalism are most visible in the immediate commodification of terrorist acts, and the rush to condemn (or support) the ideology by producing and distributing a multitude of symbolic products, turning the tragedy into a further spectacle to be consumed. Immediately after the Charlie Hebdo atrocities, for example, the "Je suis Charlie" slogan was mass produced, distributed, and consumed through "Je Suis Charlie items retailing on Etsy (seven pages of products, from bracelets to pendants), Amazon, Spreadshirt (34 different T-shirts, sweats and mugs) and Zazzle."[81] Importantly, both the agents of terror and anti-terror played roles in the production and consumption of these products. As more aspects of daily life become increasingly subjected to market forces, increased commodification practices serve to complicate matters to the point where it is not entirely clear where terrorism ends and where the market begins.

Terrorism and the war on terrorism have become staples of daily discourse—at once alarming, and yet increasingly normalized. The study of terrorism is usually event-driven and policy-driven,"[82] and, unsurprisingly, peaks at specific periods of time and especially in the wake of political unrest and spectacular attacks. To date, the sheer volume of research published in the aftermath of September 11, 2001, is indicative and unprecedented.[83] The literature is inundated with research dedicated to decoding, describing, defining, and deconstructing terrorism as a phenomenon, with many academic studies working in tandem with government departments to support, enhance, or steer government policies towards a more stringent characterization of terrorism.

Other studies, such as this one, take a less deterministic approach by arguing that terrorism remains the product of discursive forces and can be considered as much a creation of the anti-terror discourse as it is of particular attacks and atrocities. This approach provides a necessary complication of often simple and artificial binaries by engaging in a more critical reading of terrorism "both as a social relation and as embedded within a wider set of social relations."[84] Complex contemporary concerns require critical social research from perspectives other than those espoused by the politically powerful and economically dominant institutions. In this way, critical investigations yield narratives that challenge those relayed by corporate media networks and other official or government-influenced sources that attempt to frame terrorism as the antithesis of capitalism and neoliberal practice. This is despite neoliberalism's many inherent contradictions, its enactment of institutional and industrial violence as an inexorable part of production and expansion processes, and its deliberate or inadvertent appeal to symbolic violence, especially through the media.[85] Still, neoliberalism is portrayed as the symbol of an idealized Western notion of individual freedom, while terrorism is portrayed as its opposite, even though both, in many cases, lead to displacement, disarticulation, and death all around the world.[86] An analysis of the characteristics of corporate capitalism and terrorist activity in the current globalized economic environment shows how they are not only similar, but indeed often working in tandem.

The opposition between modern global capitalism and modern global terrorism is reinforced in discursive constructions of difference that do not necessarily exist in practice. By denying any wrongdoing, the "genuine anxieties brought about by an unstable economic system whose victims are almost invariably the most vulnerable in society are thereby displaced onto a host of threats disconnected (or apparently disconnected) from the chronic instabilities of post-industrial capitalism."[87] It is only by deflecting or projecting internal contradictions and rogue elements upon others, whether the subcontractor or the terrorist, that the monist institutions of corporate capitalism are able to represent themselves as lucid, coherent, and functional entities.

Such complexity and incoherence, multiplicity of discourse, and supplementarity of logic are subject to a particular type of epistemological violence in that they must be excised in order to fit into a singular meta-narrative that defines corporate capitalism as a positive norm, and any attack upon it as a necessarily negative disruption.[88] It is only by subscribing to a binary logic that it becomes possible to mark clear delineations between the borders of the supposedly holistic ideologies of capitalism and those of terrorism.

The ensuing analyses in this study, including how neoliberal capitalist practices, and by implication shopping malls, assist in the propagation of unequal power relations, should be read as adding nuance to a subject that has become increasingly bound by oppositional and binary discourses. Understandably, as authorities attempt to appease a frightened citizenry, and as publics attempt to grapple with the brutality of terrorist violence encroaching into everyday urban spaces, they shape the discourse of the "war on terror" according to sharp binaries. This allows for a necessary intellectual-abridgement in which terrorism falls outside of the realm of comprehension. Many news articles and reports on the Westgate Mall attacks, for example, do not count the four terrorists in the casualty list of deaths at the mall. In many ways, the politically-charged anti-terror discourse means that the debate remains truncated, making further investigation into the many surrounding stories, histories, and discourses not only necessary, but critical.

This study presents readers with an opportunity to engage in a more critical examination of the events that were the focus of limited media attention, and that passed without a more thorough examination of the underlying complexities regarding the relationship between capitalist and terrorist practice in metropolitan settings. While this study cannot fully explain the many atrocities and acts of violence perpetrated by extremists in urban settings, it does attempt to provide a contextual framework for these contemporary contestations. The various critiques of capitalist structures and landscapes of consumption articulated in this study are an important part of the history of shopping malls in general, and Westgate Mall in particular, and should not be read as a distraction from, but rather an elaboration on, the atrocious circumstances in which many people lost their lives.

With the reopening of Westgate Mall in 2015, there was no mention of the tragedy in any of the mall's public pronouncements, website, or social media sites. Westgate Mall's Facebook page shows a two-year gap between the last abrupt post on September 20, 2013—the day before the attacks—inviting people to "come and enjoy the Westgate Get-away fair," and the new celebratory post about the commencement of the mall's activities on July 1, 2015.[89] There is no explanation for why there was such an extended gap in communication, and why the mall was closed for so long. Westgate Mall's silence on the attacks is a strategic public relations elision of the events, and, with it, a deliberate forgetting. While the Kenyan public and government encourage annual memorials, the mall itself displays no official commemoration of the victims in its communication efforts. Since recalling a tragic event will, undoubtedly, interfere with sales, "the mall suffers an amnesia without which the smooth advancement of its business would be impossible."[90]

The specter of al-Shabaab's Westgate Mall attack is woven throughout this study, serving as a local conduit for the play of global forces. These analytical passages from Westgate to the world, and back, integrate particular socioeconomic contestations into a wider reading of the shopping mall in twenty-first century transnational society. The next chapter addresses the rise of the shopping mall in the context of emerging economies in tandem with these nations' attempts at prompting neoliberal development. It emphasizes how the shopping mall has become a symbol of national pride as well as a supposed testament to successful national economic development. In charting the rise of the prestige mall, the chapter draws attention to the simultaneous development of a new urban underclass. Defined antithetically by the shining steel and gleaming glass of a new imported modernity, many inhabitants of this new social paradigm react to it with a not altogether unexpected social violence. The chapter provides an overview of the history and development of the shopping mall both as a site of commerce and consumption as well as a site of encroaching security concerns, such that it remains a prime indicator of ideological contestation.

2. Developing the Shopping Mall

Countries considered to be "developing" on the prescribed scale of global economic growth—a status used to describe many African nations—are encouraged to promote themselves as active partakers in the global economy. The identity of the post-colonial nation as projected by contemporary corporate and government discourses is one that is increasingly based on such a globalized imaginary—a nation that has overcome its past colonial disarticulation and become resilient enough to compete in the new world order of economic globalization.[1] Entry into the global economy, however, is only accessible by emphasizing business-friendly and open markets and demonstrating increased middle-class wealth and disposable incomes—the hallmarks of the modern state. Developing nations are thus obliged to conform to a pervasive neoliberal institutional framework that is largely "characterized by private property rights, individual liberty, unencumbered markets, and free trade."[2] Citizens of developing economies are central to globalization processes, and are encouraged to partake more actively in a shared consumerist culture.

In response to these demands, developing countries have created strategic policies to prompt economic growth within a targeted period of time.[3] Kenya's development plan over the next two decades, for example, has been spelled out in its strategic Vision 2030, which is the developmental constitution of the nation, aiming "to increase Kenya's global competitiveness, to promote growth based on efficiency, and to attract more investment locally and internationally."[4] In Kenya, like most other developing nations, there is an indoctrinated ideology of nation-building that requires governments to keep pace with the global trends of progress exhibited by wealthy nations. Following the paths set by industrialized predecessors is a key step taken by postcolonial nations in their attempt to compete on an international scale. Kenya's Vision 2030 openly states that it emulates other "developed" countries, and follows their set patterns of growth couched in terms of strengthening the economy. This is achieved through a neoliberal agenda with an "emphasis on the deregulation of markets and the new priorities awarded to private business interests in the formation of policy and the delivery of public services."[5]

As colonial governments and militaries began their withdrawal, many newly independent governments were obliged to retain the already existing structure of economic advisement. In the African context, "imperial businesses did not collapse alongside colonialism, but instead successfully adapted their operations by highlighting their role in the economic development of the continent" by cooperating with the newly formed independent governments as well as with local business elites.[6] To this day, the single largest source of foreign direct investment in postcolonial nations often comes from the former colonizer. For both Kenya and Egypt, for example, most foreign direct investment comes from the United Kingdom.[7] Many postcolonial nations "are today part of the Commonwealth of Nations, an intergovernmental organization that facilitates political, commercial, and cultural ties with the United Kingdom. All that makes it easier for businesses to set up shop abroad, send employees to work as expatriates, and hire local talent. Companies are also better able to negotiate special commercial ties and preferential access to markets."[8] It follows that contemporary investments in former British colonies will allow for the former colonizer to have a direct mimetic influence on the ways in which elements of postcolonial economies operate—a global imaginary facilitated by historical transnational ties. Thus, many developing countries must perform a balancing act as they attempt to reconcile the burdens of a colonial history with the demands of a global economy.

The Making of a Middle Class

Capitalist cultural competency is, in many ways, an extension of the ways in which the colonial empire positioned itself as the hegemonic locus of wealth and power, and the center towards which colonies gravitated, and of which colonial societies were expected to frame their imaginaries. Whether celebratory or begrudging, discourses of development are a crucial frame of reference, with many complex colonial inheritances being extended into the contemporary period under the guise of free market globalization, creating a strong progressive link between colonial legacies and contemporary neoliberal policies.[9] Even today, the same type of colonialist language is utilized by international investors who perceive of developing countries as "virgin" ground ripe for economic exploitation, and as "the *Next Big Thing*."[10] Developers are calculating the benefits accrued from investing in emerging economies where a "young and connected middle class is growing fast and still deciding on its favorite brands. In short, it is brimming with potential."[11] Market researchers report that "institutional investors now regard Africa's emerging middle class and its growing consumerism the most attractive aspect of investing in Africa, more than its commodity wealth."[12]

In order to attract international investment and "to transform Kenya into a newly industrializing, 'middle-income country providing a high quality of life for all its citizens by the year 2030,'"[13] the Kenya National Bureau of Statistics (KNBS) has "re-classified" Kenya as a "middle-income" country, rather than a "low-income" one. This is a deliberate discursive rearticulation of the state of Kenya's economy that is not necessarily reflected in economic reality. Kenyan Minister for Devolution and Planning, Anne Waiguru, admitted "that an increase in GDP per capita does not necessarily mean that Kenyans will be better off nor does it imply that the existing social economic challenges have ceased to exist. Kenyans will be just as poor—or just as wealthy—as they were a year ago."[14]

This "reclassification" of Kenya as a middle-income country is thus largely symbolic and is meant to position the country as more internationally competitive, and as more attractive to foreign direct investment rather than instigating any real form of poverty alleviation.[15] As part of the "trade, not aid" strategy, inflating the public's purchasing power means that countries like Kenya will have to forgo specific international aid quotas set for social development in favor of appealing to more foreign investment directed towards economic development. Symbolically increasing the purchasing power of a nation serves to entice foreign investors with "increasingly attractive opportunities to supply goods and services to consumers with rapidly increasing disposable incomes."[16] In such ways, "consumers" are being discursively created with the anticipation that this will lead to action in the form of increased consumption.

Now that developing countries have "created" a middle class and have proposed people's increased purchasing power, there must be a place specifically designed to capture this wealth and to circulate it within the global economy. That place is the shopping mall; the portal between developing countries and the global economy. To share in the consumerist codes of a global corporate capitalism, "from Nairobi to Johannesburg, major urban centers across the continent have seen a construction boom take hold—and the world of shopping is at the heart of it."[17] Neoliberalism in the guise of shopping malls has infiltrated most, if not all, global markets, where investors and governments have eagerly adopted the design and marketing successes of these commercial venues. By encouraging increased "consumer confidence," new national identities are constructed on the basis of economic performance, inviting citizens to find consolation in consumption. This is despite the fact that poverty is endemic in many developing countries, and only a fraction of the population is able to partake in this new consumer identity.

The Globalization of Consumption and Contestation

Every era is defined by an architectural testimonial that physically locates prevailing elements of its collective social state. As an international signifier of a globalized modernity, shopping malls rate high on the list of important landmarks defining the contemporary era. The progressivist hopes of a nation have long been pinned to the concept of the shopping center, where the commercial establishment has served as a sign of progress for decades. As early as 1878, department stores were billed as "a place where almost anything may be bought," a boast that has been systematically repeated in the contemporary era.[18]

Similar to how shopping malls are currently characterized as harbingers of globalization, the establishment of the Selfridges department store in 1909 "was considered a 'monument to modernity' and was one of the most frequented tourist venues in London."[19] This sentiment was echoed almost verbatim in Ghana in the 1950s, over half a century later, when the United Africa Company (UAC) was tasked with the "duty" of developing "a modern department store in time for independence,"[20] as a sign that the nation had arrived into its modern incarnation. The Kingsway department store was duly erected in Accra, and, in the language of its developer, was a symbol of "future peace, progress, prosperity and stability."[21] Thus, a direct correlative link was created between the notion of independence and the act of shopping. Another half a century into the future, when the Accra Mall was established in 2008, its founder, Joseph Owusu-Akyaw, noted that the commercial complex would usher the nation into a hitherto unknown age of modernity.[22] In the contemporary period, the opening—and reopening—of Nairobi's Westgate Mall was geared towards embodying and exhibiting these developmental ideals.

The surge in popularity of this commodity form is exemplified by its rapid growth. In the immediate post World War II period, "there were only eight shopping centers in the United States,"[23] a figure that had grown to 114,485 in 2013.[24] In the developing country context, nations are encouraged, and increasingly obliged, to become educated in the language of progress, and to become literate in its associated codes by building shopping malls as a sign of socioeconomic development. Nigeria opened its "first modern shopping mall in 2005," and, in Rwanda, "the construction of shopping malls is changing the retail market from high street trading to enclosed centres which is gradually becoming popular with locals adapting to formal retailing under one roof."[25] Although there were only 40 malls in Kenya in 2014, a figure that might seem low compared to the number of malls in the United States, this is, in fact, a relatively rapid increase, with scores more shopping malls being planned.[26]

Cosmopolitan marketplaces, trading traditions, consumption practices, identity formations, and international networks of communication underline a rich and varied history of global connectivities. While traditional market forms exist in many nations, the shopping mall as the architectural epitome of corporate capitalism has superseded these in importance as a symbol of globalization, a signifier of economic progress, and a ready-made commodity form and spectacle. As an essential sign of a nation's social and economic progress, within the discourse of globalization, the mall is seen as a sophisticated urban necessity, regardless of how it fits within existing—and resisting—social, economic, and urban formations. The wholesale importation of the contemporary shopping mall is especially extolled in developing nations, since it can be transplanted, with little modification, into whatever local market exists.

Governments and investors all over the world have been enthralled by the idea of erecting shopping malls as self-enclosed and profit-generating miniature cities that are capable of operating on their own terms and with little connection to traditional marketplaces. In most contemporary urban environments, the shopping mall is promoted as "a point of reference, making the city accommodate its presence."[27] Many shopping malls introduced into the developing country context do not have to work their way into the existing social and market structures since they are being built as "mixed use complexes" complete with hotels, houses, private services and infrastructure, and can often even be accessed by private roads.

Because of the significant investments necessary to develop and construct shopping malls, there is only a handful of international architectural firms that specialize in mall construction. This monopolization has meant that shopping malls follow an "international standard," and do not need to fit into the local existing market structure; they can be "transplanted" fully formed with little need for interaction with their surroundings. As can be seen in many developing countries, the design of the urban mall can—and in many cases does—appear fully formed.[28] This transplantation prevents—and protects—shopping centers from growing organically over time to encounter, be shaped by, and overcome the many social, economic, and political pitfalls and problems associated with urban growth.[29]

When the Kingsway department store in Accra was accused of monopolizing the market and sidelining African retailers in the 1950s, its developers responded by noting that "department stores formed no part of the indigenous system of trading in West Africa," and that they thus did not "trespass in the field of the African trader."[30] Clearly, department stores, as precursors to shopping malls, were considered a uniquely Western phenomenon transplanted into a racially segregated African context. With their own rules of business, distribution systems, and customer base, such stores claimed to be divorced from the broader environment. Even though the mall does not always fit, and is not always welcome, in some urban contexts, where it is assembled onsite and introduced in its wholesale form, it remains socially and economically successful for those who can afford to partake in the social world offered within its walls, and for those who can afford to invest in it.

Standardization of Consumption

The concept of the contemporary enclosed shopping mall, as a product and an agent of globalizing forces, is an exercise in homogenization that demands to be uniformly understood and adopted all over the world. Out of the perceived chaos of modernizing nations, the mall is heralded as a mark of certainty and familiarity—a commercial comfort of a dominant consumer culture. Such standardization is meant to ease the process of doing business in countries with highly variable legal cultures, urban environments, infrastructures, and levels of economic and urban growth. Since generating profits is central to mall design, they are custom-built according to similar design principles all over the world, making them "ageographic."[31] Testament to the "global" and simultaneous "placeless" ideology of the contemporary shopping mall, the world is full of homogenous Westgate Malls—none of which are related. In the United States alone, there are Westgate shopping malls in Minnesota, South Carolina, Ohio, Massachusetts, California, Texas, and Pennsylvania, to name a few. Elsewhere in the world, there are Westgate malls in Shanghai, Zagreb, Ottawa, Singapore, and Oxford.

As a representative of the modern, global city, the shopping mall fulfills many of the requirements of globalization by facilitating the standardization of international business so that foreign entities do not have to deal with the overwhelming differences between each nation's legal cultures, structures, and requirements. To facilitate this regularity, and to promote a recognized "international standard,"[32] shopping mall developers have banded together into powerful trade associations, such as the International Council of Shopping Centers, with strong global influence and lobbying leverage.[33] These consortia provide international representation of real estate firms specializing in the wholesale design and installation of malls, ensuring that the many diverse cultures, markets, languages, and wealth disparities in developing countries do not impose unnecessary barriers to global retail expansion. Within the language of globalized business operations, this is a key benefit. In many developing country contexts, however, this can become a source of contestation. While Westgate Mall's establishment was an appealing prospect for many who could afford to shop there, it did much to disrupt the livelihoods of others in the surrounding informal markets and settlements.

Although the evolutionary histories of these commercial spaces and how they fit within their social surroundings are multiple, the homogenizing forces of global corporate capitalism have meant that commercial forms are being progressively standardized and unified. In developing countries, "international architectural firms replicate models first tested in the United States or Europe, which are then filled with globally identifiable chains and brands."[34] Specific points of reference and design that emerge from a dominant Western consumer culture are then universalized.[35] For example, "people who have worked their way around a mall once can use any other in a different city, even abroad, without ever having to learn the local language or customs."[36] Malls are built with the same kinds of tried and tested homogenous features to enhance functionality and efficiency.[37] This ubiquity of design has also meant that the security responses are also made homogenous, and "a strategy to reduce the risk of terrorism will be similar for most shopping centers" regardless of their particular socioeconomic or political contexts.[38]

Neoliberalism and the City

Cities like Nairobi, considered to be "emerging" on the scale of global economic development, have become beholden to private investors to construct the urban landscape in a manner that it becomes indicative of economic viability, attractive to foreign investment, facilitative of a strong tourist trade, and protective of middle classes.[39] As governments and private interests attempt to attract foreign investment "they must market the city itself as a commodity."[40] With increased global connectivities, many "cities have become more like city states, no longer tied to local or national borders but linked into an international network of urban economies and cultures. And the cities themselves are splintering into a multitude of semi-autonomous zones, creating murky regions of private/public partnerships and commercial interest."[41] Such emerging cities are being actively positioned as nodes of modernity that have more in common with—and can better connect to—other globalized cities, rather than with the impoverished districts in their own surrounding vicinities.

Many developing postcolonial cities have been shaped by a long history of private interests, causing sharp rifts and contestations between communities. There is a continuation of a colonial legacy formulated on capital accumulation in certain urban areas at the expense of the majority of poorer populations. While many public spaces in postcolonial cities remain fractured along historical racial and economic divides, these segregations are often enhanced in the contemporary period. The postcolonial city is geared to represent "a market-driven urbanity; it is a city shaped more by the logic of Market than the needs of its inhabitants; responding more to individual or corporate interests than public concerns. It is marked by an increasing deregulation and privatization of production, collective consumption, and urban space."[42] By concentrating investments in some areas of the city while ignoring other poorer ones these developments serve to enhance segregation and polarization. These tensions are "most evident in the gated communities of the middle- and higher-income neighbourhoods" that often border slum areas, causing direct visual and communal frictions between the two types of daily lived experience.[43]

Nairobi's Deep Sea slum is one such example that is located in the upcoming and wealthy Westlands district, home to Westgate Mall. The slum hosts approximately 12,000 people, many of whom have settled there since 1963.[44] The Westlands neighborhood is thus home to some of the richest and poorest areas of Nairobi that must sit side by side and tolerate the daily friction this juxtaposition entails.[45] Even though the growth of shopping malls is expected to promote job creation and better infrastructure, these urban developments do not complement other demographic factors. The population growth of Nairobi is increasing at a rate that "is not commensurate with the country's capacity to create jobs, not only in urban areas, but also in rural economies. The issue has led to proliferation of slums and gross inequalities. About 60 percent of Nairobi's 3.5 million residents live in slums where provision of public services are inadequate."[46]

As economic and infrastructural development projects reshape markets and landscapes, "urban poverty appears to be increasing as life in the city has become more expensive. Unemployment in the formal sector has risen, while real wages have not kept up with price increases,"[47] causing a variety of hostilities directed towards places of consumption, and especially the shopping mall. To become part of a culture of consumption, "urban lifestyles require cash; which is difficult to access legally in countries with high unemployment levels. As a result, crime rates are higher in cities."[48] Frustrations are increased when those most excluded from the distribution of wealth are still required to aspire to acts of conspicuous consumption. The growth of the economy and the increasing popularity of shopping malls do little to hide the uneven processes of development and unequal capital flows creating the sharp divide between rich and poor.[49]

The signifiers of modernity, including open markets, luxury shopping malls, and credit card systems, are erected and established in many developing countries even before the public's ability to become integrated into these systems or to partake in them in any meaningful way. Despite evidence to the contrary, the shopping mall is still billed by developers and advertisers as a space that can be universally enjoyed. However, such a seemingly democratic ideal can only be achieved through equity in purchasing power. As a point of comparison: in a country where "more than 45% of Kenyans live below the Kenyan national poverty line,"[50] and where "more than 43% of Kenyans live on less than USD 1.25 per day,"[51] a burger at Westgate's Gourmet Urban Burgers "sold for between $8 and $9."[52] A consumerist culture is being actively encouraged in places where shopping malls will be frequented by only a fraction of the population, and envied, endured, or opposed by many others.

Make Way for the Mall

Governments, property developers, retail chains, and marketers, to name a few entities promoting a neoliberal ideology, are converging to create a "formal shopping culture" in many developing countries where the retail landscape is often dominated by informal markets.[53] While some slum residents might find employment as security guards and other service staff at formal shopping centers and malls,[54] others are often absorbed into the surrounding informal markets—ones that are often regarded as illicit and criminal. These are defined by a "diversified set of economic activities, enterprises, jobs, and workers that are not regulated or protected by the state," in which independent stores, kiosks, cottage industries, and open markets, account for a large share of retail.[55] Despite providing a large variety of market forms, traditional and informal markets are not only marginalized by expansionist policies, but are often discounted by investors who argue that "as incomes rise across Africa, there remain relatively few retail options."[56]

In order to address this supposed lack of retail spaces, many governments have formally enshrined the shopping mall in their future developmental plans. Kenya's relationship with the mall has been etched into its 2030 Vision, with Westgate Mall serving to satisfy some of these economic objectives along with the construction of a variety of other shopping and mixed-use complexes in the coming years.[57] A largely privatized infrastructure of roads, housing developments, and shopping malls are in the process of replacing—and displacing—informal markets where the majority of the population operates,[58] and igniting a variety of hostilities along the way.

Increasingly, traditional market forms are being gradually marginalized as antiquated and outdated. As phrased by one retail consulting organization: "most African cities lack the existing shopping infrastructure of other markets, so malls are likely the only way organized retailers can open new stores."[59] The Kenyan supermarket chain Nakumatt—Westgate Mall's anchor store—attempts to formalize grocery retail and entice customers away from informal and traditional markets, causing contestation in the process.[60] Nakumatt was the scene of many of al-Shabaab's atrocities during the attack, and it was in the Nakumatt storeroom packed with potential products and profits that the terrorists took refuge. The supermarket became an outlet for imported goods and imported terrorism, both of which followed similar global distribution routes to arrive at the destination of the shopping mall.

In rapidly developing cities, polarization, confrontation, and hostility are on the rise, and "the unfolding pattern is one of disjointed, dysfunctional and unsustainable urban geographies of inequality and human suffering, with oceans of poverty containing islands of wealth. Socio-economic conditions in African cities are now the most unequal in the world."[61] In Kenya, like many other developing countries with radically unequal wealth distributions, the poor "are encroaching and stretching their heavy presence into the streets and other out-door public spaces, where they appear as if 'they are everywhere.'"[62] Since informal markets and settlements are often regarded as "a spatial problem rather than a social one,"[63] the day before the Westgate Mall attacks, on September 20, 2013, Kenyan media announced that Nairobi was set to unveil an "anti-Hawking squad."[64] The Inspector General of Police, David Kimaiyo, organized "a team of 450 officers to help get rid of hawkers from the streets of Nairobi,"[65] riling up public anger in the surrounding slums. The informal settlements that have grown around the Westlands district have regularly come under attack by the Kenyan authorities, with many residents experiencing brutality and intimidation over the years, resulting in violence enacted on both sides.[66] Describing the struggle over a prior forced eviction from the informal Westlands market, one trader notes: "We used street children. We trained them to fight. We made petrol bombs, and we had bows and arrows" to defend against forced evictions.[67]

Informal traders "are a part of the economy that spurs consumption, yet they function as quintessentially vagrant figures requiring discipline."[68] Through increasingly restrictive government and corporate policies, crime and poverty are being made synonymous and a conceptual link is being created between informality, illegality, and, increasingly, terrorism.[69] In order to separate formal and informal markets, and to take control of the discursive boundaries between them, there are sustained attempts at formalizing markets into government approved corporate entities. Informal market activities come under constant threat by authorities in their attempt to clean up the city and rid it of all kinds of crime.

In cities that are in the act of reconstituting themselves according to modern infrastructures, existing informal settlements are routinely destroyed to make way for new developments. Governments' neoliberal policies have assisted "in pushing the poor with insecure tenure rights out of city centers to grab high-value lands to hand over to corporations in pursuit of mega projects like shopping malls, leisure sites, or office buildings."[70] The informal markets around Westlands are prime real estate,[71] and so are being eyed by developers who designate these areas as "undeveloped land."[72] Such designation is the classic justification for colonial takeover of foreign assets, where "British imperial ambitions engendered a process of violent enclosures beginning in the early 1890s."[73] Ironically, such rhetoric is now being revived by post-colonial governments claiming to resist the history of such colonial manipulation.

As global corporate networks become increasingly powerful in their spheres of influence, governments and national policing efforts are gradually withdrawn as part of an ideology that "advocates the economy and society be freed from the state regulations, and be controlled, instead, by individuals and corporate bodies in accordance with their self interests, mediated through the invisible hands of the market."[74] In many cases, governments all over the world, but especially those of developing countries, are often only too willing to give up, and give up on, social services and welfare programs, and to pass on infrastructure projects to private interests. This situation poses serious questions for the ethics of business, and blurs the boundaries between legitimate and illegitimate modes of capital accumulation. In many ways, "global governance has failed to keep pace with economic globalization. Therefore, as unprecedented openness in trade, finance, travel and communication has created economic growth and well-being, it has also given rise to massive opportunities for criminals to make their business prosper."[75] A combination of capitalist production, open markets, poverty, organized crime, and terrorism becomes embroiled in a complex global network.

Transnational Networks of Capitalism, Terrorism, and Poverty

In al-Shabaab's native Somalia, the collapse of the government and formal economic system has provided a space for all kinds of businesses to flourish and for terrorist networks to profit, whether defined as legal or illegal.[76] A series of catastrophic historical events led to the current unstable political situation in al-Shabaab's native Somalia, and the rise of a particular type of militant Islamist ideology. Somalia's civil war is over two decades old, and has been defined by the breakup of the country into a variety of locally-ruled territorial enclaves, and the onset of a deadly drought and famine forcing many to seek refuge in neighboring countries, including Kenya, and further afield.[77] The Islamic Courts Union (ICU) took control of the country in 2006, with al-Shabaab as their militant wing,[78] displacing the warlords and forming a fragile political unity based on an ideology of militant Islam. This nascent stability was welcomed by many Somalis, but not by Western nations, especially the United States who orchestrated the demise of the ICU by supporting an Ethiopian military invasion.[79] While a Transitional Federal Government was created and propped up with foreign aid and troops, al-Shabaab managed to take control of much of Somalia as well as the capital. During this time, "Mogadishu earned its reputation as the most dangerous city on earth. In a harbinger of the Islamic State's ambitions, al-Shabab administered territory, provided services, and levied taxes—none of which the Western-backed Somali government could manage."[80]

Despite al-Shabaab's power being much reduced in recent years, it still managed to create international networks with similar terrorist organizations, including al-Qaeda, and to attract a number of foreign fighters. In many ways, terrorist organizations work to better their own organizational practices, whether in terms of surveillance, internal communications, outreach to external markets and audiences, marketing and branding, or engaging in profit making through both legal and illegal means. As necessary sources of income, terrorist networks rely on a range of businesses and learn from the corporate model and its means of accumulation, production, and distribution.[81] Employing a variety of methods, "terrorists and their abettors utilize existing traditional frameworks—such as companies and nonprofit entities—to raise funds, receive support, and integrate themselves into the community."[82]

The encouragement of both material and imaginary global exchanges has had a variety of other consequences, and has simultaneously paved the way for global networks of terror to operate, communicate, spread, and converge. Globalized and diffuse corporate and terrorist networks capitalize on the same form of flexible organizational structures. Importation of global business practices is not just something that governments and corporations practice; terrorist networks and other forms of organized crime are also products of economic globalization and liberalization of international markets.[83] Even as terrorist networks disavow the corruption and trappings of Western modernity in many of their ideologies, they simultaneously emulate global capitalist ventures in their structure, commercial activities, and their use of technologies of warfare and digital communication.[84] Terrorist networks have learned from global capitalist networks and follow tried and tested business models to finance their operations. There are estimates that al-Shabaab's attack in Westgate Mall "cost the group 'close to $100,000,' calculating the price of the automatic rifles, bullets and grenades that were used, along with training costs."[85] While this figure is speculative, it does pose interesting questions regarding the terrorist group's financial capabilities. There is further evidence of collaboration between corrupt elements in government and terrorist organizations, as they "build alliances with political leaders, financial institutions, law enforcement, foreign intelligence, and security agencies."[86] For example, many "reports from United Nations investigators have found Kenya's forces involved in an illicit charcoal trade from which the Shabab and local administrators shared revenues."[87]

Increasingly, there is a blurring of clearly defined lines separating legal and illegal activities, and there are many actors who muddle the distinction and confuse any notion of the legitimate. In many instances, "connecting these converging threats are 'facilitators,' semi-legitimate players such as accountants, attorneys, notaries, bankers, and real estate brokers, who cross both the licit and illicit worlds and provide services to legitimate customers, criminals, and terrorists alike."[88] Criminal transnational "networks rely on industry experts, both witting and unwitting, to facilitate corrupt transactions and to create the necessary infrastructure to pursue their illicit schemes, such as creating shell corporations, opening offshore bank accounts in the shell corporation's name, and creating front businesses for their illegal activity and money laundering."[89] With Kalashnikov weapons, for example, produced "at the rate of a million a year," many of the weapons used by terrorists "are manufactured—legitimately, for international trade—in more than 30 countries, with China leading the way. But legal weapons can quickly become illicit contraband. China exports principally to African states. There, they can end up on the illicit market either because underpaid soldiers sell them on, or because states supply rebel forces in other countries."[90]

In its global business transactions, al-Shabaab is known to have "benefited from several different sources of income over the years, including revenue from other terrorist groups, state sponsors, the Somali diaspora, charities, piracy, kidnapping, and the extortion of local businesses,"[91] as well as profits accrued from Somalia's Kismayu port, which "not only accorded al-Shabaab regular income in terms of port fees and taxes but was the main export point of charcoal to the Middle East, which earned the group some $25m a year."[92] While any figure related to terrorism profits and financing is difficult to calculate accurately because of the opaque and clandestine nature of many of these organizations, it does highlight how capitalism and terrorism are strange bedfellows, with one supposedly oppositional ideology morphing into the other—even as they denounce each other. The easing of border restrictions for the promotion of global trade has simultaneously contributed to the diffusion and globalization of a variety of legitimate and illicit networks of capitalism and terror.

Many of the profits made through international terrorist business networks are used to entice people in poor communities to join terrorist groups. Attraction to terrorist organizations is often, directly or indirectly, linked to poverty as well as "other factors that may cause support for terror, such as economic inequality or low levels of education," rather than purely as a result of religious ideology.[93] For those who do join al-Shabaab, analysts report that "salaries of $100-$300 per month are offered, joining bonuses of $400 are paid for the new recruits to hand to their families, and the family of a suicide bomber can receive 'a couple of thousand' dollars. This contrasts with a gross [Somali] national income per person of a mere $107 per annum in 2011."[94] Although al-Shabaab's rhetoric is steeped in religious discourse, the assault on Westgate Mall was not simply religiously-motivated, and, from the outset, was also framed as a response to economic inequality among other social and political grievances.

By appealing to an anti-imperial consciousness, al-Shabaab has attempted to tap into a global network of ethnic Somalis and others who respond to the group's rhetoric against past colonial injustices and contemporary neocolonial ones. Through divisive discourses, al-Shabaab attempts to encourage financial support from sympathizers to engage the media to circulate their ideological stance. In a worldwide campaign to attract supporters who share sentiments of exclusion and marginalization, al-Shabaab attempts to attract ethnic Somalis at home and abroad, including the large refugee population in Kenya as well as those further afield.[95]

Al-Shabaab's reach and threats against targets all over the world, including the Mall of America, have become increasingly international. True to the tenets of global connectivities and the international movement of goods and people, the Mall of America is relevant to the Westgate Mall story, not only because it has often been heralded as the shopping mall par excellence, but also because "Minnesota is home to the biggest Somali population in the United States." These various international connections between Somalia and Minneapolis has meant that "Minnesota's population has proven to be a ripe recruiting ground for al-Shabab."[96] Indeed, "some of the young men who volunteered to fight in Somalia had grown up in the Cedar-Riverside neighborhood of Minneapolis, which is one of the poorest places in the United States" where Somali-American family incomes are low and unemployment rates are high.[97] As economic migrants become trapped within a global cycle of poverty, many of those who migrate from conditions of poverty or conflict in their homelands end up living in continued disadvantaged conditions far from home.

In order to attract global funding and recruits, al-Shabaab engages in global media campaigns, including one titled "Minnesota's Martyrs: The Path to Paradise," aimed at a Somali-American population.[98] In another promotional campaign, the group released a video, using Donald Trump as a reason to join the cause. "Citing 'historical injustices' against African-Americans, including police brutality and racial profiling, the video urged them to convert to Islam and engage in jihad at home or abroad."[99] In the communication war that arose during, and in the aftermath of the Westgate Mall attacks, some corporate and government-news networks retaliated to al-Shabaab's recruitment messages by initiating the "Outreach to Foreign Muslim Audiences" program on the Voice of America (VOA) channel.[100] Through similar forms of promotion, targeted members of the public have been subjected to a tug of war between the official anti-terror efforts and al-Shabaab's simultaneous recruitment campaigns to join its international network of terror.[101]

In order to "transnationalize" itself,[102] al-Shabaab has positioned itself as a globally-identifiable brand by attracting international funding and foreign recruits, pledging allegiances to al-Qaeda and to the Islamic State as an extension of its franchise, and maintaining international connections with other like-minded terrorist networks.[103] Ironically, however, even as they benefit from globalizing practices, and modern technologies, groups like al-Shabaab simultaneously appeal to an anti-imperial consciousness in order to tap into an international network of sympathizers. Their message of rectifying past colonial injustices and fighting against contemporary neoliberal grievances that are progressively inequitable, unbalanced, and exploitative is delivered through information and communication technologies with a significant and often sophisticated know-how.[104]

Extremist organizations often heed the rules of marketing and publicity, even utilizing the same language and terminologies to address their audiences as "consumers," and to publicize their "brand."[105] The language and logic of capitalist practice has entered into the casual everyday speech of its alleged opposite. The infiltration of corporate language into everyday terrorist practice helps to highlight the porous boundaries between the ideologies of terrorism and capitalism, and debunks their supposed mutual exclusivity. The twin phenomena of capitalism and terrorism cannot always be separated, and just as the inequalities exacerbated by capitalism are addressed by a violent militant response, so too do terrorists use the very mechanisms of the capitalism they seek to destroy.[106]

Westgate Mall provided a space in which al-Shabaab terrorists traversed this discursive separation to not only do harm to people and property, but to damage an imagined community of consumption even as they engaged with it. The importance of malls to the global circulation of corporate culture and their centrality to the contemporary urban experience means that they have inevitably become both icon and beacon: icon of consumption for some and beacon for disgruntlement for others. Despite the hostility of the attack on Westgate, al-Shabaab was enticed by the idea of the shopping mall as a target, and became caught somewhere in between these coinciding elements of attraction and aversion.

In cities marked by ever increasing hostilities, security-oriented "shopping centres have filled a void to become one-stop-shops for those who yearn to feel 'safe.'"[107] In these gated communities, there is an "intensely privatized and quasi-anarchic vision of urban growth,"[108] in which privatized living and shopping complexes are coming under an increasingly militant security paradigm. In many areas, it becomes impossible for some people to access certain parts of the city, escalating proactive and reactive fears and animosities. Those marginalized by neoliberal economic policies are exploited, and even at times recruited, by terrorist groups, making the gap between affluence and impoverishment a space for justifying the many violent activities on both sides of the class divide—to secure or to contest. Westgate Mall accommodated the multidirectional flows of global exchanges with a mix of imported goods and terrorist attacks. In this sense, the space of Westgate Mall "is not just phenomenological, rooted in the presence, memory, or anticipation of dwelling. It is not just semiotic, based in the interrelation of legible signifiers. And it is not just the result of systems of social exchange, produced by flows of capital and labour. It is all of these."[109]

In order to explore some of these intersecting issues, the next chapter examines the evolutionary trends of shopping mall design, and how these have been adopted all over the world. It emphasizes the initial construction and design of mall space as dictated by the imperative to encourage a culture of increased consumption, then returns to Nairobi's Westgate as a way of measuring the degree to which twenty-first century African urban space imported and embedded a capital consumption ideal that nonetheless fed a violent anti-capital response.

3. Designing the Shopping Mall

During al-Shabaab's four-day siege, Westgate Mall became a site, both physical and metaphorical, for locating the intersection of the prevailing discourses of terrorism, capitalist practice, cultures of consumption, the security apparatus, and corporate media network competition, among a number of other issues constituting the contemporary urban experience. In order to understand how the shopping mall may host these complex relationships, it is important to map formative moments in the evolutionary and historical trends of shopping mall development and to examine the architectural impetus of its design in shaping patterns of consumption, as well as contestation.

As a sign of continuously globalizing transnational exchanges, the concept of the shopping mall has a long history of borrowing architectural forms and adopting consumption patterns. Greek agoras, Roman forums, and the souqs and bazaars of the Middle East, Asia, and Africa stretch back into ancient history as the conceptual originators of concentrated retail arenas that have been extended into the modern form of the shopping mall. These concentrated commercial forms have existed for centuries, and their designs have been encountered, exported, and emulated by disparate cultures in different geographies. The history of international trade exchanges complicates any definitive way of knowing exactly what came from where and how. A variety of converging and diverging factors and events have shaped the evolutionary trajectory of the contemporary shopping mall, none of which can be captured in its entirety. To echo the extravagant words of department store entrepreneur Harry Gordon Selfridge, written almost a century ago, "to write on commerce and trade and to do the subject justice would require more volumes than any library could hold."[1]

The history of landscapes of consumption does not follow a clear succession from one type of design to another and these spaces, whether considered traditional or modern, marketplace or mall, have existed contemporaneously and in coinciding commercial spheres. Even though today's corporate consumerist ideology in the shape of the shopping mall stems from a particular Western imaginary, it is necessarily ordained as a global phenomenon through a dominant neoliberal discourse whose focus "reflects principally the interests of its producers. In many ways, what passes for international culture is usually the culture of the economically developed world" in the progressivist lexicon.[2] The contemporary shopping mall has especially been reflective of the dominant commercial cultures of the United States and Europe.

Because the shopping mall, in its contemporary form as an enclosed, air-conditioned retail arena, has had such a long and sustained evolution in European countries, in general, and the United States, in particular, much of the research on this commodity form has concentrated on Western histories and experiences. The literature abounds with countless articles, books, journals, magazines, and trade reports dedicated to examining the history of shopping, and patterns of production and consumption, and numerous accounts analyzing in detail every aspect of the shopping mall, including its architecture, design, atmospherics, security apparatus, as well as its customers and employees and their habits, aspirations, and behaviors.[3] Since the contemporary shopping mall has existed for a long time in the European and US urban and suburban historical contexts, the relationship that has been developed between corporate and social elements in the developing country context must thus be read against this dominant history. While the origins of the contemporary shopping mall might be specific to the US and European contexts, these histories played a paradigmatic role, and are essential to understanding other market formations. Key urban and architectural transformations helped, in one way or another, shape the contours and concept of the modern mall as well as the prevailing culture of the consumption practices within it.

The concept of the contemporary shopping mall emerges from decades of research dedicated to the shaping of consumption patterns. Shopping malls, as orchestrated profit-making enterprises, are highly regulated zones where marketers, administrators, designers, and security analysts have spent vast amounts of money and time crafting, promoting, and monitoring the relationship between space, people, services, and commodities. Even as they go about their daily activities, mall visitors are ushered through a specialized history of architecture; they become the subject of decades of advertising and marketing research; and they become subjected to the latest technologies of surveillance. Because of these many moving parts, "the shopping mall cannot be described solely on the basis of its floor plan, location or size; it can only be encountered *in motion*, as a matrix of time and space through which passes a multitude of trajectories."[4] While mall visitors may not necessarily succumb to all such marketing orchestrations, the mall remains a center of contemporary life where many people are, in one way or another, implicated in the purpose of the business operation, and regularly embedded in, or excluded from, an environment engineered for consumption.

Since the histories of consumption practices stem from a variety of different geographic locations, and are shaped by specific socioeconomic factors, and since shopping malls have been developed at different stages depending on particular national contexts, instead of examining a single narrative trajectory, it is important to highlight a series of global overlaps. Examining international convergences in the history of shopping malls provides an overview of the commercial arena, with particular focus on moments of correspondence between how the shopping mall evolved in one part of the world and how it was imported and adopted in another. Over time, bottom-line financial objectives have outstripped most other contextual concerns, and have had direct influence on an increasingly standardized design of international shopping malls.

A Brief History of the Shopping Mall

While histories of consumption are multiple and varied, the industrial revolution ushered in a new era of mass production and consumption that gradually spread across the world. The novelty and mass availability of industrial goods attracted the attention of publics and captured their imaginations, steering many towards the wonders and possibilities of the mechanical age. Technological advances to systems of production, the mass manufacturing of goods, the introduction of automated transportation, innovations in lighting and ventilation, and changes to roads and urban planning, created a larger customer base that could revel in a world of conspicuous consumption once reserved for the bourgeoisie. In the context of an industrializing Europe, there was "a concomitant rise in incomes," so that "what were once considered luxury goods were now becoming widely available for purchase by a variety of different socioeconomic classes, rather than just dedicated to a minority of elite."⁵ These mass produced products needed to be displayed, and their means of production exalted. In such ways, the architecture of consumption began to take shape according to the need to accommodate, display, and protect increasingly large amounts and varieties of goods. Further social and cultural transformations of the industrial revolution overlapped, kindling a radical transformation in the relationship between people, places, and products.⁶

Exhibitions and Fairs

Beginning as temporary structures, regional and national exhibitions, festivals, and fairs, such as the World Fair, unveiled industrial goods to inquisitive publics. These quickly became centers of social awe, creating a newfound energy in the heart of growing cities.⁷ These spaces encouraged encounters with new and foreign merchandise, including a variety of "exotic" cultures and commodities imported from colonies all over the world.⁸ Although such early large-scale exhibitions catered predominantly for the publics of industrializing European cities, the movement of goods was global and multidirectional, and organized fairs, such as the International Exhibition in South African in 1877, were mounted outside of Europe albeit less frequently.⁹

Creating an early framework for today's shopping malls and the tactical combination of commerce and entertainment, the popular fairs and festivals provided a series of theatrical productions, magic shows, and spectacles in order to encourage customers to stay longer, and in order to imbue the commodity with a wide range of characteristics. Such exhibitions and fairs served to "glorify the exchange value of the commodity. They create a framework in which its use value recedes into the background. They open a phantasmagoria which a person enters in order to be distracted. The entertainment industry makes this easier by elevating the person to the level of the commodity."¹⁰

With the mass availability of goods, there was a new emphasis on the transformative powers of consumption. "Until the nineteenth century, capitalist power was located mainly in production, in the factory, and in the labour process, since the early part of the twentieth century, particularly in the developed capitalist countries, power has shifted increasingly to consumption."¹¹ Marketing industries and advertising narratives worked towards a creative awakening of desires, enticing and instructing publics on new means of identity-making based on conspicuous consumption.¹²

In the age of mechanical reproduction, "art became subject to the logic of commerce,"[13] and advertising techniques flourished in tandem with the consumption practices encouraged, and the goods publicized—all contributing to the expansion of imaginations and identities intertwined with commodities and their signifiers in a symphony of "symbolic alchemy."[14]

With the combined efforts of advertising and the creation of a carnival atmosphere, "the society of the spectacle" flourished.[15] By promoting the supremacy of the commodity, a wondrous world was being created with the power to replace a constrained reality offered through industrious labor. Commodity-based spectacles presented publics with elements of a fantastical world that reached beyond the quotidian of daily lives ruled by work. In these market-driven spectacles, the worker and regular wage-earner, became central to the industrial project, and were invited to occupy the foreground as sought-after customer, rather than the background as mere labor.[16]

With the industrial revolution in full swing, and with the public's curiosity piqued, temporary exhibitions and fairs evolved into more permanent city-central structures with input and capital provided by government entities and private entrepreneurs. Thus began the physical and psychological transformations of industrializing cities; instead of the customary congregation of urban activity around a traditional marketplace or town square, people's attentions were now redirected towards shopping arenas as the centerpiece of the city dedicated to conspicuous consumption. Urban planners set about developing new infrastructures, and city centers set their gaze towards new focal points.

Arcades

It was only relatively recently, in the twentieth century, that the term "mall" became a byword for the ubiquitous, fully-enclosed shopping arena we know today. In the eighteenth century, the word "mall" was commonly used to describe a "public area often set with shade trees and designed as a promenade or as a pedestrian walk."[17] The idea of pedestrian malls became increasingly popular as they provided islands of tranquility to cut through the increasingly tumultuous, overcrowded, and disorganized city centers of an industrializing Europe.

It was not long before the many urban leisurely strollers, or what Baudelaire and Benjamin conceptualized as *flâneurs*, became the targets of merchants selling their goods alongside the malls.[18] The strolling malls of London and Paris became lined with merchants, and many of the promenades were gradually customized in order to make them more attractive to the ambler. Physical comfort and shelter from the sun or rain were offered over time with the partial covering of walkways. By the nineteenth century, covered walkways grew in several different directions of the city as they increased in number and popularity, and were gradually transformed into a series of interconnected city-central arcades. The most notable arcades flourished in Paris and London where the narrow streets of the city were ideal for connecting the covered walkways to provide a comfortable and extended shopping experience.

Developed along with a boom in the textile trade, and as a place to store and exhibit merchandise and emerging fashions, arcades became attractive areas for shopping and strolling. Quoting from *An Illustrated Guide to Paris*, Walter Benjamin notes that the nineteenth century Parisian arcade, "a recent invention of industrial luxury, are glass-roofed, marble-paneled corridors extending through whole blocks of buildings, whose owners have joined together for such enterprises. Lining both sides of these corridors, which get their light from above, are the most elegant shops, so that the arcade is a city, a world in miniature."[19] It was in the arcades where gaslights were first used on a large scale, and for an industrial purpose, with entire streets lit up at night to allow for continuous shopping into the hours of darkness.

At a time of rapid industrial development, the arcades provided a key historical instance when industry, architecture, and consumption became decisively intertwined, leading to a consecration of the commodity therein. The arcade was "wholly adapted to arousing desires,"[20] and it was within the arcades that aesthetics and business were expertly combined, and where many art forms became coopted in "service of the merchant,"[21] creating a world filled with the wealth of surplus. This was a commercial world that would gradually gain power and influence over the purchasing habits of the public by promoting its own rules of design, advertising, behavior, and consumption.[22] "Arcades as temples of commodity capital,"[23] were the architectural predecessors of modern malls as dedicated spaces for commodity adulation.

However, as the commercial spaces of commodity display became more refined and organized, industrial waste polluted city streets, and industrial promise attracted a steady stream of rural migrants. Many of the grievances leveled against the contemporary shopping mall can be identified in the arcades, which were becoming less like public streets and more like spaces of exclusion, providing protected walkways predominantly for the wealthy and shielding them from the increasing hazards of city centers. Overcrowding, disease, crime, and impoverishment stood in stark contrast to the displays of wealth being paraded in and through the arcades. With a large variety of shops increasingly facing away from the street and towards each other across central walkways, the arcades "were built as a way to deal with the increasingly hostile public environments of urban centers"—a sentiment of safety that is still being used to characterize the modern shopping mall.[24]

Instead of constantly looking out for the hazards of the street, the protected environment of the arcades encouraged people to gaze inwards upon the many sights on offer, whether in the form of other shoppers, or increasingly elaborate shop windows to display and advertise commodities. In such spaces, filled with novel and cosmopolitan goods, "signs and appearances acquire a new importance and substitute increasingly for traditional narratives of social and geographical belonging. There is a new stress on display and the visual—on looking."[25] This new target on the gaze, became even more focused with the incremental enclosure of shopping venues to form stand-alone department stores.

Department Stores

Nineteenth century department stores were presented as spaces of elegance and entertainment, but their origins can also be read according to a more ominous history. The department stores of Paris can trace their origins to the widening of city streets and boulevards introduced by architect Baron Haussmann that aided in the "speed and free flow needs of the security forces,"[26] allowing for troops to be deployed in mass numbers. Among other infrastructural reasons, wider road systems were designed to put an end to the urban revolts and street barricades that were a common form of the poor's social resistance in the narrow, irregular streets of Paris.[27] One such altercation took place in a Parisian arcade when "the Passage du Saumon was the scene of a battle waged on barricades, in which 200 workers confronted the troops."[28] While the redesign of the city improved traffic flow and eased overcrowding, "military concerns were paramount" to the redesign of the city, and the subsequent establishment of department stores as safe, regulated spaces of commerce.[29]

With the development of automobiles and public transportation systems, notably in European cities, the intricate pedestrian alleyways and arcades were less visited, and eventually fell out of fashion. In their stead, road-facing, self-enclosed department stores rose to prominence.[30] As comfortable and convenient one-stop-shops, department stores outshone the arcades with "glittering decor, the great variety of goods on offer, and the range of additional services and entertainments that they provided."[31] A departure from the erraticism of the arcade, department stores presented clean, comfortable, indoor emporia, and an integrated commercial concept owned by a single merchant, and unified in a single architectural form. Over time, department stores expanded vertically, taking on more floors, as well as horizontally, taking over adjacent buildings and city streets,[32] all the while growing in a systematic, measured, and controlled way.

Because the older arcades grew organically over time to dominate or create a city center, they could not always be easily replicated in other cities. The department store, however, was an easy and compact model to follow and was emulated in cities all over the world.[33] In the colonial context, developers in African nations began adapting the model of the department store to suit their elite and middle-class customer base.[34] In the 1950s, for example, representatives from the United Africa Company (UAC) traveled to Europe and the United States to interview established department store managers in order to collect expertise for the opening of the Kingsway department store in Ghana,[35] accumulating such advice as what kinds of marketing measures should be implemented, as well as how to better attract customers.

Atmospheric technologies and architectonic designs became catalysts for fundamental changes on both ends of the marketing spectrum: from enhancing the tactical nature of selling techniques to the sustained influencing of buying behavior. Because the emphasis was now on "observing," department stores provided increasingly vivid and theatrical displays of merchandise. These spectacles were designed to entice the observer with more than just the product, but with the promise of the product. Department stores were dedicated to the sale of an increasing variety and abundance of commodities that were promoted in ever elaborate designs and displays. Through a rapidly revolving cycle of mass production and consumption, "the circus-like and theatrical element of commerce is quite extraordinarily heightened."[36] These early spectacles of consumption escalated within the setting of the suburban shopping center to include a combination of shopping and entertainment facilities.

Since attracting and retaining custom was among the department store's primary goals, it was in these commercial spaces that shoppers were first exposed to a variety of technological advances that were not yet instituted by the state for public consumption, including such novelties as continuous and sustained electricity, escalators, and elevators.[37] When Ghana's Kingsway department store was first established in Accra, "one of the most memorable features was the store's escalator, the first of its kind in West Africa. Older men and women reminisced about riding it for fun as children."[38] The store was lit up all night as most of the city lay in darkness, highlighting its importance as a national symbol of modernity and progress.[39]

Artificial lighting and air conditioning were introduced to department stores early in the twentieth century, removing the need for natural ventilation and light.[40] Eliminating glass windows and skylights—popular in arcades and early department store design—provided more retail space for commodity displays to fill the once empty, grand, and open-planned interiors, atria, foyers, and centerpieces.[41] With no more natural light and no direct connection to the world outside, department stores became incrementally insulated, isolated, and inward-looking worlds, and the act of shopping commenced in an increasingly self-sustaining atmosphere that needed little correlation to the outside environment. This is a dislocation that has only been enhanced in the design of fully-enclosed contemporary shopping malls, and with it an increase in friction and hostilities leveled against it.

The incremental detachment of the department store had a sustained effect on the relationship between people, products, space, and services. As these increasingly enclosing worlds slowly severed themselves from outside environments, they also created their own internal logic for the rational and efficient functioning of their operations. The Parisian Bon Marché department store, for example, reflected this rationalization in "its divisions into departments; its partitioning of Paris for the purposes of making deliveries; its files and statistics, records and data; its telephone lines, sliding chutes, conveyor belts, and escalators,"[42] among other mechanized, systematized, and streamlined ways of conducting everyday business. Department stores were growing into increasingly large and far-reaching operations and so "were obliged to introduce modern methods of management, stock control, cash handling and staff training, all of which led to further efficiencies,"[43] and began incrementally removing the personal in favor of the automated.

The relationship between the merchant and hired employees created a new service industry based on the characteristics of efficiency and conformity and subscription to particular types of behavior. In mass industries, "the constant and rapid turnover of goods demanded standardized methods of organization, subjecting employees to a factorylike order that extended beyond working hours into the carefully supervised dormitories and eating halls."[44] In Ghana, for example, the Kingsway department store's employee handbook emphasizes "the connection between physical appearance and salesmanship, implying that the more attractive a sales person appeared, the better their ability to sell. This correlation was applied to both male and female sales staff. The company instructed women on how to apply make-up and fingernail polish, and reminded them to wash their hands and feet. Men were encouraged to shave daily, wear leather shoes and 'crisp white shirts', and keep their hair short."[45] Set against the backdrop of recent or imminent colonial independence, investors framed the establishment of department stores as not only a sign of modernity and progress, but as a "public service" that would introduce "improved techniques in buying and selling, which included the use of modern equipment, like accounting machines, cash registers, and refrigerators, as well as self-service, merchandise displays, and staff training courses."[46]

In traditional marketplaces, personal relationships between customer and merchant were built on consistency of contact and the rapport created through regular banter about products and price negotiations. In the large department stores prices were fixed and visibly marked and sales were conducted methodically by hired salespeople with little room for, or intention of, forging relationships with customers. Here, "the obligation to buy implied by the active exchange of bargaining was replaced by the invitation to look, turning the shopper into a ... spectator, an isolated individual, a face in the department-store crowd, silently contemplating merchandise."[47] The department store environment began eliminating the need for any unnecessary communication between customer and salesperson, a relationship that became further eroded in the operation of shopping centers.

The Shopping Center

In the US and European contexts, there was a series of further technological, economic, and social developments, including an increase in automobile manufacturing and ownership, a surge in wage labor and concomitant rise in wages, and an increase in women entering the labor market. The growing middle classes began a gradual movement into suburbs in search of larger houses and better conditions compared to the congestion of city centers.[48] Redefining the geography of retail in order to cater to this movement, Jesse Clyde Nichols designed the Country Club Plaza in Kansas City in 1923. It was the first concentration of shops constructed at a distance from a downtown, catering to a large-scale residential development. For the orderly suburbs, now at a safe distance from the crime, grime, and overcrowding of the city, shopping centers provided "sanitized surrogate city centers" for shopping, recreation, and social gatherings, and became focal points to which suburban life gravitated in the absence of any other discernable center.[49] Importantly, within these new market forms, the idea of the social became increasingly defined by commercial activity, where "the center of community life was a site devoted to mass consumption, and what was promoted as public space was in fact privately owned and geared to maximizing profits."[50]

As department stores were gradually surpassed by shopping centers and strip malls, such arenas underwent a series of architectural and conceptual changes. A far cry from the elaborate and ornate design of city-central department stores, the new efficiency-seeking attitude born along with the more regimented shopping centers was key to stripping away excess features deemed unprofitable. Nichols reasoned: "We have found skylights are a source of trouble. They are hot in summer, cold in winter, hard to keep clean, are subject to leaking in rainy weather, and easy for robbers to enter."[51] Over the years, guidance regarding the construction of shopping centers advised developers to sacrifice "architectural perfection" in order to "serve practical needs in merchandising,"[52] resulting in increasingly ubiquitous structures. Shopping malls may have started off with beatific skylights, fountains, and floral arrangements, but the marketing impulse matured towards maximizing business efficiency with profits trumping any superfluous design considerations.

The lack of appealing outward designs or window displays was part of a new profit-maximizing attitude towards economic restructuring and cost-cutting on any element that was calculated as unnecessary to the commercial project. More purposefully, however, the lack of an exterior design helped in "guiding" shopping behavior and the movement of customers within these establishments. The lack of outward embellishments discouraged people from walking around the exterior of the shopping center and instead encouraged them to park their cars and walk directly towards the shops. It also meant that "delivery trucks could be driven right up to the building and unloaded directly into the ground-level stock rooms,"[53] thus saving on extra loading space and, importantly, saving time and increasing efficiency.

Suburban shopping centers were designed specifically to accommodate as comfortably and efficiently as possible the automobile,[54] making the "invention" of the sprawling parking lot just as important a concept as the shopping center itself. Personal automobiles freed people from the structures and constraints of public transportation and served to change the way people shopped, resulting in an increase in how much time they spent in shopping centers, how often they visited, and how many commodities they could purchase and carry home, all resulting in a surge in the popularity and profits of shopping centers.

The automobile was similarly one of the driving forces behind the urban planning schemes of many African cities in the twentieth century characterized by the machinations of colonial trade.[55] Combined with racial municipal legislation, a racially segregated urban plan for Lusaka, Zambia, by British architect, Jellicoe, for example, was designed "to cater for 'a car-owning European population and an African population that would be walking.'"[56] As colonial cities grew in the 1930s and 1940s, central business districts (CBDs) expanded. Stimulating the landscape for European settlers was to ensconce them in similar retail environments as they would experience back in the colonial centers, with names like the "Hyde Park Centre" to evoke a sense of "home."[57]

Meanwhile, municipal legislation prohibited African businessmen from conducting commercial activities in the towns. Since "the poverty of black township residents and the lack of infrastructure development made these areas less attractive to retail property developers,"[58] African traders, and customers, relied on informal markets and wagon or truck trade, contributing to the expansion of an unplanned urban sprawl, a condition that has been exacerbated in the contemporary era. By simultaneously accommodating a wealthy urban center and an impoverished periphery, cities became sharply divided between wealthy and impoverished districts. The trajectory of sharply uneven distributions of wealth and infrastructural development has continued to this day in many African cities, and is a feature of the "neoliberal city" and a major source of contemporary contestation.[59]

In many emerging economies, shopping malls are erected as signs of economic progress and take pride of place in the centers of cities.[60] In the same way that department stores were some of the first private spaces to have sustained electricity when no other public space was given the same privileges,[61] in many developing cities today shopping malls and office buildings are lit up all night in neighborhoods adjacent to slums where there is neither sustained electricity, nor running water. The well-maintained grounds and intricately designed structures of shopping malls often sit in stark contrast to the unkempt surroundings of makeshift stalls and street hawkers attempting to capitalize on wealthy mall clientele.[62] More than just attempting to capture passing trade, the informal settlements around Westgate Mall are a congregation of the poor and unemployed in the surrounding slums that predate the construction of the mall.[63] The mall's security apparatus as well as cultural and entrenched communal norms work to ensure that both physical and imaginary socioeconomic boundaries are not easily transgressed, and that cross-class encounters are kept to a minimum.[64] While the strategic location of malls can mitigate against everyday friction between the rich and poor, it can do little to stop the brazen and targeted violence of terrorist groups.

The Contemporary Shopping Mall

The evolutionary design of the contemporary urban mall emerged in large part out of the machinations of the military mindset. As many countries attempted to revive their post-World War II economies, the very same technologies of war, and some of the same factories where the machinery of war were produced, became available for the mass production of commodities. Instead of building munitions, assembly lines could now mass produce cars and appliances that could be marketed and sold to the public.[65] In the United States, especially, "products were designed by corporations with the aesthetic of advanced weaponry, embellishing a newfound sense of confidence while relating it to American military might; economy, power and visual culture were thus linked like never before. Buildings, cars, household appliances and electronic devices, for example, were outfitted in chrome-trim shells, mimicking combat machinery."[66] In post-war economies engaging in large-scale industrialization, "the new way of life depended on new ways of consuming,"[67] and households were encouraged, and expected, to accommodate a wide range of products. Mass production necessitated concerted efforts at product differentiation through targeted advertising, branding, and marketing campaigns to a mass audience via mass communication. Commodities made in bulk further necessitated that they be sold in bulk to as many people as possible: this place was an ever-expanding shopping mall, which has been described as "the delivery system of postwar abundance."[68]

The architecture and design of the first fully-enclosed shopping mall, the Southdale Center in Minnesota, was pioneered by Victor Gruen in 1956. For his conceptual design, Gruen "drew influence from the design work of America's governmental and military institutions."[69] Long before the idea of the contemporary fully-enclosed mall was made for public consumption, "the idea of combining both shopping and non-retail services (like movie theaters, the post office, churches, housing, etc.) in a single location came from the U.S. Federal Government."[70] The self-enclosed military town combined shopping, leisure, and entertainment facilities, as well as other practical stores designed to satisfy the daily needs of the stationed troops. For example, "San Diego's Linda Vista shopping center (built in 1942) was an all-encompassing installation built by the government for WWII defense workers, and Los Alamos, New Mexico, (built in 1943) was developed by the U.S. Atomic Energy Commission as a combined retail and non-retail facility at the heart of America's nuclear headquarters."[71] Thus, the concept of the contemporary shopping mall carries the trace of an underlying militarism imbued with a history of violence and was originally conceived as a space of survival, where a variety of daily social—and military—activities could be performed within the same protected, and barricaded, space.

Since early shopping malls were established, a general trend regarding the "modern" experience of shopping, and any related recreational public engagement, has increasingly, and architecturally, turned away from the public nature of the street and inwards upon itself, creating "a world in miniature."[72] Corporate advertising directed at creating new African target markets during the 1950s and 1960s are especially expressive of this shift. A United Africa Company advertisement from 1960 titled "A Change in West Africa" depicts the process of change with a "before" image of a traditional open marketplace and an "after" image of an enclosed shopping center representing the modern way of shopping in an enclosed arena.[73]

Contemporary shopping malls differ from the individually-owned and managed department stores and many shopping centers in that they are no longer built and operated according to the philosophies of a single retailer or designer, but are wholly managed by third parties who are, in most cases, real estate developers and investors with express interest in the bottom line, the mechanics of business, and calculating profits,[74] with security and control high on the list of operational activities. The architecture of commercial spaces has progressively become more insulated and isolated and their inaccessibility reflected in today's walled, barricaded, and privatized complexes guarded by an array of private security forces and technologies of surveillance.

With such detailed attention granted to the minutia of the daily commercial operation, the enclosed shopping mall performs an efficient and profitable control of private space. It synthesizes social and market research with city planning, necessitating the convergence and interaction of disparate groups of actors and institutions in order for the unified concept of the shopping center to thrive. These include, but are not limited to:

architects, planners, civil, structural and mechanical engineers, economists, developers, real estate owners, shopping center operators, department store and chain store organizations, super-market operators, owners of stores dealing in all types of merchandise, public officials, building and planning departments, zoning boards, traffic consultants, landscape architects, insurance companies, mortgage institutions, graphic designers, sculptors and artists, store designers and lawyers.[75]

This complex matrix of shopping mall stakeholders produced an increasingly systematized way of doing business in which the "highly structured system was designed to minimize guesswork," and allowed for the developer "to accurately predict the potential dollar-per-square-foot-yield of any projected mall, thus virtually guaranteeing profitability to the mall's developers."[76] Even the embellishments deemed wasteful decades earlier in suburban shopping centers were now calculated as a necessary means of attracting customers and competing against the glut of other malls offering "a range of conveniences, including light, warmth, longer hours, better security, improved store layouts, wider parking spaces, and increased self-selection, all accented by waterfalls, sculptures, fountains, landscaping, mirrors, and neon signs that downtown areas could rarely match."[77]

As a concept that could accurately predict and guarantee profits, shopping mall development went into overdrive. The enclosed shopping mall concept became so popular with both developers and shoppers that "by 1960, there were 4,500 malls in America—some open, many enclosed. By 1975, that number had risen to 16,400, and by 1987, there were 30,000 malls accounting for half of all retail dollars spent in the country."[78] This latter period was characterized by the global deregulation of markets when, in the 1980s, there began "an unparalleled period of growth in the shopping center industry, with more than 16,000 centers built between 1980 and 1990."[79] The contemporary shopping mall design was further updated and hyper-modernized in the 1980s and 1990s by Jon Jerde, the proclaimed "alchemist of the urban condition."[80] On its website, Jerde Partnership International refers to its activities as "placemaking," and recreating "the communal pedestrian experiences upon which great cities were built, while meeting the evolving demands of rapid modernization. We see each site as a potential economic and social engine that can recreate the urban experience and transform its environment."[81] The urban experience was not only transformed, but was also packaged and exported.

As US and European retail environments become saturated, investors set their sights abroad on new foreign markets, and particularly on developing countries, enshrining the shopping mall as an international phenomenon. Emerging from the shadow of colonial disarticulation, many African nations opened up their economies to attract international development and dedicated prime city center real estate to the construction of a variety of private enterprises with a strong emphasis on shopping malls.[82] However, there is only a handful of large-scale developers who can invest and compete in such mega retail and entertainment projects. In the 1980s and 1990s African context, for example, the active agents of neoliberal growth and "this new wave of African 'modernization' were South African retail multinationals. Wittingly or unwittingly, the South African retailers followed the path of European colonial traders who inscribed the earlier geographies of retail in the region."[83] Unsurprisingly, South Africa has the strongest retail sector in Africa, one that is matched by the length and strength of its colonial experience.[84] Today, "a single South African development company is currently building some 50 mega-malls with grand names like the Mall of Kigali, the Mall of Mauritius, the Mall of Mozambique, and the Mall of Zimbabwe."[85] Eyeing this initial growth, international property developers are targeting African cities as untapped markets for expansion of standardized shopping malls.

Architectonics of Entrapment

The design of the ubiquitous shopping mall is an attempt to create a self-enclosed world, and one that can be replicated and recognized all over the world. The architectural and architectonic designs of shopping malls are highly scripted and have been perfected over the decades to encourage, produce, and predict a variety of behaviors, whether purchasing behavior, crowd interaction, or the speed and direction of movement. The many design features of shopping malls have been enhanced and refined over the decades. In the language of the architectural design of the contemporary mall, the "anchor" store is a large tenant store that stabilizes the entire operation and serves as the main attraction. In larger malls, there are typically two or more competing anchor stores strategically placed at opposite ends of the building. In this way, the architectural design of the building assumes control over the flow of movement by encouraging shoppers to traverse the length of the mall between the main anchor stores and directs them to visit other stores along the way.[86]

When escalator and elevator technologies were still at a nascent phase, early shopping center developers did not believe in having a second floor, where they thought people would be less inclined to visit. They considered the possibilities of installing escalators to guide people to shops on different floors, but felt that "this would not pay its way."[87] Since these early days, the installation of escalators has done much to expand the size and appeal of shopping malls, and to further entice the public to engage more regularly in the act of shopping in a comfortable, yet highly orchestrated environment.

Escalators play a central role in the movement of motion through the mall where "free wandering through the space is curtailed, not only by the walker's inability to orient him or herself, but by the secondary role the walker plays; the escalator has become autoreferential, and the individual, rather than choosing a path, is directed along a designated route."[88] Alfred Taubman, an architect of the archetype of the mall illustrates the ways in which the structure of the mall encourages the circulation of shopper: "We put our vertical transportation—the escalators—on the ends, so shoppers have to make the full loop" of the mall.[89] A 1976 shopping mall patent illustrates "the way judicious design can combine with human nature to even out the split of how many shoppers will take" one of two paths, by placing "the 'up' escalator further from the entering shoppers than the 'down' stairs to make the mode of level transfer that calls for more effort easier to reach than the mode that calls for less effort."[90] Thus, mall visitors are architecturally encouraged to take the long way around, since "the more time someone spends in a mall, the more stores they visit and the more things they buy."[91]

Ironically, in the Westgate Mall attack, the location of escalators and other profit-oriented designs of the mall, engineered to keep customers walking for longer, meant that those trying to escape had longer to travel. Similarly, the open atria and the panoptic design of the mall designed for optimum surveillance turned Westgate into a hostage space where people found it hard to escape without being seen as they attempted to escape through the exit routes.[92] In the enclosed and defamiliarized space of Westgate Mall during al-Shabaab's attack, the architecture of the building served its purpose to the fullest as a "customer trap."[93] The Westgate Mall's anchor store, Nakumatt supermarket, became the scene of much carnage during the attacks, and a central site where the two forces of corporate capitalism and terrorism colluded as complementary global agents, both simultaneously attempting to influence and retain mall visitors.

Contemporary mall designs have creatively and strategically devised a number of physical, atmospheric, and psychological procedures and performances to regulate movement, and to ensure that mall corridors are used for constant movement. In addition to looking out for the dangers of terrorism, theft, and unauthorized entry, the "CCTV Operational Requirements Manual" lists "crowd control" as a key public safety concern as well as a way to measure the link between walking speed and "shopping ambition"—faster for the determined shopper, and slower for the casual ambler.[94] The architectural and architectonic design of malls encourage an "optimal" speed at which people should navigate the commercial space; two oppositional types of movement—too slow or too fast—are both discouraged. Coming to a complete standstill in a non-designated rest area, or breaking into a run are flagged by the security apparatus as causes for concern.

Within the world as defined by the mall, stopping in a non-designated rest area is characterized as "loitering" with signs all along mall corridors warning people against this "non-action." The word "loitering" is carefully selected to associate a person who stands still with an underlying sinister intent. In non-designated rest areas, "people staying still are not people circulating money; consumption *is* circulation."[95] In the mall, "complete stasis is not permitted; one cannot simply sit and concentrate but must move through the store, and through the commodities," and "even when stopping to purchase, the consumer is still caught in the movement, but at the level of fiscal circulation." Restaurants and cafes provide rest stops, but ones where items must still be purchased for consumption. Shoe shops, for example, "provide seating insofar as it will be used as a part of the movement of the stores' goods," and the few benches dotted along the aisles of the mall are strategically placed opposite shop fronts, providing only momentary respite for the malls visitor to gather strength for the shopping ahead.[96]

In the contemporary mall environment, even reflective surfaces have been strategically used to ensure that on a slow day, or time of day, a shopping mall feels populated and busy. "Mirrors reproduce and recirculate commodities in stores, but also reproduce the crowd as models for and purchasers of those commodities. Moreover, the crowd itself may be considered as part of the commercial goods, sold to and as commodities. As an attraction to would-be merchants and other mall visitors, the crowd parallels the audience, sold by television executives to advertisers."[97] This is yet another aspect of shopping mall design that was disadvantageous to the victims of the Westgate attack; as they attempted to stay out of view, the multiple reflective surfaces threatened to give them away. A shopping mall's "steel, glass, chrome, plastic, and mirrors serve to double and redouble images of plenitude, adding further to the cornucopian image of abundance."[98] During the Westgate attacks, however, these images of plenitude would have served to multiply representations of terrorists and victims, affecting the sensory perceptions of each as they were looking out for signs of the other. Even if people do take cover during such attacks, and avoid being seen through or mirrored in the many glass and reflective surfaces, the National Counter Terrorism Security Office reports that "many injuries in urban terrorist attacks are caused by flying glass, especially in modern buildings."[99] Mall visitors are advised by the office: "Remember, out of sight does not necessarily mean out of danger, especially if you are not ballistically protected."[100]

In addition to the physical architectural designates of standardized shopping malls, music has also become essential to a mall's overall design and has been acknowledged "as a form of architecture. Rather than simply filling up an empty space, the music becomes part of the consistency of that space. The sound becomes a presence, and as that presence it becomes an essential part of the building's infrastructure."[101] In many ways, the music can be thought of as "another layer of packaging laid over commodities. This packaging contains the real instructions for use—how to *feel* when using the products in the store."[102] The music played in malls is highly orchestrated and is delivered as complementary accompaniments to particular shops and products.[103] Piped music in malls is specifically designed and suited to specific times of the day, to regulate people's movement, as well as a "stimulus progression,"[104] that ultimately aids in the prolongation of shopping. "Programmed music in a mall produces consumption because the music works as an architectural element of a built space devoted to consumerism. A store deploys programmed music as part of a fabricated environment aimed at getting visitors to stay longer and buy more."[105] Underlining the militarization of contemporary consumption, "stimulus progression was invented to combat worker fatigue in weapons plants during World War II, functioning on a principle of maintaining a stable stimulus state in listeners at all times."[106] Experimental stimulus progression of music to help prolong a continuous activity was thus originally conceived on the production side, rather than on the consumption side, of an emerging corporate capitalist industry.[107]

During the Westgate Mall siege, the sound of grenade blasts and gunshots suddenly and acutely disrupted the enclosed orchestrated fantasy of the mall where the "music system kept on playing throughout, interspersed with the shooting."[108] Witnesses reported the eerie displacement created as the music emanating from shops continued to echo in some parts of the mall and as silence descended elsewhere with customers quietly hiding from the roaming al-Shabaab terrorists. Arnold Mwaighacho, a waiter at Urban Gourmet Burgers, recalls how he lay bleeding on the terrace of the restaurant. "He smeared blood across his face and played dead. He prayed and concentrated on the Justin Timberlake song 'Mirrors,' which looped over and over again on the restaurant's sound system."[109] With a "continuous, nuanced, and highly orchestrated flow of music to all its parts," even with so much death and carnage during the attacks, "it is as if a sensorial circulation system keeps the Mall alive."[110] Without the regular Westgate crowd noises to fill the void of the mall's atria and aisles, "the ringing of the unanswered mobile phones of the dead and wounded" was amplified, giving away many of those seeking shelter.[111]

Al-Shabaab's invasion of Westgate's space and ideology defied many of the designated rules set by the mall's design. As people spent hours hiding, and as the terrorists themselves were holed up in the Nakumatt storeroom, "without the circulation of consumers, the space ceases to function as a commercial center; moreover, it loses its dynamism and architectonics are reduced to static architecture."[112] However, even though the terrorists deliberately refused to enter the scripted flow of the mall, and challenged it by producing their own flow—the movement of people running, or being motionless for hours—al-Shabaab inadvertently "agreed to make the mall the space in which they act, and thus help constitute the crowd."[113] Westgate was rearticulated and displaced, but only for a limited period of time—the four days of the attack, and the two years after as the mall was being rebuilt. Westgate Mall now employs an extraordinary security arsenal, is open for business, and defiantly reclaims its original meaning as a spectacle in the center of the city.

Atmospherics of Enchantment

Since shopping malls have become so central to social life, they have acquired the status of "cathedrals of consumption" and often replicate the aura of enchantment by emulating the traditional architecture of churches and places of worship, with such designs as stained glass windows, high ceilings, and arched domes.[114] In many instances, the shopping mall has directly replaced the place of worship as the central focal point of a city's urban planning, a community's attention, and the means by which to guide or control social behavior.[115] In many Western contexts, towns "were defined by either a church or a center of government (depicting the coalition between Church and State in the production of order that characterizes morally based regimes)."[116] In one case, the switch between church and shopping mall is more literal: the Westgate shopping center in Oxford, UK, is currently being built on the site of a thirteenth century medieval church, which lies buried "beneath what is currently the Sainsbury's supermarket."[117] Constructing a mall on the ruins of a historical church is the ultimate embodiment of a cathedral of consumption dedicated to worshiping a consumerist culture.

The merging of worship and commerce has been taken to another level in some countries, where both types of venue have been combined within the same retail space. "The scene may appear an unlikely combination but in the Philippines the Catholic Church has successfully set up shop where millions increasingly spend their leisure time" in the mall.[118] Father Rufino Sescon said that "it was Jesus who went to market places to preach the good news of salvation. We must go where our people are."[119] Other than providing a place of and for worship, shopping malls are now the primary centers of most towns and cities all over the world and are geared to satisfying social and commercial needs, and, increasingly, dedicated to all kinds of entertainment activities.

Since some malls have replaced the traditional communal city center, they provide much more than just a place to shop. The engineering of mall atmospherics has evolved over the course of the modern shopping mall's existence, and is the product of years of marketing research, studies in psychology, architectural scholarship, and security studies, among other targeted disciplines, including demography, political geography, and urban planning, all geared towards the design, as well as the prediction, of consumption practices.[120] All these fields have dedicated research geared towards the optimum functioning of the shopping mall, making it a cross-disciplinary project, and a central concern of contemporary culture. Over the decades, a variety of intricate modifications have been made to the architecture and design of shopping malls, all geared towards calculating and controlling the relationship between product, space, marketing, and purchasing behavior.

Designed to appeal to different gender and age demographics, the contemporary shopping mall can simultaneously appease the various desires and demands of every family member. Over the years, shopping mall developers have added an array of other functions and services, mostly geared towards entertainment but also others that propose to satisfy a variety of practical daily needs. Not only can people expect to purchase most of their groceries, engage in conspicuous consumption, and go about their daily activities, as malls develop in size and scope they are increasingly equipped with a variety of different leisure and entertainment activities.

In 1945, J.C. Nichols identified the relationship between shopping and entertainment by advising mall developers that "recreational types of business can bring a lot of desirable traffic to your center—such as theaters, bowling alleys, and dancing schools."[121] By strategically combining the areas of commerce and recreation over the years, "malls have developed an amazing arsenal of new devices to attract consumers," in what has being labelled "shoppertainment," in order to create a new type of economy based on "experience."[122] The Mall of America, for example, proudly states that Minnesota was "once known mainly as a vacation destination for outdoor activities, tourists now flock to the state for shopping,"[123] thereby directly substituting free, outdoor action with the profit-oriented activities housed within the enclosed world of the mall.

Adding to the contemporary shopping mall experience are cinema complexes, restaurants, gaming arenas, ice rinks, post offices, banks, aquaria, theme parks, sports facilities, hotels, health spas, medical clinics, post offices, live theater venues, and business forums, to name a few amenities.[124] By placing all these facilities under one roof, this "proximity has established an inescapable behavioral link between human needs—for recreation, public life, and social interaction—and the commercial activities of the mall."[125] By creating a continuous actual and conceptual thread between daily practical needs and activities of conspicuous consumption, these different spheres of lived experience imbue each other with associative meaning, and become indelibly associated with the other.[126] Such cross-commodification is also able to "incorporate fantasy, juxtaposing shopping with an intense spectacle of accumulated images and themes that entertain and stimulate and in turn encourage more shopping."[127] Shopping mall designs try to ensure that the act of shopping is not perceived as a chore, but is associated with an enjoyable and recreational activity. After years of experimenting with styles and designs, mall developers and designers have expertly combined shopping and entertainment to satisfy the basic desire-driven elements of contemporary life.

The contemporary shopping mall's compulsion for entertainment can be located in its etymological origins. The word "mall" stems "from obsolete French pallemaille, from Italian pallamaglio, from palla 'ball' + maglio 'mallet,'"[128] and was a sixteenth century game, similar to croquet, where a ball was hit with a wooden hammer through a ring. The word "mall" became shorthand for "an alley used for pall-mall," famously preserved as London's Pall Mall.[129] The word "mall" was subsequently used to label a pedestrian walkway, and is currently most used to describe a contemporary shopping center. Thus, to walk, in the context of the shopping mall, is to shop.

One of the significant features of the contemporary shopping mall concept is its powerful merging of shopping and leisure activities into a single spatial form, and synthesizing activities—once considered disparate—under the rubric of the "commodity form" and spectacle.[130] By expertly blending a variety of retail, culinary, and entertainment activities, the contemporary shopping mall has created an "experience economy,"[131] changing the way people shop.[132] Shopping malls have become "material structures that use symbolism and mass media connections to invoke a consumerist milieu,"[133] cementing the relationship between shopping and entertainment, and promising to promote this commodified "experience" to other areas of life. Increasingly, the merging of entertainment, leisure, and work, by creating a conglomerated and concentrated retail arena with multiple entertainment and commercial outlets is replicated by other corporate, private, and public spaces, including museums, hotels, airports, sports stadia, restaurants, and increasingly in areas once considered far removed from such commodification practices, such as places of education.[134] "This logic of association allows noncommodified values to enhance commodities, but it also imposes the reverse process—previously noncommodfied entities become part of the marketplace. Once this exchange of attributes is absorbed into the already open-ended and indeterminate exchange between commodities and needs, associations can resonate infinitely."[135]

While many popular cultural codes stem from a particular US-centric history and experience, the culture of consumption is being actively encouraged and promoted all over the world, and especially in countries considered to be "modernizing." US-inspired cultural codes are exported to other countries and cultures that appropriate, integrate, and shape them according to their own local forces. This is a type of "cultural language" that is acquired by others. "What they actually say in it is a different story altogether."[136] In this sense, US cultural codes become dissociated from their specific historical grounding, as they become a shared cultural capital available for global consumption. The Kenyan Vision 2030, for example, unabashedly cites Walt Disney as a source of inspiration for the government's infrastructure modernization plans.[137] In this context, Westgate Mall demarcated the boundaries of very different real and imagined worlds. The wealthy elite frequent the controlled environment of the mall as a temporary—air-conditioned—refuge from the surrounding turmoil of Nairobi. The enclosed world of Westgate attempted to "reimagine" the city based on order, and to create a space where identities based on a shopping experience can be shared.

The Spectacle of Consumption:
A Carnival of Contested Identities

True to the tenets of the society of the spectacle,[138] one major South African shopping complex claims to be a "Gateway" from one world into another. No longer referred to as a shopping mall but as a shopping theater, Durban's aptly named "Gateway Theatre of Shopping" is the biggest shopping complex in Africa and the Southern Hemisphere, and openly claims to be formulating a new African consumer identity. Advertising for the complex warns shoppers to "prepare your senses for overload,"[139] as they traverse the threshold between the reality of the developing African urban landscape and the new world provided through the spectacle of consumption in shopping malls.

Especially in the postcolonial context of growing African urbanities, the mall is meant to provide an enclosed and safe space for the bold display and open performance of new "hard-won" modern identities based on new articulations of race, class, and gender relations.[140] In this sense, "the transformation of the mall from a space of goods exchange to a space marked by the consumption of lifestyle, entertainment, and culture has been explained as a change in the way status is socially defined."[141] In such ways, a variety of "cultural and symbolic signifiers are attached to goods so that consumption becomes related to identity and to social stratification."[142] The mechanisms of maintaining the ethos of consumption "involve the constant production of new desires and wants, generated directly through advertisement and more broadly through the culture of material 'affluence.'"[143] The shaping of desires and wants are extended to the public more broadly in which "the suggestive, imaginary reach of the mall brings the expanded global consumptive universe within the reach" of those who, even if they cannot afford the product, can still afford to imagine and to desire.[144] This is a "call of the mall" that instills simultaneous attraction and aversion in the imagination of the poorer populaces of developing nations.

In the post-WWII African context, corporate advertisements began addressing the African consumer as an emerging target market, rather than focusing solely on the European elite.[145] With slogans such as "men of tomorrow," advertisements were not only about stirring desire in this new market, but also about "educating" Africa into conspicuous consumption. A 1955 United Africa Company advertisement titled the "Colonial Customer" attempted to reverse customary divisions of labor and purchasing behavior by highlighting the postcolonial transition from traditional practice to modern consumption patterns. The advertisement depicts a young African woman, and reads: "It is no reflection on her ability that she undertakes no more than the day-to-day shopping for her family. Purchases of capital goods—bicycles, radio sets, sewing machines, cutlery—remain a male responsibility only through custom."[146] Through such rhetoric, advertisements attempted to dismantle traditional gender roles by making everyone the target of the campaign as a potential consumer.

Through constant corrective and suggestive advertising, commodities are tailored to satisfying particular wants or needs, whether actual or manufactured. In such ways, "the mall encourages 'cognitive acquisition' as shoppers mentally acquire commodities by familiarizing themselves with a commodity's actual and imagined qualities. Mentally 'trying on' products teaches shoppers not only what they want and what they can buy, but also, more importantly, what they don't have, and what they therefore need."[147] The act of shopping and the complementary power of the product promises to fill any perceived lack in identity. In the shopping mall, "identity is momentarily stabilized even when the image of a future identity begins to take shape, but the endless variation of objects means that satisfaction always remains just out of reach."[148] The mall, then, is a place of contradiction: the satisfaction of some customer desires through commodity purchase, and the simultaneous awakening of innumerable other wants that cannot be immediately addressed or gratified.

Putting on an act and trying on an identity are framed as positive steps towards creating a shared consumer culture based on global precedents, and a shared language of consumption. This identity formation is not just something that happens in "developing" countries. In order for corporate capitalist culture to be accepted as a normal part of everyday life, people all over the world are recast as "consumers," a label that defines people by a dominant characteristic: their ability to spend. Shopping malls, as self-proclaimed theaters of consumption, openly and actively encourage people to embrace their roles as consumers by performing shopping duties.

Through the architectonics of the enclosed mall and the systematized and optimized lighting, sonic effects, organized shelving, and colorful aisles, commodities come to life and signifiers run wild as they combine, contradict, play, negate, simulate, and stimulate the thousands of desires that are in turn aroused and gratified. Consumption in the shopping mall provides "a playground of subjectivity" where identities can be simultaneously created and dissolved.[149] In these playgrounds and "spaces of consumption are the articulation points of individual psychology, social pressures, the media, fashion, personal desire, the compulsion to buy, forms and structures of material culture, and the realization of group belonging."[150]

In countries where the enclosed shopping mall is a relatively new phenomenon, the contours of the civic-corporate relations defining the mall experience may still be in the process of developing. As postcolonial countries attempt to reconstruct themselves in the shadow of their past dispossession, they must struggle with the "cultural identity (shifting, variegated, and multiple...) of the postcolonial society, caught up in the throes of globalization. The vast majority of developing countries have emerged recently from the incubus of colonialism; both colonialism and globalization have in many ways fractured and distorted their cultural self-perceptions."[151]

Even though mall visitors in developing countries might not all be spending, they are still undergoing an acculturation to the mall environment and becoming familiarized with the ways in which it operates. In Santiago, Chile, many "visit malls but spend little or no money, seeking entertainment or companionship."[152] Similarly, in India, many malls are frequented by people who spend time in the mall, but do not shop. In the space of the mall, everyone is a potential consumer not only of the commodities sold, but of the idea of the mall itself and the cultures of consumption it generates. In these spaces, "consumers must be content to consume the spectacle rather than the products being sold in these malls."[153] Shopping malls, thus become sites where people can "participate vicariously in global modernity rather than fully participate via shopping."[154] In developing countries, the mall is "full of 'neo-cultural' references, which allow the uninitiated to learn a kind of 'know-how' acquired just by being there."[155] Those who cannot afford to spend, can still partake in the outward signifiers of a consumer society, and be educated in conspicuous consumption as an aspiration to a particular lifestyle. They can still enjoy the spectacle of the mall as voyeurs.

Still, there is a delicate balance that must be maintained between the mall and visitors; "when the promised footfall and conversions does not materialize, then the relationship between the retailer and the mall management sours."[156] Ultimately, however, the codes of global corporate culture can only be meaningful to those afforded entrance into the establishment. The more impoverished elements of society are subjected to screenings, and are often barred from entering shopping malls based on the outward signifiers of their appearance.[157] In its promotional efforts, Westgate Mall states that it "attracts a highly cosmopolitan and sophisticated clientele, and reaches a well-defined and attractive demographic audience."[158] Sectors of society whose members lack the very basics are further disadvantaged and barred from reading the signs of modernity, even though it reveals itself to them in all its bold and brash signifiers in the shape of the shopping mall.

Just as malls are theaters for encouraging and displaying consumer identities and public acts of consumption, they are also spaces where counter narratives can also be performed, and where oppositional identities can be enacted. Westgate Mall exhibited similar theatrical features of the typical structure of a shopping mall, where, upon entering the premises, visitors are faced with a large, central, and often empty atrium, heightening the expectancy that "something is just about to be exhibited or performed."[159] The mall became a theater where al-Shabaab staged their drama for local and international audiences, which was further publicized by the local and international media. In this tragic sense, the mall fulfilled its purpose as a space of spectacle. In the spirit of the Bakhtinian carnival,[160] the shopping mall, then, becomes an ambiguous space where identities are performed and contested. As with other forms of contemporary rioting in urban areas, these public performances of social unrest often have a dual, and contradictory, purpose: to destroy symbols of affluence and exclusion, and to simultaneously engage in looting, and thereby in the coveting and consumption of commodities tantalizingly advertised and displayed in shop windows. In these moments of rupture, the mall encompasses a further ambiguous and hybrid relationship between local and global forces, becoming an indeterminate space in which the ideological paradox at the heart of consumption and rejection of consumption is played out.

Since the world of the shopping mall, and its associated cultural references of consumption and spectacle, depends on the imaginary of being a safe and enjoyable space, it must be protected and secured against any alien element threatening to break this illusion. In the current climate of fear induced by the rise in terrorist violence and the intensification of the security apparatus, it has become standard industry practice for shopping malls to offer safety advice on how to react during a terrorist attack, thus diminishing some of the mall's elements of fantasy that have been strategically crafted over the decades. Increasingly, malls and other places of leisure are imbued and viewed with higher levels of trepidation.

The next chapter illustrates how, in their attempt to counter terrorist violence and disruption, advocates of neoliberalism begin an inexorable march towards a social warfare waged against the general public. The war on terrorism has become integrated into the design of the contemporary shopping mall and embedded in its architecture from a commercial venue's conceptual stage. As a result, military industrial war machinery has given way to a military industrial security architecture of which the shopping mall remains the prototype example. Increased acts of international terror, along with a heightened anti-terror response, have also led to the eager deployment of a private security industry and a growing acceptance of its infiltration into public and private spaces. As corporate enterprises enact their own policing, the governance of shopping malls and other businesses begins to take on a different shape—one that abides by its own rules and is no longer beholden to traditional state authorities.

4. Securing the Shopping Mall

When early shopping malls were being conceptualized, the various design elements were mostly geared towards creating some form of communal atmosphere and harmonious continuity between shopping, leisure, and profits. In the contemporary period, the minute elements of standardized shopping mall design have a renewed objective of incorporating the paradigm of security. In response to the prevailing terrorism discourse, anti-terror measures, surveillance, and security have become central to the overall shopping mall architecture and design. Particularly since September 11, 2001, the promotion of the global "war on terror" has meant significant increases in government and corporate spending on the security apparatus in countries all over the world. The mitigation of terrorist activity has become a feature of daily discourse and has been embedded in the very architectural design and atmospherics of public spaces, and especially in shopping malls.

Along with the rise in the number of terror attacks around the world,[1] there has been an increased militant response on the part of authorities—the effect of which is turning cities into spaces with a persistent underlying sense of warfare. Part of this "military urbanism is the paradigmatic shift that renders cities' communal and private spaces, as well as their infrastructure—along with their civilian populations—a source of targets and threats."[2] Along with the seemingly permanent threat against physical spaces, the discourse of war, especially the war on terror, has become "the perpetual and boundless condition of urban societies."[3] Increased fears and security measures work towards instilling notions of war into everyday life and spaces of everyday encounter. Over the years, the security architecture of public space, with particular emphasis on shopping malls, has evolved along the lines of increasing fortification and surveillance in large part driven by increased security concerns.[4]

Since the concept of the shopping mall is presented as a homogenous transnational corporate space, anti-terror responses in one commercial venue become applicable to another, regardless of their specific national contexts. The US army uses al-Shabaab's Westgate Mall attacks as a training case study regarding how terrorist attacks can happen and how to protect against them, noting that "the complexity of four attackers operating in synchronized fashion guided by a central command and control arguably represents the most dangerous scenario should a similar attack occur in the United States."[5] In 2015, "more terrorist attacks have been carried out with Kalashnikov-type assault rifles this year than with any other device. In the 13 November Paris attacks, suicide bombers killed few but gunmen killed many. Further afield, in Tunisia and Kenya, it was also automatic weapons that did the damage."[6] Recent terrorist atrocities have involved small coordinated groups of extremists patrolling the hallways and atria of hotels, malls, and restaurants, causing mass casualties. In the military lexicon these are termed "swarm attacks," and "are high-risk, coordinated assaults sometimes directed against multiple targets or building complexes, using mobile groups to circumvent security measures, allowing attackers to inflict casualties, garner news coverage and, in recent years, to inflict considerable damage prior to neutralization of the assailants."[7]

For all public spaces, government and security agencies offer advice on a variety of protective measures that people can employ depending on the attack scenario, and especially if it involves explosives and other hazardous devices. However, they acknowledge that a weapons assault like the one that occurred at Westgate Mall is difficult to predict, control, or avoid.[8] Westgate Mall's security measures could not forestall al-Shabaab's attack, and the mall's carefully crafted sonic signifiers, architectonics, and systems of circulation designed to control the flow of people were rendered inoperable by the brutal simplicity of the terrorists' use of handheld weapons. Still, the US Federal Bureau of Investigation (FBI) has worked directly with US shopping malls "to test the readiness of SWAT teams by staging fake attacks during hours when malls were closed,"[9] thus using the mall as a space for rehearsal of impending violence. It has become the norm for organizations and large-scale public events to hold regular anti-terrorism rehearsals.[10] Within this context, shopping malls are increasingly subjected to a variety of military technologies, advanced video analytics, and facial recognition systems.[11] Monitoring the mall's population from an unseen and yet all-seeing position, the security apparatus becomes an automated system that not only observes, but also records and retains information for immediate or future use.[12]

The United States, especially, has been keen on influencing international partners, and is active in transferring its own security strategies to governments of developing countries. Since the Westgate Mall attacks, the US government has been instrumental in shaping the security apparatus of Kenya. The US "Department of State's Antiterrorism Assistance program focused on building law enforcement capacities in the areas of border security, investigations, and crisis response, and on the institutionalization of counterterrorism prevention and response capabilities."[13] The Shopping Center Security Terrorism Awareness Training Program offers further courses and trainings developed by the International Council of Shopping Centers and the George Washington University Homeland Security Policy Institute in collaboration with the National Center for Biomedical Research and Training (NCBRT), among other such security-focused programs.[14]

The relationship between the United States and its allies in the war on terror is a strategic one revolving around the central pillars of neoliberal trade and security, and this stance has been adopted by many other supporting institutions. In fighting the war on terror, there has been an increasing affinity between state and private institutions, and business interests are often aligned with government mandates so that "advocates of the neoliberal mindset now occupy positions of considerable influence in education (universities and many "think tanks"), in the media, in corporate board rooms and financial institutions, in key state institutions (treasury departments, central banks), and also in those international institutions such as the International Monetary Fund (IMF) and the World Trade Organization (WTO) that regulate global finance and commerce."[15]

By promoting the same anti-terror stance, combined with a neoliberal ideology, the forces of these various institutions are united in strengthening the anti-terror discourse, and promoting security as an integral feature of public spaces. Under the Nationwide Suspicious Activity Reporting Initiative in the United States, "public attractions such as sports stadiums, amusement parks and shopping malls report suspicious activities to law enforcement agencies."[16] Shopping malls often coordinate with national anti-terror stances and surveillance schemes, such as Operation Lightening in the United Kingdom, which is an intelligence gathering operation that records, researches, investigates, and analyzes suspicious sightings and behavior in public places in order to interrupt or monitor "hostile reconnaissance" missions.[17]

In order to further aid in anti-terror campaigns, private businesses have been encouraged to take matters into their own hands by investing in and employing an entirely private security apparatus. Because the security industry has become such an internationally lucrative venture, the contemporary discourse of terrorism is being actively shaped by terrorism opponents. With the privatization of security, there is an increased tendency towards the militarization of shopping malls as they attempt to enact their own protection and guard against terrorist, and other, threats. At the time of al-Shabaab's attacks, Westgate Mall was regularly guarded by forty private and unarmed security guards who were stationed at various entrances of the building, and who roamed around the mall. Additionally, the mall's banks and casino employed their own armed private security forces. Westgate's overall security mechanism and surveillance systems, like the private security guards, were outsourced to third-party organizations, among them the Securex Agencies private security force.[18] Since al-Shabaab's attack, the number of private security guards in Kenya has shot up to 300,000 "making them the country's biggest private sector employers. A booming trade has also emerged in closed-circuit television (CCTV) and access control systems."[19]

By comparison, although terrorist acts were rampant in the 1970s,[20] a 1978 Burns Security Institute report on security in shopping malls in the United States makes no mention of terrorism, indicating that this particular discursive fixation and its applicability to securing public space is a recent formulation.[21] At one time, shoplifting and fraud were emphasized as the primary security concerns to be guarded against in shopping malls. The 1978 report notes that "no segment of the business community is more susceptible to or provides more opportunities for thievery, fraud and other crimes than retail stores."[22] The crime of shoplifting is followed by other security issues related to loitering and vandalism.[23] Tellingly, not all the malls surveyed in the 1978 report had "contingency plans—written programs that define courses of action in responding to emergencies, accidents and crimes."[24] The lack of a contingency plan is inconceivable in the current climate where the security architecture has become an integral part of commercial structures, and a central concern of most industries. Through the design of early shopping centers a new relationship developed between how the architecture of a commercial establishment influences other areas of commerce, including transformed techniques of marketing and retailing, and a revised relationship between the organization and the customer.

The Architecture of Security

Over years of trial and error, shopping center entrepreneurs developed a series of standard practices regarding architecture and design that are constantly being updated and refined in the contemporary era. In J.C. Nichols' 1945 guide for standard shopping center practice, shopping center pioneers identified a multitude of "mistakes" made when first erecting these venues, and gave advice for optimum design, including standardizing ceiling height, temperature control, store front design, signage size, types of lighting, basement usage, width of sidewalks, and width of parking spaces, down to minute details, including advice that "exterior switches for street floor shops should be provided so a night watchman can turn off and on the lights."[25] These original security suggestions were amended and improved upon over the years leading to a more or less "standard" for the design of the contemporary shopping mall instituted all over the world.

Today, security is architecturally built into the very structure of shopping malls, from the planning and design phase and even before construction, through such paradigms as Crime Prevention through Environmental Design (CPTED), which is "a multi-disciplinary approach to deterring criminal behaviour through environmental design. CPTED strategies rely upon the ability to influence offender decisions that precede criminal acts by affecting the built, social and administrative environment."[26] The stated goal of these principles "is to prevent crime by designing a physical environment that positively influences human behavior. The theory is based on four principles: natural access control, natural surveillance, territoriality, and maintenance."[27]

Intricate features of the security apparatus have become increasingly integrated into the very architecture and design of shopping malls and other business complexes, including the installation of "shatterproof windows and bomb-resistant trash cans."[28] In such ways, inventions intended to bolster war efforts are harnessed for commercial use and enter into the civilian realm. For example, E. R. Weidlein, director of Mellon Institute of Technical Research, proposed that shopping malls should avail of a new liquid being used by the armed forces that "could be applied to show windows and showcases, which enables them to be kept clean for a period of three months by simply rubbing with a dry cloth."[29] Further, the CCTV monitoring systems in place in most shopping malls have their origin in military technology, and utilize "near infrared detection systems that are sensitive to 'light' beyond human vision."[30]

The placing, degree, and type of lighting was once standardized for aesthetic purposes and to add enhanced visual effect to the commodities on offer, but, in the structure of the contemporary mall, lighting has an added duty: it is key to CCTV monitoring and becomes a prerequisite for effective camera capture. In the contemporary shopping mall, intruder alarms, CCTV, and lighting "systems must be integrated so that they work together in an effective and co-ordinated manner."[31] A mall's anti-terror effort further merges aesthetics and security, where "pruning all vegetation and trees, especially near entrances, fence lines and boundaries" are key to the surveillance operation.[32] In the construction of new shopping malls, lighting and CCTV security systems must be installed in tandem to "ensure that appropriate lighting complements the system during daytime and darkness hours."[33] As such, shopping mall developers are advised that "measures you may consider for countering terrorism will also work against other threats, such as theft and burglary. Any extra measures that are considered should integrate wherever possible with existing security."[34] In the same vein, parking spaces in older shopping centers were aligned according to calculable metrics of traffic congestion and average car size. Today, the parking lot must also answer to how it can mitigate terrorist activity. The UK's National Counter Terrorism Security Office advises shopping centers to "keep non-essential vehicles at least 30 metres from your building," as a precautionary measure.[35]

In addition, mall developers capitalize on combining architectural design with security requirements for increased profits. For example, a deliberate lack of seating areas in malls plays a dual role: to keep people moving—and shopping—and to ensure that explosive devices cannot be hidden if furniture is kept to an operational minimum.[36] However, there are instances where the security-conscious policies introduce elements of "irrationality" into the shopping mall setting, including such impractical measures as "avoiding the use of litter bins" to prevent the possibility of terrorists placing explosives within them.[37] In addition, to fully enact security measures behind the scenes, the mall's security apparatus must also promote vigilance as an outward signifier.

Despite these threatening stances, however, the security apparatus of the mall must find a balance between securing and surveying the premises at the same time that it does not disrupt the flow of commerce or inconvenience customers in any way; it must allow shoppers to go about their activates unhindered. A RAND report on terrorism and shopping malls identified potential security measures that can be implemented, but warns that "some of the high-priority security options identified in the analysis are expected to have negative collateral effects that, if great enough, may cause some shoppers to shop elsewhere. On the other hand, were the threat from terrorism to be perceived as increasing, the psychology may be reversed and customers may feel safer in centers with increased security."[38] The report further points out that "screening checkpoints, in particular, could have strong negative collateral impacts if they cause people to wait in line to enter a shopping center."[39] As is evident, within the profit-margin calculus of the private sector business, ensuring the security of customers becomes a question of weighing costs and benefits. "As for more elaborate security improvements, those run into bottom-line resistance. Like all businesses, retail operations have limited dollars. Every mall will be asking itself, 'Do you invest $100,000 in security or do you use it to promote an upcoming sale?'"[40] As such, most shopping malls must balance costs and effects of security measures and check points.

Asymmetrical power relations are increasingly at work in the mall environment, from "minor" to "major" surveillance techniques, whether "voluntarily" through information and communication technologies—credit card data, mobile phone geolocations, personal cameras, and social media updates—or involuntarily through pervasive, and perhaps unseen, private surveillance mechanisms that are turning these venues into latter-day panopticons.[41]

The Panopticon of Shopping: Discipline and Purchase

Similar to how the panoptic design of the prison was used to control the behavior of inmates, so thoroughly examined in Michel Foucault's *Discipline and Punish: The Birth of the Prison*,[42] the panoptic architecture of shopping arenas attempts to induce certain behaviors. The panoptic design was introduced by Jeremy Bentham to the prison system as a means of "efficient" surveillance: a single, central and elevated observation tower could effectively survey the prison in its entirety, without the guards themselves being seen.[43] This suggestion of constant surveillance was a means of controlling and shaping inmates' behavior; they, in turn, internalized and self-administered the disciplining principle.

While the panopticon was perfected in the prison system, it was originally conceived in the workplace as a means of enhancing efficiency according to a "'central inspection principle' which would facilitate the training and supervision of unskilled workers by experienced craftsmen,"[44] and "the atrium construction, with surrounding galleries, had already become an established principle of industrial architecture" of the factory.[45] There are many similarities that can be drawn between the birth of the panoptic prison and that of the shopping mall, where "the genealogy of the penitentiary parallels a broader order of social differentiation and control within society," including the "desire to instill capitalist work habits and ethics on the working classes. Accordingly, the birth of the modern penitentiary was linked to other social mechanisms that ensured the systematic operation and overall success of capitalism."[46]

The surveillance impulse of the panopticon began to permeate other venues, and was being gradually applied to control certain social behaviors. However, as opposed to the panoptic effect on the penal institution, and the proposed rehabilitation of inmates, the private security apparatus's dictation of human behavior in shopping malls is not "the redemptive soul-training of the carceral project,"[47] and is not directed at ensuring or encouraging ethical behavior, but is designed to encourage approved consumerist activities. The purpose of surveillance in shopping arenas is not only to guard against criminal or disruptive acts, but is simultaneously aimed at shaping and disciplining behavior towards the smooth and uninterrupted perpetuation of a consumerist culture.

Since the early days of the department store, the panoptic design and the atmosphere of constant surveillance worked towards influencing buying behavior. It is in the enclosed department store that the first concrete panoptic principles of the contemporary shopping mall can be identified, along with how the architecture of a commercial establishment can be used to influence people's behavior. Those frequenting nineteenth century arcades were advised that "entrance to the galleries is strictly forbidden to anyone who is dirty or to carriers of heavy loads; smoking and spitting are likewise prohibited."[48] A few years on, the open plan of the department store further increased the threat of constant surveillance, and was used to deter shoppers from criminal activity. In the contemporary period, surveillance and security have become integral concerns of architectural design, where counter terrorism efforts are simultaneously used to deter other types of crime and unwelcome behavior. As with most other public or private spaces, panoptic observation stems from the particularities of the built environment, but also via the integral, indispensable, and all-pervasive—and invasive—technologies of surveillance.

The management of shopping mall environments can be seen as a form of "governance,"[49] one that is extended beyond the walls of the mall through a variety of partnerships between the mall and its stakeholders, and the collaboration between the private security industry and a nation's police force. The ultimate goal of mall atmospherics is not only to work towards increasing profits, but to create an enclosed world that abides by its own established rules and principles to be respected with little interference. The surveillance architecture employed in shopping malls is geared towards ensuring that visitors act like "normal" consumers and do what consumers should ideally do: engage in the culture of consumption. Behavior in shopping malls is highly regulated, much more so than in the street or other public places that must often cater to the "abnormal" elements of social life.

This is not to suggest that people who visit malls have no agency, and that they are unwillingly and unwittingly subjected to the mall's circulation of consumption, but that the design of the mall is carefully orchestrated to encourage, if not produce, certain types of purchasing behavior and movement. The mall functions as a world in miniature, and comes with a series of rules and regulations. Within this architectural logic, "to come to the mall with no intention to shop is counter-consumptive and thus makes the non- or anti-consumer a possible target of suspicion, regulation and even expulsion."[50] To this end, the Shopping Center Security Terrorism Awareness Training Program was launched to train security personnel and employees on terrorism awareness and response in which "the first goal in the training program is to recognize people who are acting out of character for a shopping center."[51] Malachy Kavanagh, a spokesperson for International Council of Shopping Centers (ICSC), explains that "everyone acts pretty much the same when shopping... So part of the training teaches people to look for anomalous behavior—who is not acting like a shopper."[52] Within the enclosed world of the shopping mall, there is a tacit agreement between the mall and visitors to engage in certain accepted and agreed upon types of behavior—with such "homogeneity of intention comes safety."[53] Unification of purchasing purpose "is the lulling effect of the mall—you are surrounded only by fellow shoppers, all drawn together in a communion of consumption."[54] The shopping mall becomes "an exemplar of modern private corporate policing,"[55] where control strategies are embedded in both environmental features and structural relations."[56]

In order to familiarize people with the ways in which they should function within the mall,[57] it is common to have normative prescriptions for required behavior, including postings and display notices listing what is deemed to be inappropriate behavior.[58] The following are examples of prohibited actions listed on the Mall of America website:

- Conduct that is disorderly, disruptive or which interferes with or endangers business or guests is prohibited. Such conduct may include running, loud offensive language, spitting, throwing objects, fighting, obscene gestures, gang signs, skating, skateboarding, bicycling etc.
- Intimidating behavior by groups or individuals, loitering; engaging in soliciting; blocking storefronts, hallways, skyways, fire exits or escalators, and walking in groups in such a way as to inconvenience others is prohibited.
- Picketing, demonstrating, soliciting and petitioning are prohibited.
- Guns are banned on these premises.[59]

The list of prohibited behavior in enclosed, privatized spaces may be as detailed as Disneyland's prohibition of anyone—child or adult—walking barefoot.[60] Behavior correction through constant policing can usually induce certain behaviors, but cannot fully predict or guard against the shopping mall's security façade being attacked using brute force, as was the case with Westgate Mall.

The surveillance system of shopping malls has a simultaneous and dual purpose: to watch people at the same time that it watches out for people. Surveillance of criminal activity, potential and actual terrorist attacks, and shopping behavior has been uniformly integrated using the same security apparatus. Subjecting all these activities to the same system of surveillance effectively muddles the distinction between potential criminal activity and shopping as both become subject to a single observant security system. The UK's National Counter Terrorism Office advises shopping malls to ensure that "the CCTV cameras in use for the protective security of your shopping centre [are] integrated with those used to monitor customer movement."[61] In this sense, disciplinary practices are spread evenly across the public, and surveillance once reserved to deter crime is "targeted at those simply *capable* of transgressing social norms and laws."[62] The mall's visitors are observed by the same surveillance apparatus that does not, initially at least, distinguish between shoppers, criminals, and terrorists. In the contemporary language of the security industry, suspicious behavior becomes framed as "activity inconsistent with the nature of the building" that is performed by "the same or *similar* individuals" who might engage in such suspicious bevavior "as staring or quickly looking away," or who might take more significant interest in observing "parking areas, delivery gates, doors and entrances."[63] Other possible suspects are regarded as "people taking pictures—filming—making notes—sketching."[64] Thus, omnipresent surveillance systems becomes justified when any form of behavior that is unrelated to shopping is the subject of suspicion.

In some cases, the surveillance apparatus is the very first concern and is installed before the mall is even constructed. For example, the potential customer can watch Oxford's Westgate shopping centre being built through a "new development webcam, giving you live pictures of progress on site every 20 minutes from 7am to 7pm."[65] Such a benign example of surveillance shows the increasing "blurring distinction between the surveillance and social control practices of the official justice system and those existing in the everyday lives of ordinary people."[66] Here, the potential customer is given the opportunity to be inspector of the mall as it is being constructed. Once the mall is complete, this surveillance relationship will be reversed, and targeted at the customer.

During times when the threat, and anticipation, of terrorism is especially high, the profiling and monitoring of the public are greatly enhanced, and lead to the deployment of extra security measures.[67] In February 2015, a highly publicized threat was issued by al-Shabaab via a video message posted on a variety of social media platforms and circulated by international news networks.[68] In the footage, the terrorists named several international malls, including the Mall of America and London's Westfield shopping center, as forthcoming targets. In response, the Willis Retail Practice, a UK insurance and risk advising organization, released a "Security and Terrorism Guidance for Retailers" stating that "it is important to raise awareness and make sure that everyone (including cleaning, maintenance, contract and concession staff) is vigilant," and, further, that "all staff should be trained in bomb threat handling procedures or have ready access to instructions, such as a bomb threat checklist."[69] By involving all employees in the general surveillance of the mall as well ensuring that they are educated in the technical aspects of explosives—how to deal with bombs and bomb threats and how to evacuate people in emergency situations—the entire labor force of the mall becomes implicated in surveillance and monitoring.

Paradoxically in this case, the staff becomes versed in the accoutrements of terror, and become themselves subject to suspicion. In this regard, to ensure that staff are vigilant of other staff members, the report notes that "some external threats, whether from criminals, terrorists, or competitors seeking a business advantage, may rely upon the cooperation of an 'insider'. This could be an employee, a contractor or an agency staff member who has authorised access to your premises."[70] In the complex web of heightened vigilance, everybody is under surveillance at the same time that everyone is in the service of the surveillance industry. Even the control room where the CCTV footage is monitored and does not escape observation.[71] Such all-pervasive panoptic structures produce a similarly panoptic atmosphere wherein everyone becomes implicated in the elaborate choreography of surveillance, with mall management observing security personnel and employees; security guards observing employees and shoppers; employees observing contractors and shoppers; and shoppers observing each other and simultaneously gazing upon the spectacle of the mall. It is within systems of surveillance that skewed power relations and "information asymmetry" become most apparent,[72] "where one person, group, or organization gains important information about a person and uses it as leverage to modify their behavior."[73] The mall's surveillance structure keeps a constant watch on patrons, even as patrons gaze upon the mall, albeit from different vantage points and within different structures of power.

Within increasingly media-saturated spheres, the difference between technologies of surveillance and personal cameras and mobile technologies is further erased, as all are in the service of recording the surrounding environment. Shoppers are further encouraged to not only watch out for signs of suspicion, but to contact the mall's central security and even to publicly communicate their suspicions through social media.[74] The Mall of America has set up an Enhanced Service Portal—aptly named ESP—

which centralizes its "website; social media channels; telephone, text and dispatch teams; guest services and security into a newly designed space that will allow the ESP team members to actively listen to consumers and retailers and promptly respond to them."[75] In the climate of fear induced by terrorism and the concomitant anti-terror discourse, the "duty" of surveillance is ultimately passed on to the shopper. Additionally, installing security systems is expensive, and "invariably, mall operators pass those costs on to their retail tenants, which then pass them on to the shoppers."[76] The cost of security is also passed on to the customer in many other forms of business. For example, "the Passenger Fee, also known as the September 11 Security Fee, is collected by air carriers from passengers at the time air transportation is purchased."[77] Thus, the general public must simultaneously bear the violent brunt of terrorism as well as the costs associated with marketing anti-terror measures.

Marketing Violence

Technologies of surveillance are used in the mitigation of terrorist activity, but have also been coopted for marketing purposes. Much of market research stems from technologies of surveillance in shopping malls, the results of which are used to track pedestrian and purchasing behavior, with the ultimate goal of increasing sales.[78] Retailers watch video analytics for clues on purchasing behavior, monitor CCTV footage, and analyze credit card data to not only record which products have been bought, when, where, and by whom, but to also predict preferences and future purchasing patterns.[79] In this way, the architecture of the contemporary shopping mall encourages a number of "predatory, often dubious tactics (such as customer tracking devices and focus groups) that allow retailers to sustain consumer demand despite volatile markets and trends."[80] Ultimately, generating profits is the key for any corporation, which must align its overall security operation to ensure the smooth running of the business, and the compliance of its clientele. Thus, it is not only the economically weak, or those exhibiting "abnormal" shopping behaviors, who are subject to the disciplining effects of surveillance. In the shopping mall, those who enjoy economic benefits of the corporate system are especially courted, studied, and observed by the marketing discipline.

Through blanket surveillance activities, mall visitors can be "considered as both potential terrorists and a vast consumer market."[81] Mall visitors are thus treated as both a potential target market to be enticed, and as a potential target threat to be excised. This inherent duality of the term "target market" serves to reveal the underlying violence of marketing activities, even as they attempt to attract custom. In marketing literature, people are recast as objects of study in order to quantify behavior and turn it into data to be used for experimentations geared towards profit maximization. CCTV operations manuals list specific regulations for the monitoring of shopping malls, and, in the hostile language of militarization of public space, refer to the people under surveillance as "targets" and "objects."[82] The marketing discipline displays a combative attitude towards conceptualizing the public, and is awash in symbolic violence. When marketers analyze CCTV footage of people in shopping malls, they engage in "object counting" and "object recognition;" societies are segmented into "target markets;" retail arenas too close to each other engage in "cannibalization;"[83] and in various studies on markets in Africa, and especially in South Africa, populations are segmented according to race, with black populations termed "black markets"—a term that is shared with illegal markets and all the negative connotations this terminology entails.[84]

The synergizing of violence and consumption has long been a feature of the shopping center. An early shopping center developer, J.C. Nichols, experimented with introducing a shooting gallery as a recreational activity in 1945, but admitted that this was a mistake. The idea was abandoned, not because of the shooting gallery's association with violence, but because of the noise.[85] While modern malls might not provide sanctioned shooting galleries, large department stores like Wal-Mart are the United States' prime retailers selling firearms and ammunition to the public.[86] Unsurprisingly, the biggest sale day for firearms in the United States is "Black Friday"—the nationwide sale day after Thanksgiving.[87] As customer fight over discounted products, Black Friday sales have produced a cycle of frenzy in the shopping spectacle and especially in the media spectacle that accompanies—and encourages—the histrionic purchasing behavior. The injurious, and sometimes fatal, rough and tumble violence of Black Friday sales have become normalized incidences, a form of organized chaos, that shoppers and television audiences have come to expect. Testament to the globalizing flows of corporate capital practice, and the increasing connectivities of international markets, while the tradition of Black Friday is specific to the United States, and to the Thanksgiving holidays, it is being introduced to other countries, including the United Kingdom, Brazil, and

India.[88] These countries have adopted the same formula, and conduct the same sales on the same day as the United States, and with it the attempt to garner the same buoyant economic effects.

During such orchestrated special events in shopping malls and other commercial arenas, there is always the possibility of "violence erupting over sneakers or a chance to see a favorite celebrity."[89] Even though there might be serious casualties and consequences emanating from these types of events, they are nonetheless framed as not only acceptable, but are geared towards increased publicity of the corporate capitalist model, and are used to spur the notion of consumption as a most coveted contemporary cultural act. Violence, in this case, is good—the epitome of enacting the ideology of consumption at the expense of others. When it is connected to promoting economic activity and is in service of the capitalist project, violence is endorsed by the structure of the mall and by the ideology of the market.[90]

Surveillance for Terrorism

Just as marketers and mall management study the behavior of shopping mall visitors, and isolate particular characteristics for study to mitigate against terrorist activity or to turn such surveillance data into profit-oriented results, the al-Shabaab terrorists used their knowledge of shopping malls to strike Westgate at a day and time—a Saturday at lunchtime—when they could be guaranteed higher numbers of casualties. In this sense, both marketers and terrorists heed the same industry advice by tracking mall visitors, or "target markets," during times of highest traffic; in the case of marketers, for increased publicity and sales, and, in the case of al-Shabaab, for increased publicity and carnage.[91]

While the growing security industry is indispensable for policing authorities and profitable for private enterprises, many of the same technologies of surveillance used in the war on terror are being simultaneously utilized by terrorists to plan and execute their attacks. For example, "open-source intelligence is readily available via the Internet and with the advent of web-based interactive maps and web-sharing media (e.g., photos of public crowded spaces) terrorists can actually view targets at street level."[92] The al-Shabaab terrorists "had scouted Westgate before the attack,"[93] and, during the assaults, communication and coordination were key features of the operation. CCTV footage of the Westgate Mall attacks show the terrorists communicating, presumably with each other or with others coordinating events from outside the mall, over mobile phones. Similarly, during the 2008 Mumbai terrorist attacks, "authorities were caught off guard in a well-orchestrated assault by commandos with superior firepower and technology."[94] In the Mumbai attacks, emulated by the Westgate terrorists,

> the commandos employed digital technology to conduct preoperational surveillance of the target properties, traversed the Arabian Sea using global positioning systems, quickly located their targets from Google Earth satellite images, and used satellite telephony and voice over Internet protocol to remain in constant contact with their handlers. Instantaneous communication enabled the handlers, watching the events unfold on live television, to alert the commandos to the movements of security forces, thereby prolonging the attack.[95]

In a world in which the corporate capitalist mode of production and consumption defines the structure of everyday life, terrorists cannot but use "business services to advance their operations."[96] In an obvious example of the capitalism/terrorism matrix, the September 11 terrorists purchased airline tickets,[97] but, more profoundly, they also paid fees to rent planes at a flight school.[98] Similarly, the al-Shabaab terrorists premeditated their attacks on Westgate Mall by utilizing a variety of businesses, both legal and illegal, to aid in their operations: they withdrew money from a bank, they rented a car, they purchased mobile phones and activated sim cards, they obtained weapons, ammunitions, and related military-style gear, they surveyed the mall, and they used social media to publicize the attack.[99] In a chilling distillation of this regimen of exchange, at one point during the Westgate Mall attacks, those still alive and hiding behind the meat counter of Nakumatt supermarket were approached by one of the al-Shabaab terrorists. Before killing one of the mall employees, the terrorist asked: "where do we find Safaricom scratch cards?"[100] In addition to intricate pre-planning and use of sophisticated surveillance technologies and strategies, terrorists must also engage in everyday acts of consumption to aid in the execution of atrocities.

Shaping Employee Behavior

Constant policing is not just about mitigating crime and controlling customer behavior. Since power is productive, as Foucault has argued,[101] surveillance systems in malls are designed to be much more than instruments of repression.[102] Those who work within the mall are especially subjected to the watchful gaze. The disciplining structure of the mall places employees under constant observation in an attempt to modify their behavior according to the particular needs of the institution. Efficiency is high on the list of desirable characteristics, which in turn is translated into greater productivity, predictability, and, ultimately, higher profits for the operation.[103]

Shoprite Holdings, a South African retail multinational, is a major investor bringing shopping malls to countries all over Africa, and with them a new sense of business ethos and integration into the global capitalist economy. In the shopping malls of developing countries, "working in this 'space of consumption' puts the employee in the midst of this promise of modernity."[104] A study of Shoprite employees in Zambia examines how their tailored uniforms serve to distinguish them from the poverty of their surroundings. "Unlike the dreary smokestack environs of the factory worker, the mall employees' labour power is consumed under glamorised conditions."[105] The uniforms set Shoprite workers apart as privileged members of a global capitalist culture that extends beyond Zambia, and into a shared global consumer culture.

Similarly, during the Westgate Mall attacks, the uniforms of the Nakumatt supermarket staff served to distinguish them as mall employees and to set them apart from the terrorists. The Kenyan security forces entered the mall with little information about what was happening on the ground—much of which was distorted by the corporate news media networks reporting an inflated number of attackers. Since "there were just a lot of men without badges or any other identification waving guns in different corners of the mall,"[106] it was difficult to know who was a civilian and who was a terrorist. Emerging from their hiding place behind the meat counter, Nakumatt supermarket staff, Edwin Omoding, Daniel Mwongela, and Jared Odhiambo, drew attention to their uniforms for the security forces to see that they served the shopping mall and not the terrorists.[107]

Many allegiances to Westgate Mall, however, were short-lived during the attacks, with security guards abandoning their posts and refusing to engage any further in protecting the mall. Private Kenyan security guards do not always have weapons, body armor, or portable radios,[108] and whatever safety mechanisms were in place during al-Shabaab's attacks—guard force, bomb screenings, CCTV system—proved to be mostly cosmetic. The only confrontation the terrorists faced "was from a policeman guarding a bank on the first floor who had fired, wounding Sudani [one of the al-Shabaab terrorists] in the lower right leg, leaving him limping."[109] While security service corporations are some of the fastest growing and lucrative enterprises, security guards themselves are often poorly paid and, in many cases, come from poorer neighborhoods to work in upscale shopping malls and other private complexes. Maurice Adembesa Ombisa, a security guard who died during the Westgate attack, commuted to the mall from the Kawangware slum. Similar to many other "private security guards in Nairobi, Ombisa worked 12-hour shifts, six days a week for the minimum wage of 10,912 shillings ($123 [per month])—without overtime or sick pay. It was a thankless job that ultimately cost him his life."[110]

Especially in the context of developing countries, even though shopping mall workers are employed in a highly consumer-driven environment, many cannot themselves afford to engage in acts of conspicuous consumption. As mall employees are promised entry into a consumer culture, their uniforms simultaneously discipline them into corporate-approved behaviors and salaries. "The suggestive, imaginary reach of the mall brings the expanded global consumptive universe within the reach of the retail worker. Any perceived or real deprivation due to wage levels is thrown into sharp relief when working in such commodity havens."[111] Even though retail employees share the space of the mall, they are often excluded as consumers.[112]

The Westgate atrocities highlighted the disjuncture between the world presented by the mall and the engulfing environment of poverty and political struggle that define much of Kenya and neighboring Somalia.[113] Kenyan "police officers are badly paid (about $200 a month) and often deeply corrupt. There is no 911 to call, and even if there were, it might not have mattered ... because most officers do not have cars."[114] A lack of training for government forces meant that there was a total lack of coordination and communication between the Kenyan army and SWAT teams who entered Westgate three and a half hours after the attacks began. When they did arrive, they began shooting at civilians as well as at each other.[115] The Kenyan military and the Kenyan police also shot at each other across the corridors, killing a police officer, and wounding two more, in what official reports stated were acts of "friendly fire."[116] It is within the shopping mall and the sharp divisions of the urban environment that "the relations of capital, technology, labor, and the unequal distribution of wealth engender ... conflict,"[117] such as we have seen in the case of Westgate Mall located within the rift of the affluent Westlands neighborhood and surrounding slums.

These complex socioeconomic backgrounds give more context to why, in the aftermath of the Westgate siege, CCTV footage showed several Kenyan soldiers stealing merchandise, and exiting the mall with plastic bags full of goods.[118] Ultimately, what was captured by the recorded footage served to reveal much more about the attacks than the simple binaries of victims and terrorists, and terrorists and authorities. The recordings revealed the many complexities that existed within the space of the mall, including the simultaneous abundance of privilege and poverty, the disillusion of the mall's capitalist imaginary, and the ambiguous fidelities of the privately hired security apparatus and state authorities.

Within the panopticon of the shopping mall, behavior is under constant surveillance and control. The security apparatus becomes absorbed and integrated into the mall's architecture along with the omnipresent CCTV surveillance systems, which, at times, feeds into the wider media. During the Westgate Mall attacks, there was a wealth of footage captured via the CCTV surveillance system, from wide-shot crowd control angles to high definition close-ups of events on the ground.[119] Before al-Shabaab struck the mall, the CCTV footage broadcast on corporate news networks revealed that the cameras were in a "monitor" position, where people could be observed, at some distance, going about their activities. As the attacks commenced, news networks broadcast footage from camera angles that moved into an "identify" setting, where the al-Shabaab terrorists were given close-up treatment as they fully embodied their central role for the cameras as protagonists of the Westgate Mall drama. By analyzing the video footage, it is clear that the CCTV operators followed the surveillance guidelines prescribed by the official CCTV operation requirements manuals.

Ultimately, the Westgate Mall attacks were presented to international audiences "through the mass media in video imagery that has become the primary source of our cultural knowledge."[120] The next chapter examines how both state authorities and terrorists use media to broadcast their messages, with an emphasis on "the spectacle of terrorism."[121] The Westgate Mall tragedy illustrates the degree to which contemporary terrorist organizations compete with mainstream media for a market share of the promotion and publicity of terror attacks. Even as al-Shabaab broke the "commercial contract" of the shopping mall by disturbing the consumption patterns therein, their actions served to disrupt only the particular, localized capitalist node of the shopping mall. Outside Westgate, the commodification of terror, the deployment of media networks, and the stimulation of the security industry meant that the wider capitalist structure went into overdrive, compensating for the shopping mall's temporary financial loss.

5. Spectacles of the Shopping Mall

Over the four days of al-Shabaab's Westgate Mall attacks, the movements of the terrorists and their victims were captured on a multitude of recording devices, including by over 100 CCTV cameras, and scores of personal phone cameras, and news cameras. Audiences all over the world watched as corporate media networks competed for minute-by-minute scoops, as al-Shabaab announced the success of the operation on their social media sites,[1] and as government forces entered into the fray, also claiming victory.[2] International audiences watched as the mall became a microcosm for the intersection of international terrorism, corporate news networks, and the military-industrial complex, as each attempted to grapple with the events and take control of the emerging narrative. All these elements coalesced, turning the tragedy into one of the most viewed—and sustained—media spectacles of recent times, with footage being constantly broadcast over the four days of the attack, and for some time after.

In addition to inflicting mass casualties, with the increasing availability of, and access to, information and communication technologies, even poorly-equipped and poorly-funded terrorist organizations can produce media "spectacles" to publicize their ideological messages. Through the media, terrorists wield a power that "is judged not by their actual numbers or violent accomplishments, but by the effect these have on their audience."[3] The casualties resulting from the 2008 Mumbai attacks, the 2013 Westgate Mall attacks, and the 2015 Paris attacks were able to have detrimental effects on international publics, even though these atrocities were perpetrated by a small group of terrorists. The shock of such terrorist spectacles reverberates through corporate media networks as well as through a variety of social media channels.[4] If communication is considered to be at the heart of human activity, then extremist communication is no exception, and terrorist attacks can be read as acts of political communication. These ideological conflicts are taking place as much in the media as they are on the ground, and, in this sense, "terrorism *is* communication and, as such, is really aimed at the people watching."[5]

The pervasiveness of mobile technology, social media connectivity, and corporate media network competition meant that the Westgate Mall attacks were inevitably turned into a global media spectacle that served both the terrorists, whose message was circulated around the world, and media networks, which were provided audiences and advertising revenues.[6] Because of this interdependence, "the relationship between media and terrorists is often described as a 'symbiosis.'"[7] Corporate news networks compete for audience share often by broadcasting sensationalist information, with terrorist acts providing a steady stream of content—especially for 24 hour news networks. In a perverse paradigmatic shift, "news organizations supply terrorists access to their audiences in exchange for the right to publish information about events that will entice consumers to purchase their products."[8] Similarly, terrorist organizations make full use of information and communication technologies to connect with each other, with other international networks, and, to communicate their various messages to authorities and international audiences. Modern terrorist networks understand the need to create synergies with international news organizations in order for their message to be picked up and disseminated further across media platforms. This has become a relationship of mutual interdependence "since both terrorists and news organizations benefit when information about terrorist attacks is turned into the commodity of news."[9]

Increasingly, the conditions in which news media and entertainment media operate are aligning, especially in cases where the same parent corporation owns both news channels and entertainment channels.[10] Such sharing of business plans and content strategies means that previously unique areas of media are being integrated, making their products similar in style and substance.[11] The fierce competition between media networks is largely a result of the structures in which they operate and the many commercial pressures they face. In order to streamline the operations of media conglomerates, "many top media executives today come from the corporate world, and no longer from the ranks of journalists. They are less sensitive to the quality and truthfulness of pictures. In their eyes, the market for information, the news business, is first and foremost a means of making profits."[12] The ways in which corporate news networks choose to cover tragic events, such as terrorist attacks, are often "formulated to prolong the salience and news-worthiness of the event. This is done, in part, by frame-changing the evolving news story and by raising controversial issues."[13] Entertainment and "news formats, or the way of selecting, organizing, and presenting information, shape audience assumptions and preferences for certain kinds of information,"[14] and the ways in which news is packaged and presented influences the way audiences are expected to think about an event. It is becoming standard practice for media networks to turn stories into protracted dramas in which "violence is not something to be condemned but to be appropriated,"[15] a key feature of how the Westgate Mall attacks were represented by news networks all over the world.

While the proliferation of alternative sources of information may be regarded as more inclusive, and even more democratic, they remain largely unaccountable to the notion of media ethics. As news media rush to broadcast their latest findings regarding a media-saturated event, they often release not only unverified information, but sensitive pieces of information—ones that could ultimately have consequences for the victims and their families, as well as impacts on steering police operations and terrorist actions in such situations. In many instances, reporters attempting to cover the active Westgate Mall attacks interfered with or influenced police operations. Outside the mall, crowds of reporters gathered and shared a variety of information, footage, and photos, regarding the whereabouts of Kenyan security forces, which may have "endanger[ed] the lives of the responders, and might have contributed to the prolonged siege, as the terrorists received live information detailing the armed response against them and were able to use this information to enhance their response."[16]

Similarly, the media's compromising of victims occurred during the Hyper Cacher supermarket siege in Paris in 2015. A number of media networks, including 24-hour news channel BFMTV, delivered a live broadcast during the siege revealing the location of six people who were hiding in the supermarket's cold room, and endangered their lives in the process. As a result, in the aftermath of the events, victims and their families resorted to suing these channels, arguing that "the working methods of media in real time in this type of situation were tantamount to goading someone to commit a crime."[17] Similarly, in the aftermath of the Westgate Mall attacks, the Media Council of Kenya released a report criticizing media coverage of the events, stating "that journalists, in their bid to report from the scene, breached the Code of Ethics by publishing graphic pictures of the dead and injured."[18] The Media Council further found that the Kenyan media failed in its duties of informing the public, and made no attempts to give a "historical, cultural and social explanation of terrorism and instead focused on [the] dramatic, most violent, bizarre, tantalising and brutal accounts of the attack magnifying the impact of their horrifying brutality."[19] In an attempt to call for unity in the face of public anger and confusion, the Kenyan government promoted the Twitter hashtag "we are one," which was subsequently subverted into "we are wondering" when no official reports were forthcoming in the aftermath of the attacks.[20] To date, there is still no definitive official report that comprehensively explains the details of the Westgate Mall atrocities.

Digital Media and the Globalization of Terror

The reach of international terrorists extends into new parts of the world with the expansion of globalization processes, the proliferation of information and communication technologies, and extremists' access to these media tools. Terrorists are "no longer geographically constrained within a particular territory, or politically or financially dependent on a particular state, they rely on technologically modern forms of communication" to create global communities and connections.[21] In this sense, terrorism, is "one side of a globalized modernity made possible by advanced technology, geographical mobility, open flows of communication, and the breaking down of territorial divisions."[22]

With the help of media networks, terrorists broadcast their unprecedented efforts at producing content, creating a cache of media texts.[23] Al-Shabaab is adept at digital communication, and delivers its message through a variety of media, including a radio station, Radio Andalus, with presentations and programs delivered in the English language, and its media center, the al-Kataib Foundation for Media Production, regularly produces high quality films and documentaries that are fluent in the visual grammar and cultural codes of professional media texts.[24] In today's media saturated environment, terrorist organizations use the internet as the primary form of communication to release their messages to the world, whether to eager subscribers, to oppositional authorities, or to horrified publics. During the Westgate Mall attacks, al-Shabaab's media, and especially its social media accounts, were operating at full force with multiple and constant communications over the four-day siege.[25] The terrorist group live-tweeted "258 times between September 21 and September 25"[26] in order to claim direct responsibility for the attack, referring to it as the "Westgate spectacle."[27] This was the first time that a terrorist group used Twitter to make such an announcement.[28]

In the aftermath of al-Qaeda's September 11, 2001 attacks, terrorism supporters had to seek out specific clandestine websites in order to express their solidarity, and the terrorist group was beholden to traditional and mainstream media for the global dissemination and recognition of its messages. The form and structure of traditional mass media, including television and newspapers, meant that stories and footage needed to be verified by researchers and fact checkers at these networks. For a story to be publicized largely depended on editors and network owners, and whether they dared to engage in unverified sensationalization, or whether they upheld strict gatekeeping media principles of informing and educating the public. In the early 2000s, al-Qaeda was obliged to fax statements to corporate news networks with a hope that they would be noticed and circulated publicly.[29] Even though some networks responded, other broadcasters were able to simply ignore the extremist message, making it more difficult for supporters to access these pronouncements.[30] In many ways, while traditional media forms still reported on terrorist activities, they served to withhold the circulation of terrorist messages.

With increased accessibility and ubiquity of digital media networks, "social media has changed the dynamic fundamentally. It has eliminated the terrorists' dependency on mainstream media, reversing the relationship by making mainstream media dependent on" terrorist media content.[31] Making full use of information and communication technologies, "terrorists have direct control over the content of their messages by constructing and operating their own websites and online forums, effectively eliminating the 'selection threshold.'"[32] With the advent of digital media networks, all information and communication technology users, whether terrorist or otherwise, gain new controls over the dissemination of their own messages and publicize their own news without having to wait for the necessary permissions from editors and network owners. Those afforded the technological means are able to gain access to international audiences through digital technologies which, in many ways, are "designed to account for the entry of nonstate actors into the fields of war and diplomacy and to describe how information works as a weapon within this extensive field of combat."[33] Social media platforms offer open access to the public domain and allow for extremist ideologies to be shared with audiences beyond specific support groups of like-minded people. Terrorist ideologies, and "messages posted to social networking sites reach audiences immediately, and are extremely easy to access and redistribute, exponentially multiplying their audience."[34] Where once media was defined by gatekeepers, it is now beset by gatecrashers.

Through digital communication technologies, terrorists and their supporters are able to engage with other audiences on a number of fronts, where the "internet contributes to several activities of terrorist groups, such as fundraising, networking, and coordination, as well as information gathering."[35] Terrorists are able to communicate their messages, to engage in their own research regarding best practices on their violent activities, to educate others in their ideologies, and to build radical global communities of like-minded people.[36] The rise of online extremist activity correlates directly with the rise of digital global networks and access to these technologies. In 1998, there was a total of fifteen officially defined terrorist organizations that had some kind of online presence. In 2005, extremist related online sites mushroomed to over 4,000.[37] Most terrorist organizations use a multitude of digital technologies and are active on a number of media channels, including Facebook, Twitter, Whatsapp, YouTube, Google Earth, etc.[38] In 2014, the Islamic State terrorist organization even managed to create an Arabic-language Twitter app, translated into English as "The Dawn of Glad Tidings," which posted tweets directly from the group's account to users' personal accounts after soliciting their personal information.[39] The app was seemingly straightforwardly uploaded to Google Play, the official application store for Android mobile devices, and was instantly and easily downloaded by many of the terrorist group's supporters.[40] It was used to channel "40,000 tweets in one day as ISIS marched into the northern Iraqi city of Mosul," making the story "trend" due to the large and sustained volume of online traffic.[41] The application has since been removed by Google.[42] Communication through digital media has become the norm for people all over the world, provided they have access to the means of communication, and terrorist groups are no exception.[43]

Extremists are especially active on the internet as various digital platforms provide the requisite anonymity for their messages to be publicly dispersed, and also shelters these actors from the reach of authorities as they are able to better obscure their identities and locations.[44] The ability to operate multiple accounts is an integral feature of contemporary social media platforms allowing anyone with access and ability to operate numerous accounts with a high degree of anonymity. When and if an account is reported and shut down, this causes only a temporary disruption, and users are able to easily open alternative accounts. During the Westgate attacks, for example, al-Shabaab used five different Twitter handles.[45] Any time one of these was taken down and made inactive, news media "reporters received an email from the group's press office informing them that they could now follow" a new Twitter handle.[46]

At times when there is an ongoing investigation of suspected terrorist activities, authorities and network owners will deliberately keep these social media platforms and accounts open in order to better monitor the online messages and to gather information regarding the identity and locations of those communicating.[47] Consequently, in many instances, those policing terror and opposing terrorist ideology are "liking," "friending," and "following" known terrorists' Facebook and Twitter accounts, and adding to the audience and follower numbers of extremists. At one point, one of al-Shabaab's Twitter accounts boasted more than 15,000 followers, including journalists and terrorism analysts.[48] Thus, the anonymity afforded by digital media platforms has served to complicate discernable divides between terrorists, their supporters, policing authorities, and inquisitive members of the public.

Information technologies have allowed for both terrorists and antiterrorists to communicate back and forth with each other on a regular basis. Since waging war on the battlefield of the media has become a paramount concern for counter-insurgency operations, government efforts have been targeted at online message battles and promoting a direct counter-narrative to terrorist ideologies. At one time, the traditional stance of authorities was to not deal with terrorists in any way. However, this denial of communication, or even acknowledgement of terrorist messages, is unsustainable in the age of digital communication, significantly changing the paradigm. The US State Department has even created the Center for Strategic Counterterrorism Communications (CSCC), which is a government unit dedicated to communicating with terrorist supporters in an effort to counter their ideologies with alternative messages.[49] In the age of digital media, there has been a crucial transformation in the stance of authorities, with communication at the heart of the contemporary anti-terror strategy.

In order to speak directly to all these disparate audiences, terrorist networks have taken to communicating in a variety of different languages, with an emphasis on English. In this way, terrorists respond to the contemporary tenets of globalization, and especially the global culture promoted by Western power holders. Communication in English belies two different trends. The first is that, since modern terrorist networks are made up of a collection of foreign fighters hailing from a variety of different countries and linguistic backgrounds, English then becomes the common language of communication for these disparate group of actors. The second is that the audiences of terrorist messages, whether willing or unwilling, are also global, and so many of the "official" and centralized terrorist communication channels use English as a unified narrative trend. The Islamic State's Al Hayat Media Center, for example, "is specifically aimed at non-Arabic speakers, particularly younger viewers, and its output is closer to mainstream broadcast standards than" that of any other terrorist group.[50] Similarly, al-Qaeda publishes an English language online magazine called *Inspire*, and factions of the Taliban post English language retorts online with the aim of communicating a message to international audiences and to speak directly to Western authorities.[51]

During the Westgate Mall attacks, al-Shabaab released a barrage of social media messages, mostly in English, with the aim of connecting with, and appealing to, an international audience.[52] During the attacks, many of the messages and tweets emanating from al-Shabaab's social media accounts showed a sophisticated use of the English language with phrases such as "reap the bitter fruits of your harvest,"[53] and "#Westgate: a 14-hour standoff relayed in 1400 rounds of bullets and 140 characters of vengeance."[54] The widespread use of English on social media channels is interesting insofar as it complicates the normative figure of the terrorist—once largely defined as a provincial, regressive other—who now appears more global, connected, and educated, and thus more difficult to define.[55]

Social Media and Personal Narratives

Especially during times of upheaval and unrest, and in emergency situations, reporting on active events, including live reporting on platforms such as Twitter, has become a common feature of online news gathering and dissemination. Most recently, Twitter has proved its importance as the source of breaking news, rather than just an optimal medium for reporting breaking news, in what is termed "real time." During the Westgate Mall attacks, Twitter emerged as the main social media accompaniment to the tragedy, and its specific method of communication suited the needs of many of those involved.[56] Twitter was key to relaying short, rapid messages from inside and outside the mall, and, importantly, was the chief communication platform used simultaneously by the terrorists and their supporters, the victims and their families, the local public, the news media, government officials, and international audiences.

Because social media channels allow for a fast and efficient means of communicating news, people from outside and inside the mall were the first to raise the alarm about the unfolding tragedy, with many commenting on the sound of gunshots and explosions. The first public alert that something was amiss at Westgate Mall was relayed through Twitter within minutes of the first explosions by someone from outside the mall at 12:38 pm, a few minutes after al-Shabaab launched the attack.[57] In quick succession, the next few tweets came from people within the mall, directly experiencing the attacks, followed by a barrage of tweets exchanging queries, concerns, fears, prayers, and other snippets of information—both true and false.[58] These user-generated exchanges of information created a matrix of questions and answers regarding events on the ground, and established narratives of the attacks long before the Kenyan authorities and the news media became involved.

During the first few hours of the Westgate Mall attack, it became apparent that not only was there little coordination between the Kenyan security forces on the ground, there was also poor coordination between them on digital communication platforms. The Kenya Police and Kenya Military were new to the platform having "joined Twitter less than ten days prior to the attack,"[59] and many of the government departments were not connected to each other, leading the Ministry of Interior to publicly ask the Kenya Military account to "follow" it back on the second day of the siege. These disorganized attempts at communicating through the platform prompted Twitter itself to ask Kenyan government units to verify their accounts.[60] The National Disaster Operations Centre (NDOC Kenya) was the first government body to tweet about the Westgate attacks at 1:05 pm, and "the first (local) media house to tweet about the incident was K24 TV at 1.11 PM, 33 minutes and 17 seconds after the first tweet."[61] This was followed by a tweet from an international news organization, Associated Press, at 1:15 pm.[62] Thus, ordinary people were the first in the chain of communication to break the news about what was happening at Westgate Mall, followed by a government unit, then confirmed by a local news network, and, finally, circulated by an international news organization.

After the news about al-Shabaab's Westgate Mall attack became public and was broadcast on local and international news channels the story gained worldwide momentum, and social media channels were abuzz with multiple messages posted by those hiding in the mall, along with those posted by al-Shabaab and their networks in Somalia and abroad, government authorities, emergency responders, and the general publics in Kenya and abroad. Westgate Mall became a site for the production, consumption, and commodification of terror, where corporate news networks, extremists, and government authorities all competed for control of the public story. There was an extraordinary array of messages volleyed back and forth from a variety of perspectives, arguing from a diversity of ideologies, pleading for prayers, asking for assistance, accusing, justifying, boasting, gloating, and informing—and misinforming.

With over 67,849 tweets posted over the four-day attack, the chaotic multiplicity of voices, opinions, and information relayed through Twitter made it increasingly difficult for authorities, terrorists, witnesses, and news networks to maintain a coherent narrative.[63] The PSCU Digital Kenya Twitter account, the official communications channel of the Kenyan Government, tried and failed to control the flow of information, tweeting: "We are appealing to Media to avoid showing photos of our @kdfinfo soldiers. Kindly, Only tweet what you are absolutely sure about #Westgate."[64] In another tweet, "the Kenya Police asked a Twitter user to delete a message that contained pictures of military helicopters preparing to launch an attack on the mall,"[65] and the Kenyan Disaster Operation Center contacted a news channel asking it to delete a story. Through these failed attempts at controlling information, it becomes apparent that in the sphere of digital communication "censorship and regulation are alien to the nature of social media,"[66] and unverified stories receive the same circulation and publicity as official pronouncements, further eroding the concept of media gatekeeping.

Despite the Kenyan government's attempts at separating fact from fiction, it too was guilty of releasing a great deal of false information.[67] Many of the news items released, even though false, were capitalized upon by anti-terror authorities at home and abroad, and were used to align with wider political interests and foreign policy concerns, especially in the formation of the global narrative of the "war on terror." For example, in the aftermath of the attacks, there was an immediate backlash against Somali refugees in Kenya, with the Joint Committee on Administration and National Security, and Defence and Foreign Relations recommending that the Dadaab and Kakuma Refugee Camps "be closed and resident refugees repatriated to their country of origin."[68] The Westgate Mall attacks became a blank slate upon which a multitude of fears were projected. Some of the unsubstantiated information relayed by witnesses, the media, and government sources, included: there were ten to fifteen terrorists; the attackers took hostages and tortured them; one of the terrorists dropped his gun, changed his clothes, and slipped into the crowd of people escaping the mall; and that the terrorists were a coalition of Somalis, Kenyans, and Arabs, led by a white woman.[69] Even Interpol became embroiled in the circling of misinformation and "issued an international arrest notice for Samantha Lewthwaite, a British woman who is the widow of one of four London suicide bombers."[70] When news of Lewthwaite's implication was created through false social media stories and on news networks, it was al-Shabaab who later made the correction, tweeting: "We have an adequate number of young men who are fully committed & we do not employ our sisters in such military operations #Westgate."[71] Thus, through social media platforms, terrorists are afforded the opportunity to directly oppose official pronouncements with their own personal narratives.

Information and communication technologies allow for users to generate their own narratives and social realities, and these same privileges are extended to terrorist organizations and their supporters. Through a variety of online communication platforms and social media campaigns, terrorists "can directly share their positions—on their own terms and in their own words—to shape media coverage of their actions,"[72] even as they perform heinous acts. During the Westgate Mall attacks, al-Shabaab's tweets repeatedly attempted to justify their actions by constantly referring to atrocities perpetrated by Kenyan troops in Somalia. They also attempted to highlight themselves as protagonists taking center stage in the Westgate Mall story by live-tweeting the events,[73] and by announcing a series of heroic justifications, including: "The Mujahideen entered #Westgate Mall today at around noon and are still inside the mall, fighting the #Kenyan Kuffar inside [sic] their own turf."[74] The term "Mujahideen," meaning holy warriors in Arabic, was used repeatedly in al-Shabaab's online postings to imbue the Westgate gunmen with a heroic status. In another tweet posted on one of al-Shabaab's accounts, the attackers were further hailed as "Westgate Warriors."[75] The seminal phrase coined by Jenkins in 1974 that "terrorism is theater" has never sounded louder than in the contemporary media-saturated environment, where extremists have positioned themselves as protagonists in their own mediated dramas.[76] During the Westgate attacks, al-Shabaab said as much, tweeting that "the mesmeric performance by the #Westgate Warriors was undoubtedly gripping, but despair not folks, that was just the premiere of Act 1."[77]

Commodification of Terror and Media Productions

As with most ideological battles, narrative construction and opposition take center stage, and play out in a variety of available media and digital platforms. Modern terrorist identities are created through a multitude of different media platforms, including self-produced films, social media campaigns, applications, and videogames. Much extremist video footage is expertly filmed, edited, and distributed, and shows a sophisticated understanding of the medium of film, including the use of dramatic license and synchronization of music and image. One al-Qaeda supporter, Younis Tsouli, identifies as "Irhabi007,"[78] meaning Terrorist 007 in Arabic, in order to endow himself with elements of spy thrillers and movie culture. Despite terrorists' outspoken disavowal of the corruptions of Western culture, the connection between popular cultural artifacts such as movies and videogames and terrorist activity can be read in many of their online narratives, and terrorists are fluent in the language of media texts.

In the contemporary era, it has become the norm for terrorists to record themselves before an attack in order to validate their actions and to leave behind a record in the form of an autobiography. In the age of digitally-enabled international terrorism, audiences are key to the action, and have become privy to viewing an event from a variety of different angles. Advances in digital technology and ubiquitous CCTV footage has meant that audiences are not only able to witness footage from "within" a terrorist attack, but often footage that is recorded by the perpetrators themselves as they commit their atrocities. For example, French extremist Mehdi Nemmouche used a GoPro-style camera when he killed four people at the Brussels Jewish Museum in 2014,[79] as did Mohamed Merah who recorded "a series of attacks in which he killed seven people" in 2012.[80] Following the trend, during the attack on the Hyper Cacher supermarket in Paris in

2015, Amédy Coulibaly wore a GoPro camera as he took hostages. Audiences confronted with a terrorist's first-person point of view footage, are obliged to, willingly or unwillingly, become part of the spectacle. Producing subjective-view footage, terrorists simultaneously shoot weapons and camera footage, while those watching become the simulated shooter, seeing what the attacker sees and doing what the attacker does—techniques normally employed in videogames.

Such comparisons between terrorist activities and video game content have become a discursive norm. In first-person-shooter videogames "conflict is experienced from an embodied, subjective viewpoint, rather than from the detached overhead view that is common in other types of games. The simulation of embodiment connects players to a character and encourages them to identify with the character's experiences and motives."[81] The structure of a videogame has even been utilized in terrorist recruitment and training methods whereby in some clandestine operations recruits are required to pass "through a series of tests in password protected websites and restricted chat rooms before [being] accepted and joining the terrorist group."[82] Abu Sumayyah Al-Britani, a British fighter for the Islamic State, describes the act of shooting as being: "better than, what's that game called, Call of Duty? It's like that, but really, you know, 3D. You can see everything's happening in front of you."[83] Thus, everyday cultural practices and videogame enthusiasm and proficiency can then be used in the enactment of violence outside of the mediated text.

Through mediated communication, and especially through cultural texts, both terrorists and anti-terrorists communicate in a shared language based on similar cultural media codes. The US government similarly uses entertainment products to bridge the gap between real and symbolic violence with appeals to mainstream commercial media forms. Films and videogames "work like advertisements for the military lifestyle, interpellating players into a military mind-set and turning them into 'virtual citizen-soldiers,' ready to accept the legitimacy of hard power and willing to apply it to virtually any social problem."[84] The US government produces its own videogames, including the US Army's *America's Army* and the US Marines' *Full Spectrum Warrior*. These games "allow players to slay terrorists in fictionalized and Orientalized cities in frameworks based directly on those of the US military's own training systems."[85] In these forms of popular entertainment, the distinction is blurred "between virtual entertainment and remote killing,"[86] and to make these games more appealing "control panels for the latest US weapons systems—such as the latest control stations for the pilots of armed Predator drones [...] now imitate the consoles of PlayStations, which are, after all, very familiar to recruits."[87] Both the terror and the anti-terror stances justify their particular forms of mediated violence and encourage the dissemination of these texts across media platforms. In this sense, "the spectacularization of fear and the increasing militarization of everyday life have become the principal cultural experiences shaping identities, values, and social relations"[88] where the "threat of terrorism and violent crime provides the state with the legitimating power to increase its security and militaristic directions."[89]

The war on terror has been actively promoted as a communication and military strategy in a variety of cultural texts serving to "position militarism at the center of public policy and social life."[90] In many ways, such Western media efforts "only seem to be providing more raw material for Isis's image library. Hollywood has even been accused of setting the tone, with its dark, doomsday scenarios, not to mention its own expensive recruitment films, from Top Gun to Transformers, made with the cooperation (and conditional approval) of the US military."[91] Similarly, the US Department of State often overlays its own anti-terror messages edited with violent extremist footage, creating a hybrid collage of terrorist brutality, including "gruesome images of beheadings and executions."[92] The US Department of State's Twitter site, Think AgainTurn Away, regularly "links to Isis-related news stories" to highlight their depravity, but in doing so also gives the terrorist group further publicity. This strategy only helps to normalize violence, and anti-terror media efforts often engage in the creation, circulation, and consumption of terrorist violence. For example, when the Islamic State released a recruitment video using snippets of the *Grand Theft Auto* videogame, the US Department of State parodied this very same footage with their own anti-terror message that reads: "Don't let Isis be your controller!" Over time, "Isis supporters have parodied Think AgainTurn Away's parodies. It becomes a hall of mirrors."[93] Since "the spectacle of terrorism trades in moral absolutes whether it makes such claims in the name of religion or human rights,"[94] representations of violence in the media escalates as each side of the war on terror rationalizes its actions even as they produce more violent media content.

Previously, one of the key differences between how this violence was represented on both sides of the divide was typically through the art direction and choice of camera angles: messy, blood-splattered close-up shots of death favored by extremists, versus clean and detached wide shots favored by state authorities, and often delivered by technologies of distance such as drones and satellites.[95] This distinction is gradually changing, and corporate media networks are increasingly pandering to more violent depictions of terrorist events. In a world defined by ideologies of globalized economic liberalization, the ideational forces of marketization and commodification shape value systems and extend "beyond the commercial realm into other spheres of human society,"[96] and media coverage of atrocity is no exception. In such ways, "as image-based technologies have redefined the relationship between the ethical, political and aesthetic, they are largely used to service the soft war of consumerism and the hard war of militarism."[97] The ideological dovetailing between the state and cultural industries can be seen most acutely during times of conflict, when it becomes especially pertinent to construct particular ideological allegiances and to counter others. The communication strategy wherein the state appeals to the expertise and persuasive skills of the entertainment industry has been prevalent since the early twentieth century. "American military propaganda was transformed during World War II when Hollywood directors went to work for the government and injected a sense of drama into documentary formats. The Why We Fight series, in particular, is well known for its rousing tone, appeals to the emotions, and, above all, its Walt Disney animation sequences."[98] Today, the war on terror is being "mediated through an overwhelming array of visual forms and media, including photography, sculpture, painting, film, television, advertisements, cartoons, graphic novels, video games, and the Internet."[99] The formal articulation of terrorism has, in many ways, been propagated as much by the counter-narratives of the media and government authorities as it has by acts of terror.

The discourse of terrorism is propagated from multiple angles and players, including the terrorists who enact violence in public space; the militarized response that engages in counter violence; the security apparatus that locates, observes, and monitors; the corporate news and social media networks that circulate and sensationalize; and the authorities that capitalize on terrorism for creation of policy and deployment of retaliatory action at home and abroad. The narrative of terrorism is being fed by the input of all these actors and activities, and, with the aid of information and communication technologies, "is constantly retold and re-evoked by wider audiences."[100] As the US enacts such tactical operations as "Burnishing the Steel,"[101] audiences all over the world have grown accustomed to a seemingly unending cycle of mediated violence, obtrusive surveillance of public and private spaces, intensified militarization of spaces of consumption, and increased commodification of terror. Although the militarism of everyday spaces since September 11, 2001 has been most actively promoted by the United States, the powerful anti-terror discourse has become global in its reach and influence.

Through mediated cultural texts, the parallels between corporate capitalism and terrorism can be read most acutely at the symbolic level and in many of the images and recorded footage that emerges during global tragic events. "While the merging of terror, violence, and screen culture has a long history, a new type of spectacle—the spectacle of terrorism— has emerged in the post-9/11 world, inaugurated by the video images of the hijacked planes crashing into the World Trade Center,"[102] and all the subsequent cultural texts these images engendered. Nowhere was the intersection of corporate capitalism and terrorism more symbolically manifest than in the spectacle of terror produced on September 11, 2001, which, as has been mentioned countless times, "looked like a disaster film."[103] Because most international audiences experience terrorist atrocities through the media, a common initial reaction to the brutal images and footage emanating from disastrous situations is to associate them with the fiction of film.[104] Moreover, during major contemporary terror spectacles, news media networks provide all the hallmarks of a film production, and expertly provide and set up cameras, personnel, sets, newsrooms, editing suites, pundits, reviews, interviews, and audiences. In similar fashion to the highly orchestrated visual culture of terrorism produced in the wake of September 11, 2001, footage of al-Shabaab's Westgate Mall attacks was repetitively circulated in a steady stream of images that were instantly consumed by audiences struggling to understand the sudden penetration of violence into the predictable everyday backdrop of a city central urban commercial venue.[105]

The confined space of Westgate Mall provided a camera-ready action set for al-Shabaab's attacks, and became a microcosm for the filmed action viewed through the lenses of hundreds of cameras, beamed into the centralized command station of a remote security office, and then via media networks. During the attacks, there was an extraordinary amount of footage recorded by "more than 100 security cameras inside the mall, video from television crews and modest cellphones, as well as still photographs."[106] Audiences watching the tragic scenes unfold on the news were presented with the precise moment when shoppers, only a few minutes ago engaged in all kinds of commercial activities, were transformed into frightened captives attempting to escape from view.[107] With omnipresent CCTV security cameras, not much could escape being recorded, and the architecture of the typical mall designed as an open, panoptic space worked against those trying desperately to avoid detection.

The CCTV cameras rolled for most of the first day of the attacks like a reality television show in which audiences all around the world were taken inside the mall to watch what was happening on the ground.[108] News organizations released streams of video from the multiple security cameras and from personal cameras, capturing much of the rampage, including victims being killed or others hiding in the private areas reserved for staff and not normally traversed by mall visitors: in ventilation shafts, toilets, stairwells, and storerooms. The cameras also recorded the more quiet moments taking place "behind the scenes" when the attackers seemingly decided to no longer pursue any more victims, and to take refuge in the Nakumatt supermarket's storeroom. The security cameras recorded several hours of the attackers' actions, including relaxing and temporarily putting down their weapons, tending to one of their wounded accomplices, eating and drinking, taking turns to pray on a mat on the ground, and audio-free hours in which the perpetrators idled while waiting to be confronted by government forces.[109]

The acute juxtaposition of extreme violence and the everyday colorful commercial products and advertising billboards of the shopping mall presents some of the most memorably shocking images to emerge from the Westgate massacre. After the attacks, Reuters photographer Goran Tomasevic described the scenes at Westgate Mall as a warzone, and that although he had "been stationed in Syria during the worst of their devastating civil war, not to mention Libya, Kosovo, and Afghanistan," Tomasevic said "the massacre in the upscale mall was still more shocking."[110] Instead of the generic placeless familiarity and predictability of the commercial surroundings, Westgate Mall became imbued with the signifiers of war ricocheting through its fantasy-laden corridors.

The atrocities, combined with the ways in which the public and the international news media covered the events, produced powerfully evocative images that transformed the ordinary and everyday space of the mall into a defamiliarized world where the boundaries of reality became increasingly blurred. There is a surreal quality to much of the footage and many of the photos that emerged from the attacks, and an acute contrast between the world of the real—frightened and injured people cowering in the aisles of the mall—and the pristine world created by the surrounding corporate culture—aisles filled with colorful products and advertisements featuring smiling, happy people.[111] In an image of the Westgate attacks reminiscent of a horror film poster, it is difficult to untangle reality and fantasy wherein a body lies in a pool of blood directly under a macabre advertisement for a Halloween event due to take place at the mall the following week.[112] Highlighting the symbolic capitalism/terrorism nexus are further images of the wounded and dead being pushed out of the mall in shopping trolleys, themselves now ironically a "product" of the mall and of the massacre. The striking effect that is produced during these atrocities is the manner in which these images defamiliarize and confuse a peaceful, casual, or sunny setting with the extreme violence that has occurred. With the help of information and communication technologies, never have international audiences been presented with such a plethora of imageries of violence creeping into their everyday lives.

Except, international audiences *have* been presented with violent imagery in the media, but in different circumstantial settings and with different effects—as entertainment or news that does not elicit the same audience or government reaction. Such an intersection of different forms of violence is exemplified by an image in which armed Kenyan soldiers crouch at the entrance of Westgate Mall cinema and are framed by a poster of the film *Elysium*,[113] making it hard to separate the terrorism-induced theater from the corporate entertainment theater and the sanitized violence packaged as a blockbuster film. As the Kenyan soldiers are pictured during their disorganized rescue attempt, they are overseen by a gun-toting Matt Damon, and the unwavering certainty of commodified corporate culture. In this cinematic representation of warfare, the Hollywood hero is likely to be successful, translating into the victory of corporate cultural hegemony. French philosopher Jean Baudrillard reminds us that even though the Vietnam War signaled a colossal moral and tactical loss, the United States was able to not only recoup, but to achieve success in the many films made subsequently and to be victorious at the box office.[114]

Two days into the siege, Kenyan security forces detonated a rocket-propelled grenade, effectively destroying the mall, shutting down the power, and wiping out the camera feeds.[115] Without a complete visual reference from which to construct a narrative of events, what could not be seen on screen either did not exist as part of the Westgate Mall attacks narrative, or could not be verified—especially since witness testimonies, news reports, and government statements were often contradictory and even false.[116] By sifting through recorded footage gathered through CCTV surveillance, news networks, and personal mobile cameras, one can begin attempting to piece together how the events unfolded. However, even then, the story of the Westgate Mall attacks, like any film, can only be represented as fragmentary and refractory, and its interpretation subject to edits and camera angles. To date, a documentary film titled *Terror at the Mall* contains one of the most comprehensive collections of footage and images that emerged from the attacks, and includes a variety of witness interviews. The director, Dan Reed, and his team sifted through more than 2,000 hours of footage, witness testimonies, and "information that none of the investigating authorities had reached."[117] One of the survivors of al-Shabaab's attack notes "that the film offered the first true depiction of what had happened that afternoon in Nairobi, a story that was muddled and meddled with by [sic] conflicting reports coming from media, government, and foreign intelligence agencies."[118]

Not to be outdone by official media networks in the aftermath of the Westgate Mall attack, al-Shabaab's own dedicated media unit, al-Kataib Foundation for Media Production, released a feature-length film titled *The Westgate Siege: Retributive Justice*, which was "distributed on Twitter on February 21, 2015 in two versions: one in Arabic and another in English."[119] Information and communication technologies have thus enabled terrorists to not only present their own propaganda and versions of events, but to do so in a highly professional and packaged way and to compete with official media networks. Additionally, with the prevailing capitalist forces encircling Westgate Mall, it is unsurprising that the tragedy was commodified almost immediately after the attacks, with street hawkers in Nairobi touting "different movies depicting the attack and hundreds of copies were sold on the first day they became available."[120] One of these documentaries was titled *Terror Attack at Westgate*. It "has little in the way of a plot or commentary, [and] was manufactured by a group called Titanic Videos,"[121] an organization that pirated the MGM lion logo as part of its branding.

The wealth of visual material and the abundance of recordings that emerged from the Westgate attacks were used by the various sides of the war on terror, as well as by opportunistic others, in their efforts to condemn, congratulate, or profit from the atrocities. The fluid combination of different types of commodities and marketing activities within the same space of the shopping mall suspends and decontextualizes the normative and discursive differences between capitalism and terrorism, imbuing them with attributes of other objects strategically placed around them so as to create a complementary and commerce-driven continuous narrative. The next chapter concludes with an examination of how the constant threat of terrorism has been similarly commodified in the form of the ubiquitous security apparatus. Under the rubric of neoliberal practice, terrorist activities are rendered profitable for both terrorists and those opposing them.

6. Conclusion: Specters of the Shopping Mall

"Westgate is back, shoppers said with their shillings."[1]

Spectacular and contemporary architectural symbols of modernity—whether skyscrapers or shopping malls—that have been scarred by terrorist attacks or that are considered likely targets are infused with a curious mix of exhilaration and fear. Affected venues are defiantly reconstructed or injected with renewed fervor and people are encouraged to visit or revisit these spaces as a way to defy terrorist ideologies. In the hope of returning to these everyday places of work and leisure a semblance of the normal, people are persuaded to enter these specter-filled city central sites, but they do so in the knowledge of the history of violence that has befallen these spaces and are troubled by the possibility of future attacks. These public venues "become places 'in terror,'" and the surveillance apparatus and security services deployed to protect them do "not alleviate this terror in place, but rather re-assert it."[2] While such fears may be overcome with time, "terror is inscribed upon places" and "produces and reflects a kind of cultural neurosis."[3] The constant reminders of past and potential violence are issued by both terrorists aiming to instill public fears, by authorities striving to win the war on terror, and by private interests attempting to profit from the security industry.[4]

Westgate Mall has now been "reconstructed using government funds as a symbol of the resilience of Kenya's capitalist path."[5] This is testament to how shopping malls, and the act of shopping, continue to be politicized, and how consumer cultures are being actively promoted through the combined efforts of government and private interests. The new Westgate Mall cannot afford another terrorist attack and so economic and ideological differentiation and exclusion policies will be more forcibly enacted, further feeding many foundational problems and exacerbating the grievances voiced against such private developments. As expected, the reconstructed Westgate Mall has invested heavily in a more robust security architecture by installing "x-ray machines, explosive detectors and bullet-proof guard towers,"[6] and by complying and collaborating with international anti-terrorism standards and organizations.[7] In the aftermath of the attacks, "IRG, the Israeli security company hired in 2014, insists that with its overhaul, Westgate is the safest mall in Nairobi today. Managing Director Haim Cohen's team of ex-Israeli commandos has trained the mall's security personnel assiduously."[8] This new security-minded environment of the shopping mall requires "a geography of fortifications and enclosures; increasing demand for spatial and social insulation; and reliance on technologies of security, control, and surveillance."[9] While these increased security measures may work towards mitigating against future terrorist attacks, they simultaneously work towards the exclusion of many other kinds of activities and people considered undesirable to the commercial world of the shopping mall.

In order for the military-industrial complex to continue being profitable, terrorism is a constant threat and is perpetuated as such. In this regard, terrorism is good for business and keeps the security industry buoyed as it continues to construct ever more impregnable structures that require constant improvement by both security agents and security technologies. In an ultimate form of exchange that is exemplary of market forces, the fear of future attacks encourages people to trade their civil liberties for increasingly pervasive forms of security, and all the panoptic invasions these entail. Investing in the security mindset promotes both a culture of vulnerability as well as "a belief that personal security can be purchased; that with the right accessories, [people] can make themselves impervious to foreign threats."[10]

Since al-Shabaab's 2013 Westgate Mall attack, the number of private security guards in Kenya has swelled "and there are now about 300,000 employed by some 429 private security firms—vastly outnumbering Kenya's police force of 60,000."[11] These security features have been extended from the shopping mall into other areas of public life, and the Kenyan government is working with telecommunications company Safaricom "to lay out a national surveillance programme, including the installation of tamper-proof CCTV cameras in most major streets in Nairobi and Mombasa. While such projects might trigger an outcry about privacy, in Kenya reaction has largely been muted, driven in part by shock over al-Shabaab's tactics."[12] Terror and the war on terror provoke a state of permanent fear among international publics, each achieving its specific objects by capitalizing on the same discourse. Promoted through the constant media focus, people encounter a normalized and entrenched daily narrative "that is inextricably tied to the spectacle of terrorism and the move toward a state of emergency."[13]

As the dust settles over Westgate Mall, other large-scale developments are being constructed within the ever expanding influence of capitalist acquisition to offer far more than Westgate ever did in terms of commodities, entertainment, services, and security. One of these, "Migaa—a 20-minute drive from the rubble of the Westgate shopping centre in Nairobi, Kenya—is a new development complete with a private hospital, conference centre, 'shop till you drop' mall facilities and a 200-acre executive golf course."[14] In addition are a variety of other mixed-use complexes springing up all over Nairobi, including Garden City and The HUB.[15] A few miles down the road from Westgate Mall, the Two Rivers Development is billed as "the largest lifestyle centre within Sub Saharan Africa, outside of South Africa,"[16] and features "$10m in security technology, which has become a major concern for shoppers following the 2013 Westgate mall attack."[17] The new incarnations rising from Westgate Mall's ashes are self-enclosed mega developments guarded ever more closely by an all pervasive—and invasive—security apparatus.

Privatizing Public Space

In a series of hybrid private-public partnerships, and by instituting their own private security apparatus, corporate private spaces are no longer under the control of, and in many ways no longer answerable to, local authorities. In many cases, "by resorting to private methods of order maintenance rather than relying on assistance from the police, property owners… ensure that policing strategies within their territories complement their profit-maximisation objectives."[18] Privatized spaces, from shopping malls and mixed-use complexes have "been removed from the hands of the local authority, and hence the public domain."[19] While the commercial property itself is often privately funded and financed, the public services around it in terms of public transport hubs and surrounding roads are often government- or publicly-funded. Once people cross the private property threshold of the shopping mall, they become consumers governed by the rules and regulations of the mall. Contemporary shopping malls are architecturally designed to create a reality that operates according to the logic of capitalism—one that can sideline the practicalities of the outside world.

Paradoxically, shopping malls are insular worlds that deliberately distance themselves from prevailing economic, political, and social challenges, even as they respond to the dominant anti-terror discourse in order to strengthen their security apparatus. The critical analysis of shopping malls serves to highlight the increasingly fractured meaning of the "political." While malls do not tolerate disruptive forms of political behavior, they revel in other overtly "political" displays of patriotism, especially during times of crisis and as a response to terrorist activity. The active politicization of shopping enacted by governments and businesses is despite the fact that the typical shopping mall expressly prohibits any form of challenging political activities like protests and worker strikes. The mall is simultaneously politicized and depoliticized depending on the prevailing discourse. Within the world of the shopping mall, both terrorist strikes and labor strikes are equally prohibited. Thus, within the space of the shopping mall, the very notion of the "political" is being rearticulated by private interests: to spend money is framed as political, but to protest low wages is a subversive breach of mall regulations.

Most shopping malls have a strict policy of barring any form of overt political behavior despite the fact that, in some cases, malls may provide government services such as the "City Hall in the Mall" office in Florida's Coral Springs mall, which provides passport services and fingerprinting.[20] In the case of the Mall of America, "although parts were designed to mimic Main Street and it benefited from public financing when built,"[21] it was officially designated as private property in the 1999 Wicklund case when animal-rights activists protesting the sale of fur-coat were declared trespassers.[22] In 2014, this designation was challenged by around 3,000 "Black Lives Matter" protestors who targeted the Mall of America for protest and disrupted the busy Christmas shopping period to highlight racial injustice.[23] The organizers of the protest argued that the mall occupied an ambiguous space between public and private, giving people the right to protest there.

People are likely to regard a mall as a public space if they are obliged to visit these arenas to engage in a variety of necessary daily activities such as government services, health checks, and postal services. The strategic veering between public and private activities and facilities only serves to make further opaque the relationship between government and private interests and to further complicate the public's relationship to shopping malls. The mall provides a space for social life, and the satisfaction of daily needs, but within a very narrowly defined sense of community. Its gravitational pull is fashioned from its own unique form of community engagement predicated on commercial rather than social or political ideals. As shopping malls purport to offer everything under one roof, the conflict between private and public is accentuated.[24] While the mall promises *the* world, it delivers *a* world—one that is shaped and dictated by specific market forces at the expense of other social needs.

Social Contract vs. Commercial Contract

Along with the reconstruction of Westgate Mall in the aftermath of al-Shabaab's attack, there have been simultaneous calls for the demolition of the neighboring Deep Sea slum in order to rid the city center of the visual pollution of poverty and to clear the way for a new road project termed the "missing link,"[25] a name that symbolically highlights its evolutionary imperative in the context of a modernizing Kenya. The development is funded by the European Union—an entity that has distanced itself from any human rights issues resulting from the project, with representatives from the EU stating "that their role was limited to financing and supervising the road construction and that responsibility for any eviction and resettlement lay with the Kenyan government."[26] For such modernization projects to be realized there is a basic violence, actual and symbolic, that must be enacted. Such acts of "creative destruction" are argued to be necessary to fulfill a nation's economic visions of urban expansion in which reforms are "accelerated in order to create a better environment for doing business."[27]

In their attempts to modernize and fit into a new liberalized global economy, developing nations are undergoing a series of urban growth schemes that are highly profitable for some, while they are decidedly dismissive of others—especially those who are unable to share in the new economic ideology. The poor and the disenfranchised figure little in these grand economic plans. As urban planners and corporate enterprises capitalize on middle-class fears of urban crime, cities are being reoriented according to the dictates of the security industry, with increasingly enclosed and gated urban complexes comprised of "mixed-use" facilities complete with shopping malls, offices, hotels, and recreation centers. As such complexes are increasing in number and size they are being connected by private walkways and roads linking these islands of tranquility at the same time as they are being separated from more chaotic urban areas, further eroding the notion of public space, and increasing hostilities against them.[28] In this sense, the new shopping malls do not pretend to represent public spaces; "these privately owned emporia encourage discreet forms of economic exclusion and social regimentation. As entertainment and tourist landscapes, they are open only to those who can pay."[29] Increased private takeover of public spaces and resources has become especially active in the aftermath of terrorist activity and in the name of security.

In many instances, governments in developing countries are only too happy to be released from the responsibility—and with it the accountability—of providing for their citizenries and are eager to pass on any developmental and infrastructure requirements to private interests.[30] If a government is unable "to provide the requisite infrastructure for a growing population, it is no surprise that private developers have stepped in."[31] With the liberalization of markets, crucial urban infrastructures and government functions are then necessarily privatized to come under the purview of profit-making corporations. The result, in many cases, is that people become "progressively unable to question corporate influence, challenge public officials, or engage in political dissent."[32] With the reformulation of the government's social contract into a private economic contract, public services, like transportation and sanitation, once considered the responsibility of the state, are only provided for those who can afford to pay for them. Because many people pay high fees in order to live in gated communities, they expect that the privately managed housing estates will furnish them with a range of basic services, such as street maintenance and garbage collection. In these private spaces, "paying high fees, in effect taxes, in their local communities, members of these communities are apt to vote against new taxes that support the needs of the larger society."[33]

As national interests become privatized under corporate control, these must abide by whatever particular corporate laws govern space and behavior, including particular types of taxation and legislation.[34] The government's relinquishing of responsibility and "the partial retreat of public authorities from the provision of collective consumption has left the people's everyday necessities to either the whim of private capital, the reach of the NGOs, or the mercy of charitable institutions."[35] Since the idea of "development" is often heavily skewed towards "economic" development rather than any other form of social development, preferential treatment is given to investors, and various funds previously aimed at aid have instead been injected into the capitalist infrastructure. In Kenya, for example, "millions of pounds of British aid money to tackle poverty overseas has been invested in builders of gated communities, shopping centres and luxury property in poor countries" such as the CDC, formerly the Commonwealth Development Corporation.[36] Projects include such developments as Nairobi's Garden City, which will be home to east Africa's largest shopping mall.[37] Even as the rhetoric of corporate social responsibility revolves around the power of enterprise to solve poverty issues, businesses blame governments for the conditions of the poor, arguing that "stronger government intervention is required."[38] As the government moves aside for corporations to take over provisions in the wealthier neighborhoods, slums and other impoverished districts of developing countries are neglected by both private *and* government interests.

The poor are often expected to fend for themselves, and many do so by organizing "self-help" schemes and engaging in informal markets or illicit activities. However, "by criminalizing every attempt by the poor...to use public space for survival purposes, law-enforcement agencies have abolished the last informal safety-net separating misery from catastrophe."[39] The development vacuum left by corporate and government disinterest is quickly filled by terrorist organizations, who attempt to gain legitimacy through provision of some basic services such as ad hoc healthcare, sanitation, and education schemes—the hallmarks of communal governance.[40] Within Somalia, although largely disorganized and inconsistent, al-Shabaab has established "a range of administrative bodies that are far more effective than those of the Somali National Government and its predecessors."[41] Within this socioeconomic context, and since a link can be established "between urban poverty and terrorism, the best strategy to limit the power of militant groups to seduce recruits is to fight poverty."[42] The question of who should help alleviate conditions for the poor is tossed back and forth between the government, civil society organizations, and the market.

Escape from the Mall

The structures of malls are increasingly fortified by a panoptic security apparatus in order to keep the money flowing within the walls of the mall, and in order to keep out the undesirable and disruptive elements of modern society.[43] Increasingly, the contemporary shopping mall "epitomises this carceral city,"[44] and especially in places considered to be dangerous—unsurprisingly often found in many developing nations where there is a sharp divide between affluence and impoverishment—shopping malls ward off external threats by employing a deliberately threatening security apparatus that is intentionally visible, and theatrically exhibits security sensors and metal detectors at entrances, and guards brandishing batons, and guns in some cases. In order to guard against violence, shopping malls must themselves exhibit the outward signifiers of violence. In poorer neighborhoods, shopping malls are designed with security in mind from their conceptual stages, and according to the logic of the panopticon.[45] In this sense, the shopping mall and the prison share a common bond in many aspects of their design, and especially in the ideology of their architecture as a disciplining force.[46]

Similarities between the prison and the shopping mall are exemplified by how easily one can be morphed into the other with little reconstructive design necessary for the conversion. The Headquarters shopping center in San Diego, for example, was developed "to capitalize on the former headquarters of the San Diego Police Department."[47] The mall still retains "a prominent 68-foot tall watch tower," and original "fortress-like design."[48] When the building still housed the police department, it was already moving towards an all-encompassing mall-like concept, and so required only minor modification into its current form. Before its conversion into a shopping mall, the "state-of-the-art facility brought all police operations together under one roof; administration, courts, jails, law library, crime lab, exercise areas, vehicle maintenance, and even a pistol range. In later years the headquarters even had a four-lane bowling alley, utilizing jail inmates as pinsetters."[49] Today, the mall's website reminds visitors to "explore our fully restored 8 cell jail block which houses historic photos and police memorabilia. Also, don't forget to snap a photo at our lineup wall. Jail cell block is located in between Kitson and Madison San Diego,"[50] two of the retail stores in the mall.

Similarly, the Uruguayan Punta Carretas Penitentiary, once a notorious emblem of the historical atrocities and political grievances of a military dictatorship, exemplifies the expert rehabilitation of a prison into a shopping mall. The prison, originally built in 1895 to incarcerate mostly political prisoners was transformed into a shopping mall in 1994 with few modifications to its main architectural and panoptic elements.[51] Like Westgate Mall, and the socioeconomic pitfalls that surround it, Punta Carretas "is located in one of Montevideos's most coveted residential locations."[52] The rising real estate cost of the area was key to the government's decision to sell the land to developers, which ultimately rested on the fact that the prison was not a profit-making enterprise.

Not only was Punta Carretas Penitentiary unprofitable, the prison was unsuccessful at incarcerating inmates: in 1971, there was a mass outbreak of 111 prisoners, earning the escape a Guinness World Record.[53] Of these, 106 were political prisoners, members of the urban guerrilla group, Tupamaros, "notorious for Robin Hood-esque economic redistribution stunts."[54] Many of these ex-prisoners are still living in the area and are encouraged, through the persuasive gravitational pull of the mall, to visit the 215 stores replacing their former cells.[55] While the prisoners may have escaped the penal institution, they are increasingly engulfed by the corporate capitalist institution of the shopping mall overtaking the neighborhood.

In a deliberate act of erasing Punta Carretas's past, "there are no tour guides or plaques to inform the 1.2 million visitors each month of the mall's turbulent past."[56] Its developer, Mario J. Garbarino, noted: "We prefer not to identify ourselves with the prison, although we did maintain some of its architectural elements." The developer's elision of history is a deliberate choice in order to "associate the mall with freedom." [57] The word "freedom" in this instance is one associated with the "right" to shop. The developer continues by noting: "We have turned a prison into a space of complete freedom"—provided, of course, one buys into this particular phantasmagorical notion of freedom promoted through the shopping mall, through consumption, and through erasure of a traumatic past.[58] While the physical abuse of detainees in the building may be a thing of the past, arguably, the psychological conditioning and the carceral effect have only been enhanced through the premeditated structure—and stricture—of the captivating and panoptic shopping mall environment.

Similarly, the newly reconstructed Westgate Mall, in its promotion of an ahistorical and ageographic space, is built upon the ruins of its former scarred self, and knowingly erases its troubled history of al-Shabaab's terrorist violence. Since there is still no definitive government report on the details of al-Shabaab's 2013 Westgate Mall attack, Patrick Gathara, a satirical cartoonist for Kenya's *The Daily Nation* newspaper notes that "by rebuilding the mall, we are covering over everything that we don't know... It's a symbol of our continued and deliberate ignorance."[59] This act of elision has been extended into Westgate Mall's marketing efforts with no mention of the terrorist attack in any of its social media accounts or public profiles. Even as Westgate Mall refrains from mentioning the atrocities, the memory of the attack is instilled in the new security apparatus constructed within the mall and the surrounding areas. Urban spaces scarred by terrorist attacks "both represent and avoid this trauma, enabling a play of remembering and forgetting,"[60] depending on how useful the memory is to fulfilling a particular political or commercial agenda. Thus, al-Shabaab's attacks are remembered when it comes to extra enforcement of security, but people are persuaded to forget when the mall attempts to encourage people to shop within it. The atemporal and ageographic qualities of Westgate Mall enact a deliberate "amnesia without which the smooth advancement of its business would be impossible. If the traces of history were too evident and went beyond their decorative function, the mall would experience a conflict of functions and meanings: The mall's semiotic machinery has to be that provided by its project alone."[61]

All around the newly built Westgate Mall banners drop from the ceiling instructing customers to "Experience *Lifestyle*,"[62] and this mantra is echoed by authorities as well as the media. During the 2015 opening ceremony of the reconstructed Westgate Mall, Inspector General of Police Joseph Boinett declared to a cluster of reporters that the terrorists "will not mess up our way of life."[63] Which particular way of life was he referring to, considering Kenya's mutli-ethnic and multi-class society? The kind of lifestyle offered through the mall is one that can only be afforded by a minority of wealthy elite. After talking to the reporters, the Inspector General "went on a shopping trip in Nakumatt's entertainment store. He bought copies of George W. Bush's *Decision Points* and Malcom Gladwell's *Outliers*."[64] The Inspector General's choice of literature was strategic and symbolic—one book to promote the war on terror, and the other to promote a capitalist ethos. By promoting shopping malls, authorities, city planners, and private interests are promoting the notion of "modernity" as a type of urban lifestyle being created and sold in these commercial venues.

Chimeras of Consumption

In countries where the mall is a relatively recent phenomenon, the lifecycle of shopping centers has only just begun. However, even as shopping malls are breaking new ground all over developing countries that have eagerly adopted a neoliberal ideology to become part of the global economy, these commercial venues are experiencing a decline in other areas of the world. Even though megamalls such as the Mall of America and the West Edmonton Mall continue to thrive out of sheer force of spectacle, the concept of the shopping mall in many Western contexts is undergoing a conceptual transformation. While Victor Gruen based his original design of the shopping mall on the ideals of "the Greek agora,"[65] and had high hopes of forging enhanced civic connections in the sprawling suburbs of the United States, he became critical of the orchestrated and artificial modern formulations of these venues. He witnessed how "social change, cultural drift, economic developments, and commercial dynamics gradually eroded the original basis on which the mall was founded and this had implications for the architectural delight and community factor of malls, two of the pillars of his project."[66] After years living and working in the United States, Gruen returned to his native Austria—from which he had escaped during Nazi occupation—disappointed with what his vision had become.[67]

There are a variety of factors conspiring to transform the concept of the shopping mall, and in the United States, where the number of shopping malls grew voraciously in the 1980s and 1990s to dominate the landscapes of most city centers and suburbs, the current outlook is that "anywhere from 10 to 20 percent of malls are expected to fail in the next ten years."[68] As these venues become inscribed by fear of terrorist attacks, other spaces open up as safe, convenient, and efficient—and online. In the Western context, where organized urban and digital infrastructures allow for increased ease of virtual shopping, online stores are being promoted as secure alternatives—ones that contain a theoretically unlimited surplus of goods and services to rival the spectacular nature of any physical shopping mall.[69] As fast, efficient, nimble, and versatile, the paradigm of online shopping has rendered the idea of the shopping mall a relic of a cumbersome capitalism assembled through the needs of an old-fashioned industrial revolution. Online shopping is the ultimate triumph of a global corporate consumer culture in which shoppers, like those who practice most forms of faith, "bring the creed home, and practise it there."⁷⁰ While the traditional mall works hard at achieving a sense of wonder and entertainment, the online shopping experience is a spectacle in and of itself. Physical goods are reduced to a referent of themselves, and are purchased largely on the basis of their image qualities—spectacles of consumption that are further distanced from production processes and the many power structures and injustices therein.⁷¹

In order to fully engage in a culture of consumption, it is necessary to cultivate a "commodity fetishism—that is, the tendency to abstract material goods and the pleasures they promise from the human and environmental costs of production."⁷² This dissonance creates a space of elision so one does not have to acknowledge or concede one's own implication in how personal purchasing choices affect people in other parts of the world. This is a dissonance that is facilitated through "outsourcing" accountability in the same way that multinational corporate strategies are characterized by transferring risk, and culpability, outward upon an "other," whether it is the subcontractor or the informal trader.⁷³ By shifting the problem elsewhere, both corporate and social entities can absolve themselves of blame, both legally and perceptually.

This chimera of consumerism does not mean, however, that dominant systems cannot be changed. Indeed, the system of corporate capitalist production can be most affected by, and disciplined through, the very creature it brought into being: conspicuous consumption. If we acknowledge that "consumption and production are inexorably linked,"⁷⁴ and that one has direct effects on the other, then it follows that by changing personal consumption patterns, no matter how small or insignificant these might seem in the grand scheme, this will have knock-on effects upon the wider global corporate capitalist system. Although "economic power is deployed by dominant global actors, analysts of globalizing processes have largely overlooked how quotidian acts such as consumer demand across the globe influence economic relations, however asymmetrical those relationships may be."⁷⁵

Similarly, the relationship between corporate capitalist gains and the promotion of the terrorism discourse, as well as the relationship between terrorism practice and daily disenfranchisement, need to be made more explicit. In this context, "the debate over terrorism cannot be isolated from a larger, comprehensive understanding of the diverse threats to democracy taking place under the regime of neoliberalism."⁷⁶ Through "consumption consciousness," there can be a more effective demand for corporate accountability. It is through education of market practices, and how they affect societies, that unequal and unfair systems of wealth accumulation and power can be shifted. Herein lies the meaning of the "agora:" a marketplace where both commodities and knowledge are circulated, creating an informed public that neither worships, nor is ashamed of its consumption practices. The accumulation by dispossession practiced by many neoliberal schemes, although overpowering and dominant, have faced much resistance. These resistances need to enact dignified and measured responses in order to guard against the more extreme forms of contestations against corporate expansion such as terrorist retaliations and attacks such as those against Westgate Mall.

This study has illustrated how contemporary capitalism and contemporary terrorism inhabit the same social, political, and financial world, separated largely by a discourse that seeks to represent them as antithetical practices. This discursive formation, which suggests capitalism and terrorism occupy opposite poles on an ethical spectrum, increasingly cannot paper over the reality that these concepts inhabit, occasionally inhibit, but most often complement each other. By examining the shopping mall, with an emphasis on Westgate as a point of convergence for many of these contemporary complexities, this study localizes a variety of different global exchanges, geographies, ideologies, and consumption practices. The Westgate Mall case study, much like the contemporary shopping mall experience, offers "everything under one roof,"[77] including elements of a global corporate capitalism, as well as the various contestations—both meaningfully constructive and devastatingly destructive—leveled against it. In its desire to create a world in miniature, the mall inexorably bears the seeds of its own unraveling.

The original architects of the archetype of the mall thought "that by putting everything under one roof, the retailer and the developer gained, for the first time, complete control over their environment."[78] The shopping mall, despite its many attempts, cannot exist in isolation. Just as the mall has direct or indirect effects on the immediate and global environments, the outside world will also necessarily find ways of invading the shopping mall. Although behavior in shopping malls is highly scripted through mall atmospherics and design, and even as shopping malls attempt to control their engineered environments in a securitized and systematized manner, there are always moments of rupture that pierce through the mall's atmosphere, disturbing its illusion.[79] For all of the mall's attempts at controlling the environment, it could do little to stop terrorism from entering the confines of this capitalist stronghold. Despite the mall's preoccupation with surveillance and control, and its endeavors to create a systematized and predictable world, there will always be a breach that disturbs its carefully crafted spectacle. The contemporary shopping mall promises to provide a spectacle, and, in the case of Westgate, it was the site of one of the greatest spectacles ever seen in a shopping mall—only this spectacle was not of its own design.

Endnotes

1. Introduction

1 | Daniel Howden, "Terror in Westgate mall: the full story of the attacks that devastated Kenya," *The Guardian*, October 4, 2013, http://www.theguardian.com/world/interactive/2013/oct/04/westgate-mall-attacks-kenya-terror.
2 | Alan Cowell, "Subway and Bus Blasts in London Kill at Least 37," *The New York Times*, July 8, 2005, http://www.nytimes.com/2005/07/08/world/europe/subway-and-bus-blasts-in-london-kill-at-least-37.html; Victoria Burnett, "7 Are Acquitted in Madrid Bombings," *New York Times*, November 1, 2007, http://www.nytimes.com/2007/11/01/world/europe/01spain.html?_r=0.
3 | James Glanz, Sebastian Rotella, and David E. Sanger, "In 2008 Mumbai Attacks, Piles of Spy Data, but an Uncompleted Puzzle," *The New York Times*, December 21, 2014, http://www.nytimes.com/2014/12/22/world/asia/in-2008-mumbai-attacks-piles-of-spy-data-but-an-uncompleted-puzzle.html; "Tunisia attack on Sousse beach 'kills 39,'" *BBC News*, June 27, 2015, http://www.bbc.com/news/world-africa-33287978; "Burkina Faso attack: Troops battle to end deadly hotel siege," *BBC News*, January 16, 2016, http://www.bbc.com/news/world-africa-35330169.
4 | Tom Keatinge, "The Role of Finance in Defeating Al-Shabaab," Royal United Services Institute Whitehall Report 2-14, 2014, https://rusi.org/sites/default/files/201412_whr_2-14_keatinge_web_0.pdf; Lars Eriksen, Robert Booth, Mark Townsend and Warren Murray, "Copenhagen shootings suspect was 'known to police'," *The Guardian*, February 15, 2015, http://www.theguardian.com/world/2015/feb/14/copenhagen-cartoonist-charlie-hebdo-style-attack; "Sydney siege: Hostages held in Lindt café," BBC, December 15, 2014, http://www.bbc.com/news/world-australia-30473983.
5 | "Charlie Hebdo attack: Three days of terror," *BBC News*, January 14, 2015, http://www.bbc.com/news/world-europe-30708237.

6 | Alexandra Topping, "France sieges: After Charlie Hebdo attack, how terror unfolded," *The Guardian*, January 10, 2015, http://www.theguardian.com/world/2015/jan/10/france-sieges-charlie-hebdo-gunmen-killed-print works-kosher-supermarket.
7 | For more on terrorist attacks on business, and other commercial venues, see Dean C. Alexander, *Business Confronts Terrorism*: Risks and Responses (Madison, WI: University of Wisconsin Press, 2004); Luke Harding and Kim Willsher, "'Something from Dante's Hell': Harrowing Details of Bataclan Siege," *The Guardian*, November 17, 2015, http://www.theguardian.com/world/2015/nov/17/something-from-dantes-hell-harrowing-details-of-bataclan-siege.
8 | David Kilcullen, "Westgate mall attacks: urban areas are the battleground of the 21st century," *The Guardian*, September 27, 2013, http://www.theguardian.com/world/2013/sep/27/westgate-mall-attacks-al-qaida.
9 | Philip Steadman, "The Changing Department Store Building, 1850 to 1940," *The Journal of Space Syntax* 5, no. 2 (2014): 155.
10 | Stephanie Decker, "Corporate Legitimacy and Advertising: British Companies and the Rhetoric of Development in West Africa, 1950-1970," *The Business History Review* 81, no. 1 (Spring 2007): 60.
11 | Samuel Owuor and Teresa Mbatia, "Nairobi," in Capital Cities in Africa: *Power and Powerlessness*, eds. Simon Bekker and Göran Therborn (Dakar and Cape Town: CODESRIA and Human Sciences Research Council, 2011), 137.
12 | Simon Rogers, "England riots: suspects mapped and poverty mapped," *The Guardian*, December 6, 2011, http://www.theguardian.com/news/datablog/interactive/2011/aug/16/riots-poverty-map.
13 | Tom LaTourrette, David R. Howell, David E. Mosher, and John MacDonald, "Reducing Terrorism Risk at Shopping Centers: An Analysis of Potential Security Options" (Santa Monica, CA: RAND Technical Report, 2006), xi; Although such terrorist atrocities committed against businesses and commercial enterprises have become an increasingly common occurrence, there is very little research conducted specifically on shopping mall attacks.
14 | National Counter Terrorism Security Office, "Counter Terrorism Protective Security Advice for Shopping Centres" (London, 2014), 5.
15 | LaTourrette, Howell, Mosher, and MacDonald, "Reducing Terrorism Risk at Shopping Centers," xi.
16 | Lawrence Grossberg, Cary Nelson, and Paula Treichler, eds. *Cultural Studies* (New York, NY: Routledge, 1992).

17 | United States Army, "Case Study: Terrorist Attack on Westgate Shopping Mall, Nairobi, Kenya, September 21-24, 2013," http://isdacenter.org/wp-content/uploads/2014/03/1-FY14_2Q_Final-Westgate-Mall-Attack-Case-Study-31-Jan-14-1.pdf.
18 | United Nations, "International Day of Peace," http://www.un.org/en/events/peaceday/; Jeffrey Gettleman and Nicholas Kulish, "Gunmen Kill Dozens in Terror Attack at Kenyan Mall," *The New York Times*, September 21, 2013, http://www.nytimes.com/2013/09/22/world/africa/nairobi-mall-shooting.html?pagewanted=all&_r=0.
19 | New York City Police Department, "Analysis of Al-Shabaab's Attack at the Westgate Mall in Nairobi, Kenya," November 1, 2013, http://www.scribd.com/doc/190795929/NYPD-Westgate-Report; Tristan McConnell, "'Close Your Eyes and Pretend to Be Dead': What really happened two years ago in the bloody attack on Nairobi's Westgate Mall," *Foreign Policy*, September 20, 2015, http://foreignpolicy.com/2015/09/20/nairobi-kenya-westgate-mall-attack-al-shabab/.
20 | United States Army, "Case Study."
21 | The Mall of America's website boasts that "86 hours is the length of time it would take to complete your visit to the Mall if you were to spend just 10 minutes in each store," Mall of America, "Facts," 2015, http://www.mallofamerica.com/about/moa/facts.
22 | United States Department of State, "Country Reports on Terrorism 2013," 2014, http://www.state.gov/documents/organization/225886.pdf.
23 | United States Department of State, "Country Reports on Terrorism 2013."
24 | United Nations Security Council, "Letter dated 10 October 2014 from the Chair of the Security Council Committee pursuant to resolutions 751 (1992) and 1907 (2009) concerning Somalia and Eritrea addressed to the President of the Security Council," October 13, 2014, http://www.securitycouncilreport.org/atf/cf/%7B65BFCF9B-6D27-4E9C-8CD3-CF6E4FF96FF9%7D/S_2014_726.pdf; McConnell, "'Close Your Eyes and Pretend to Be Dead.'"
25 | New York City Police Department, "Analysis of Al-Shabaab's Attack at the Westgate Mall in Nairobi."
26 | McConnell, "'Close Your Eyes and Pretend to Be Dead.'"
27 | New York City Police Department, "Analysis of Al-Shabaab's Attack at the Westgate Mall in Nairobi."

28 | Gregory Warner, "Outside Westgate," Radiolab, November 29, 2014, http://www.radiolab.org/story/outside-westgate/.
29 | Nicholas Kulish, "In this Horror Film, Blood is All Too Real: 'Terror at the Mall' on HBO Documents an Attack in Kenya," *New York Times*, September 14, 2014, http://www.nytimes.com/2014/09/15/arts/television/terror-at-the-mall-on-hbo-documents-an-attack-in-kenya.html?_r=0.
30 | Peter Bergen, "Are mass murderers using Twitter as a tool?" CNN, September 27, 2013 http://www.cnn.com/2013/09/26/opinion/bergen-twitter-terrorism/.
31 | "Nairobi Westgate shoot-out kills 11 in Kenya," *BBC News*, September 21, 2013, http://www.bbc.com/news/world-africa-24186780#TWEET897232.
32 | Tomer Simon, Avishay Goldberg, Limor Aharonson-Daniel, Dmitry Leykin, and Bruria Adini, "Twitter in the Cross Fire—The Use of Social Media in the Westgate Mall Terror Attack in Kenya" *Plos One* 9, no. 8 (August 2014): 6.
33 | McConnell, "'Close Your Eyes and Pretend to Be Dead;'" See also, The Joint Committee on Administration and National Security, and Defence and Foreign Relations, "Report of the Joint Committee on Administration and National Security; and Defence and Foreign Relations on The Inquiry into the Westgate Terrorist Attack, and Other Terror Attacks in Mandera in North-Eastern and Kilifi in the Coastal Region," December 2013, http://info.mzalendo.com/media_root/file_archive/REPORT_OF_THE_COMMITTEE_ON_WESTGATE_ATTACK_-_4.pdf.
34 | McConnell, "'Close Your Eyes and Pretend to Be Dead.'"
35 | Ibid.
36 | Dennis Okari, "Kenya's Westgate attack: Unanswered questions one year on," *BBC News*, September 22, 2014, http://www.bbc.com/news/world-africa-29282045.
37 | United States Department of State, "Country Reports on Terrorism 2013."
38 | Giorgio Agamben, *The State of Exception*, trans. Kevin Attell (Chicago, IL: Chicago University Press, 2005).
39 | Laura Petrecca, "39 Die in Kenya Mall Siege; Hostages Still Held," *USA Today*, September 21, 2013, http://www.usatoday.com/story/news/world/2013/09/21/witness-kenya-mall-attackers-target-non-muslims/2846319/.
40 | New York City Police Department, "Analysis of Al-Shabaab's Attack at the Westgate Mall in Nairobi."

41 | Archive.is, "HSM Press Office," September 21, 2013, https://archive.is/CAJCc; Archive.is, "EX HMS_PRESS2," September 22, 2013, https://archive.is/pVEkm; Archive.is, "HSM Press Office," September 26, 2013, https://archive.is/XVBeU#selection-1609.0-1609.16. Westgate mall's part-Israeli ownership was another likely reason for the attack. Kenya is no stranger to such violent attacks on Israeli targets. For example, "in 2002 militants bombed an Israeli-owned hotel in the coastal resort of Mombasa, killing 13 people; two missiles then narrowly missed an Israeli airliner as it took off from Nairobi Airport." See Jessica Purkiss, "The Westgate mall attack highlights Kenya-Israel ties," September 27, 2013," *Middle East Monitor,* https://www.middleeastmonitor.com/articles/africa/7551-the-westgate-mall-attack-highlights-kenya-israel-ties.

42 | HSM Press Office, "Transcript: Speech of HSM Leader, Shaykh Mukhtar Abu Zubayr, regarding the #Westgate Operation," Twitlonger, September 25, 2013, http://www.twitlonger.com/show/n_1rp1qpv.

43 | HSM Press Office, "Transcript."

44 | Ibid.

45 | Amnesty International, "'We are like Rubbish in this Country': Forced evictions in Nairobi, Kenya," 2013, https://www.amnesty.org/en/documents/afr32/005/2013/en/.

46 | Ibid.

47 | Hal Foster, "Bigness," *London Review of Books* 23, no. 23 (November 29, 2001): 13-16, http://www.lrb.co.uk/v23/n23/hal-foster/bigness. A. T. Kearney, reports that Wal-Mart is expanding this market expertise into the African context by opening 90 supermarkets all over the continent, "The 2015 African Retail Development Index," https://www.atkearney.com/consumer-products-retail/african-retail-development-index/2015.

48 | The International Council of Shopping Centers (ICSC), "2014 Economic Impact of Shopping Centers," http://www.icsc.org/uploads/default/2014-Economic-Impact-Kit.pdf.

49 | Gateway Theatre of Shopping, "About Us," http://gatewayworld.co.za/home/about.

50 | Naomi Klein, *The Shock Doctrine: The Rise of Disaster Capitalism* (New York, NY: Metropolitan Books, 2008), 301.

51 | Alexander, *Business Confronts Terrorism*, 14.

52 | Mike Davis, "Fortress Los Angeles: The Militarization of Urban Space," in Michael Sorkin, ed., *Variations on a Theme Park: The New American City and the End of Public Space* (New York, NY: Hill and Wang, 1992), 161.

53 | Daniel Zwerdling, G.W. Schulz, Andrew Becker, and Margot Williams, "Under Suspicion at the Mall of America," National Public Radio, September 7, 2011, http://www.npr.org/2011/09/07/140234451/under-suspicion-at-the-mall-of-america.

54 | New York Police Department, "Analysis of Al-Shabaab's Attack at the Westgate Mall in Nairobi;" Federal Bureau of Investigation, "A Conversation with Our Legal Attaché in Nairobi, Part 1," January 2014, http://www.fbi.gov/news/stories/2014/january/a-conversation-with-our-legal-attache-in-nairobi-part-1; Guy Alexander, "Kenyan mall shooting: 'They threw grenades like maize to chickens'," September 22, 2013, http://www.theguardian.com/world/2013/sep/21/nairobi-shopping-centre-terror-attack.

55 | New York City Police Department, "Analysis of Al-Shabaab's Attack at the Westgate Mall in Nairobi."

56 | Allied Barton Security Services, "Partnering with Military Assistance Groups to Hire Our Heroes," n.d., http://www.alliedbarton.com/Security-Resource-Center/Case-Studies/View-Case-Study/ArticleId/239/Partnering-with-Military-Assistance-Groups-to-Hire-Our-Heroes.

57 | George W. Bush, "President Holds Prime Time News Conference," The White House, Press Release, October 11, 2001, http://georgewbush-whitehouse.archives.gov/news/releases/2001/10/20011011-7.html.

58 | Todd S. Purdum, "After the Attacks: The White House; Bush Warns of a Wrathful, Shadowy and Inventive War," *New York Times*, September 17, 2001, http://www.nytimes.com/2001/09/17/us/after-attacks-white-house-bush-warns-wrathful-shadowy-inventive-war.html?pagewanted=all.

59 | Lizabeth Cohen, "A Consumers' Republic: The Politics of Mass Consumption in Postwar America," *Journal of Consumer Research* 31, no. 1 (June 2004): 236.

60 | Margaret Crawford, "The World in a Shopping Mall," in *Variations on a Theme Park: The New American City and the End of Public Space*, ed., Michael Sorkin (New York, NY: Hill and Wang, 1992), 11.

61 | Cohen, "A Consumers' Republic," 236.

62 | Mark Gottdiener, ed. "The Consumption of Space and Spaces of Consumption," in *New Forms of Consumption: Consumers, Culture, and Commodification* (Lanham, MD: Rowman & Littlefield, 2000), 276.

63 | Eve Fairbanks, "Africa's Obsession with Shopping Malls," September 23, 2013, http://www.newrepublic.com/article/114826/westgate-mall-attack-al-shabab-assaults-symbol-african-urban-life.

64 | Heidi Vogt and Patrick Mcgroarty, "Before Kenya Attack, a Warning on Terrorism," *Wall Street Journal*, September 30, 2013, http://www.wsj.com/articles/SB10001424052702303643304579105222268968650.
65 | Richard Lough and Abdi Sheikh, "UPDATE 3-Kenya launches probe as Shabaab leader confirms mall attack," Reuters, September 25, 2013, http://www.reuters.com/article/2013/09/25/kenya-attack-idUSL5N0HL0MS20130925.
66 | "Kenya: A Different Country," *The Economist*, September 28, 2013, http://www.economist.com/news/middle-east-and-africa/21586851-national-politics-has-shifted-response-attack-somali-terrorists/print.
67 | Ben Makori, "Kenya's Westgate shopping mall reopens after massacre," Reuters, July 18, 2015, http://www.reuters.com/article/us-kenya-attacks-westgate-idUSKCN0PS0HZ20150718.
68 | Deborah Hobden, "'Your Mall with it All:' Luxury Development in a Globalizing African City," *Perspectives on Global Development and Technology* 13 (2014): 130.
69 | Michael D. Larobina and Richard L. Pate, "The Impact of Terrorism on Business," *Journal of Global Business Issues* 3, no. 1 (Spring 2009): 153.
70 | Drazen Jorgic, "Scarred by Islamist attacks, Kenya set to re-open Westgate mall," Reuters, July 14, 2015, http://www.reuters.com/article/us-kenya-attacks-westgate-idUSKCN0PO22S20150714.
71 | International Council of Shopping Centers, "Nairobi retail bouncing back from terrorist attack," August 19, 2015, http://www.icsc.org/press/nairobi-mall-scene-back-to-normal-a-year-after-terrorist-attack.
72 | Paco Underhill, *Call of the Mall: The Geography of Shopping* (New York, NY: Simon & Schuster, 2005)
73 | David Harvey, "Neoliberalism as Creative Destruction," *The Annals of the American Academy of Political and Social Science* 610, no. 1 (2007): 23.
74 | Atwan, *Islamic State*.
75 | Jeffrey Gettleman and Nicholas Kulish, "Somali Militants Mixing Business and Terror," *The New York Times*, September 30, 2013, http://www.nytimes.com/2013/10/01/world/africa/officials-struggle-with-tangled-web-of-financing-for-somali-militants.html.
76 | Gettleman and Kulish, "Somali Militants Mixing Business and Terror."
77 | Michael Czinkota, Gary A. Knight, Peter W. Liesch, and John Steen, "Terrorism and International Business: A Research Agenda," *Journal of International Business Studies* 41, no. 5 (2010): 827.
78 | Klein, *The Shock Doctrine*, 12.

79 | Aggrey Mutambo, "Bodies of Westgate terrorists 'are with the FBI', says KDF Chief Julius Karangi," *The Nation*, February 7, 2014, http://mobile.nation.co.ke/news/Julius-Karangi-Kenya-Defence-Forces-Westgate-Attack/-/1950946/2196566/-/format/xhtml/-/r6oqhdz/-/index.html.

80 | See, for example, SITE Intelligence Group, "Shabaab Releases Video on Westgate Mall Raid, Names Western Malls as Targets for Lone Wolf Attacks," February 21, 2015, http://news.siteintelgroup.com/blog/index.php/categories/jihad/entry/363-shabaab-releases-video-on-westgate-mall-raid,-names-western-malls-as-targets-for-lone-wolf-attacks; Dan Reed, *Terror at the Mall*, 2014, Home Box Office.

81 | Vanessa Friedman, "After a Tragedy, the Memorabilia," *New York Times*, January 21, 2015, http://www.nytimes.com/2015/01/22/fashion/after-a-tragedy-like-the-charlie-hebdo-shooting-come-the-products.html; The slogan was further publicized as a fashion statement worn on printed badges by George and Amal Clooney on the red carpet at the 2015 Golden Globe awards ceremony.

82 | Jonathan Joseph, "Terrorism as a social relation within capitalism: theoretical and emancipatory implications," *Critical Studies on Terrorism* 4, no. 1 (2011): 34.

83 | A small selection of the many books on contemporary terrorism, include: Åsne Seierstad, *One of Us: The Story of Anders Breivik and the Massacre in Norway*, trans. Sarah Death (New York, NY: Farrar, Straus and Giroux, 2015); Michael Morell with Bill Harlow, *The Great War of Our Time: The CIA's Fight Against Terrorism—From al Qa'ida to ISIS* (New York, NY: Twelve Hachette Book Group, 2015); Malcolm W. Nance, *Terrorist Recognition Handbook: A Practitioner's Manual for Predicting and Identifying Terrorist Activities*, 3rd ed. (Boca Raton, FL: CRS Press, 2014); and Abdel Bari Atwan, *Islamic State: The Digital Caliphate* (Berkeley, CA: University of California Press, 2015).

84 | Joseph, "Terrorism as a social relation within capitalism."

85 | Tim Krieger and Daniel Meierrieks, "The Rise of Capitalism and the Roots of Anti-American Terrorism," CESifo Working Paper no. 4887 (July 2014): 5.

86 | Jeffory A. Clymer, *America's Culture of Terrorism: Violence, Capitalism, and the Written Word* (Chapel Hill: University of North Carolina Press, 2003), 216; See, for example, Antony Loewenstein, *Disaster Capitalism: Making a Killing Out of Catastrophe* (London: Verso, 2015); Noam Chomsky, *Profit Over People: Neoliberalism and Global Order* (New York, NY: 2011); Klein, *The*

Shock Doctrine; Pierre Bourdieu, *Firing Back: Against the Tyranny of the Market* 2 (New York, NY: The New Press, 2003).
87 | Liane Tanguay, *Hijacking History: American Culture and the War on Terror* (Montreal: McGill-Queen's University Press, 2013), 116.
88 | Jacques Derrida, *Of Grammatology*, Trans. Gayatri Chakravorty Spivak (Johns Hopkins Press, 2013).
89 | Westgate Shopping Mall Facebook page, December 8, 2015, https://www.facebook.com/westgateshoppingmall/.
90 | Beatriz Sarlo, *Scenes from Postmodern Life*, trans. Jon Beasley-Murray (Minneapolis, MN: University of Minnesota Press, 2001), 14.

2. Developing the Shopping Mall

1 | Government of the Republic of Kenya, "Kenya Vision 2030."
2 | Harvey, "Neoliberalism as Creative Destruction," 22.
3 | Many "developing" countries have adopted 2030 Visions of development. See, for example, Jamaica's Vision 2030, http://www.vision2030.gov.jm/; Namibia's Vision 2030, http://www.npc.gov.na/?page_id=210; South Africa's Vision 20130, http://www.poa.gov.za/news/Documents/NPC%20Natio nal%20Development%20Plan%20Vision%202030%20-lo-res.pdf; and Pakistan's Vision 2030, http://www.pc.gov.pk/vision2030/Pak21stcentury/vision%202030-Full.pdf.
4 | Government of the Republic of Kenya, "Kenya Vision 2030."
5 | Denis Linehan, "Re-ordering the Urban Archipelago: Kenya Vision 2030, Street Trade and the Battle for Nairobi City Centre," *Aurora Geography Journal* 1 (2007): 24.
6 | Decker, "Corporate Legitimacy and Advertising," 62.
7 | Global Impact Investing Network, "The Landscape for Impact Investing in East Africa: Kenya," August 2015, http://www.thegiin.org/assets/docu ments/pub/East%20Africa%20Landscape%20Study/05Kenya_GIIN_east africa_DIGITAL.pdf.
8 | Bhaskar Chakravorti, Jianwei Dong, and Kate Fedosova, "Colonialism's Enduring Dividends: Why European Companies Have an Advantage in Emerging Markets," *Foreign Affairs*, February 13, 2014, https://www.foreign affairs.com/articles/africa/2014-02-13/colonialisms-enduring-dividends.

9 | Timothy Burke, *Lifebuoy Men, Lux Women: Commodification, Consumption, and Cleanliness in Modern Zimbabwe* (Durham, NC: Duke University Press, 2003), 4.
10 | A. T. Kearney, "The 2015 African Retail Development Index."
11 | Ibid.
12 | Ibid.
13 | Government of the Republic of Kenya, "Kenya Vision 2030."
14 | Farai Gundan, "Kenya Joins Africa's Top 10 Economies after Rebasing of its Gross Domestic Product (GDP)," Forbes, October 1, 2014, http://www.forbes.com/sites/faraigundan/2014/10/01/kenya-joins-africas-top-10-economies-after-rebasing-of-its-gross-domestic-product/.
15 | Gundan, "Kenya Joins Africa's Top 10 Economies after Rebasing of its Gross Domestic Product (GDP)."
16 | Global Impact Investing Network, "The Landscape for Impact Investing in East Africa."
17 | Chris Borg and Earl Nurse, "Mall the Merrier: Africa's Growing Appetite for Shopping," *CNN*, October 2, 2015, http://www.cnn.com/2015/10/02/africa/shopping-malls-africa/.
18 | "The Great Sixth-Avenue Bazaar; Opening Day at Macy & Co.'s--A Place Where Almost Anything May be Bought," *New York Times*, April 4, 1878, http://query.nytimes.com/gst/abstract.html?res=9F0CE5DB143EE73BBC4C53DFB2668383669FDE.
19 | Mica Nava, "Cosmopolitan Modernity: Everyday Imaginaries and the Register of Difference," *Theory, Culture & Society*, Special Issue on Cosmopolis 19, nos. 1-2 (2002): 3.
20 | Murillo, "'The Modern Shopping Experience,'" 376.
21 | Ibid.
22 | Signifying the importance of the development, the Accra Mall was funded by "Actis, a private London-based spin-off of the Commonwealth Development Fund," Deborah Hobden, "'Your Mall with it All:' Luxury Development in a Globalizing African City," *Perspectives on Global Development and Technology* 13 (2014): 140 and 130.
23 | Jackson, "All the World's a Mall," 1113.
24 | The International Council of Shopping Centers (ICSC), "2014 Economic Impact of Shopping Centers."
25 | Broll Property Group, "The Broll Report 2014/2015."

26 | Kamau Mbote, "East Africa's Growing Middle Class Demands for More Shopping Malls," April 29, 2014, http://afkinsider.com/53224/east-africas-growing-middle-class-demands-shopping-malls/.
27 | Sarlo, *Scenes from Postmodern Life*, 13.
28 | Debord, *The Society of the Spectacle*, paragraph no. 174.
29 | The International Council of Shopping Centers (ICSC), "About," 2015, http://www.icsc.org/.
30 | Bianca Murillo, "'The Modern Shopping Experience:' Kingsway Department Store and Consumer Politics in Ghana," *Africa* 82, no. 3 (August 2012): 374.
31 | Michael Sorkin, ed., "Introduction," in *Variations on a Theme Park: The New American City and the End of Public Space* (New York, NY: Hill and Wang, 1992), xiii.
32 | "Kenya: New Mall Set to Change How Kisumu Shops," *The Nation*, July 2, 2015, http://allafrica.com/stories/201507020248.html.
33 | The International Council of Shopping Centers (ICSC), "About," 2015, http://www.icsc.org/.
34 | Jon Beasley-Murray, "Translator's Introduction," in Beatriz Sarlo, *Scenes from Postmodern Life*, trans. Jon Beasley-Murray (Minneapolis, MN: University of Minnesota Press, 2001), x.
35 | Sarlo, *Scenes from Postmodern Life*, 15.
36 | Ibid., 14.
37 | Rodrigo Salcedo, "When the Global Meets the Local at the Mall," *American Behavioral Scientist* 46, no. 8 (April 2003): 1095.
38 | LaTourrette, Howell, Mosher, and MacDonald, "Reducing Terrorism Risk at Shopping Centers," xii.
39 | Rafael Marks and Marco Bezzoli, "Palaces of Desire: Century City, Cape Town and the Ambiguities of Development," *Urban Forum* 12, no. 1 (January 2001): 44.
40 | Deborah Hobden, "A Man, A Plan, A Mall: The Role of Globalizing Elites in the Development of Accra, Ghana," *Global-e*, http://global-ejournal.org/2014/09/08/vol8iss7/.
41 | Marks and Bezzoli, "Palaces of Desire," 31.
42 | Asef Bayat, "Politics in the City-Inside-Out," *City & Society* 24, no. 2 (2012): 111.
43 | Owuor and Mbatia, "Nairobi," 128; Bayat, "Politics in the City-Inside-Out," 115.

44 | Ambreena Manji, "Bulldozers, Homes and Highways: Nairobi and the Right to the City," *Review of African Political Economy* 42, no. 144 (2015): 206.
45 | Ibid., 206.
46 | Raphael Obonyo, "Nairobi's Emerging Cities Dilemma," March 24, 2014, http://www.worldpolicy.org/blog/2014/03/24/kenyas-emerging-cities-dilemma.
47 | Owuor and Mbatia, "Nairobi," 128.
48 | United Nations Office on Drugs and Crime, "The Globalization of Crime a Transnational Organized Crime Threat Assessment," 2010, https://www.unodc.org/documents/data-and-analysis/tocta/TOCTA_Report_2010_low_res.pdf.
49 | Sadaf Lakhani, "What Does Social Exclusion Have to Do with the Attacks at Westgate, Nairobi? Asking the Right Questions," December 11, 2013, http://blogs.worldbank.org/publicsphere/what-does-social-exclusion-have-do-attacks-westgate-nairobi-asking-right-questions.
50 | Global Impact Investing Network, "The Landscape for Impact Investing in East Africa: Kenya."
51 | Ibid.
52 | McConnell, "'Close Your Eyes and Pretend to Be Dead.'"
53 | Kearney, "The 2015 African Retail Development Index."
54 | Amnesty International, "We are like Rubbish in this Country."
55 | The informal sector is often characterized by "survival" activities and coping strategies, such as casual labor and other forms of unsanctioned and unregulated forms of employment. "About the Informal Economy," Women in Informal Employment: Globalizing and Organizing, 2016, http://wiego.org/informal-economy/about-informal-economy.
56 | Kearney, "The 2015 African Retail Development Index."
57 | Government of the Republic of Kenya, "Kenya Vision 2030."
58 | Mary Njeri Kinyanjui, "Can Africa's Informal Sector Spur Growth?" April 7, 2015, http://www.worldpolicy.org/blog/2015/04/07/can-africas-informal-sector-spur-growth.
59 | Kearney, "The 2015 African Retail Development Index."
60 | Owuor and Mbatia, "Nairobi," 128.
61 | UN Habitat, "The State of African Cities 2010: Governance, Inequality and Urban Land Markets," 2010, https://www.citiesalliance.org/sites/citiesalliance.org/files/UNH_StateofAfricanCities_2010.pdf.
62 | Bayat, "Politics in the City-Inside-Out," 115.
63 | Hobden, "'Your Mall with it All,'" 144.

64 | "Nairobi anti-Hawking squad to be unveiled," News 24 Kenya, September 20, 2013, http://www.news24.co.ke/National/News/Nairobi-anti-Hawking-squad-to-be-unveiled-20130920.
65 | Ibid.
66 | "Hawkers," News 24 Kenya, 2015, http://www.news24.co.ke/Tags/Topics/hawkers; Amnesty International, "We are like rubbish in this country."
67 | Klopp quoting Njoroge Maina in an interview in Jacqueline M. Klopp, "Pilfering the Public: The Problem of Land Grabbing in Contemporary Kenya," *Africa Today* 47, no. 1 (Winter 2000): 12.
68 | Arvind Rajagopal, "The Violence of Commodity Aesthetics: Hawkers, Demolition Raids, and a New Regime of Consumption," *Social Text* 68, 19, no. 3 (Fall 2001): 91.
69 | The White House, "Strategy to Combat Transnational Organized Crime."
70 | Bayat, "Politics in the City-Inside-Out," 112.
71 | Klopp, "Pilfering the Public," 10.
72 | Ibid.
73 | Kimani Njogu, Kabiri Ngeta, and Mary Wanjau, eds. *Ethnic Diversity in Eastern Africa: Opportunities and Challenges* (Nairobi: Twaweza Communications, 2010), 202.
74 | Bayat, "Politics in the City-Inside-Out," 110.
75 | United Nations Office on Drugs and Crime, "The Globalization of Crime a Transnational Organized Crime Threat Assessment."
76 | Beekarry, *Combating Money Laundering And Terrorism Finance*; Sarah Percy and Anja Shortland, "The Business of Piracy in Somalia," *Journal of Strategic Studies* 36, no. 4 (2013): 541-578.
77 | McConnell, "'Close Your Eyes and Pretend to Be Dead.'"
78 | United States Department of State, "Country Reports on Terrorism 2013."
79 | McConnell, "'Close Your Eyes and Pretend to Be Dead.'"
80 | Ibid.
81 | Beekarry, ed., *Combating Money Laundering and Terrorism Finance*.
82 | Alexander, *Business Confronts Terrorism*, 8.
83 | Andrew Zimmerman, "Africa in Imperial and Transnational History: Multi-Sited Historiography and the Necessity of Theory," *Journal of African History* 54, no. 3 (November 2013): 335.
84 | Navin Beekarry, ed., *Combating Money Laundering And Terrorism Finance: Past and Current Challenges* (Edward Elgar Publishing, 2013).

85 | Gettleman and Kulish, "Somali Militants Mixing Business and Terror."
86 | The White House, "Strategy to Combat Transnational Organized Crime," 2011, https://www.whitehouse.gov/sites/default/files/Strategy_to_Combat_Transnational_Organized_Crime_July_2011.pdf.
87 | Josh Kron, "Report Ties Kenyan Army to Militants' Smuggling," *The New York Times*, November 12, 2015, http://www.nytimes.com/2015/11/13/world/africa/report-ties-kenyan-army-to-militants-smuggling.html?ref=topics&_r=4; The spelling of the terrorist group's name in English varies, depending on the author's preference and literature review.
88 | The White House, "Strategy to Combat Transnational Organized Crime."
89 | Ibid.
90 | Sandra Laville and Jason Burke, "Why has the AK-47 become the jihadi terrorist weapon of choice?" *The Guardian*, December 29, 2015, http://www.theguardian.com/world/2015/dec/29/why-jihadi-terrorists-swapped-suicide-belts-kalashnikov-ak-47s?CMP=Share_AndroidApp_Gmail.
91 | Jonathan Masters, "Al-Shabab," September 5, 2014, Council on Foreign Relations, http://www.cfr.org/somalia/al-shabab/p18650.
92 | Wanjohi Kabukuru, "The Business of Terrorism," *The New African*, June 25, 2014, http://newafricanmagazine.com/business-terrorism/.
93 | Michael Mousseau, "Urban Poverty and Support for Islamist Terror: Survey Results of Muslims in Fourteen Countries," *Journal of Peace Research* 48, no. 1 (January 2011): 39.
94 | Keatinge, "The Role of Financing in Defeating Al-Shabaab."
95 | The Westgate Mall terrorists, for example, are suspected to have resided, at least temporarily, in Eastleigh, a district of Nairobi home to a large Somali refugee population. See New York City Police Department, "Analysis of Al-Shabaab's Attack at the Westgate Mall in Nairobi, Kenya;" Ken Menkhaus, "What the Deadly Attack on a Kenya Mall was really about," September 22, 2013, Think Progress, http://thinkprogress.org/security/2013/09/22/2662191/deadly-attack-kenya-mall-sign-desperation/.
96 | David Francis, "Al-Shabab Threat against Mall of America Could Be a Call to Action," *Foreign Policy*, February 23, 2015, http://foreignpolicy.com/2015/02/23/al-shabab-threat-against-mall-of-america-could-be-a-call-to-action/.
97 | Peter Bergen, "Al-Shabaab's American allies," CNN, September 24, 2013, http://edition.cnn.com/2013/09/23/opinion/bergen-al-shabaab-american-ties/.

98 | Dina Temple-Raston, "For Somalis in Minneapolis, Jihadi Recruiting is a Recurring Nightmare," National Public Radio, August 13, 2015, http://www.npr.org/2015/02/18/387302748/minneapolis-st-paul-remains-a-focus-of-jihadi-recruiting; Francis, "Al-Shabab Threat against Mall of America Could Be a Call to Action."
99 | Liam Stack, "Qaeda Affiliate Uses Video of Donald Trump for Recruiting," *The New York Times*, January 1, 2016, http://www.nytimes.com/2016/01/02/world/africa/al-qaeda-uses-video-of-trump-for-recruiting.html?ref=topics.
100 | United States Department of State, "Country Reports on Terrorism 2013," 2014.
101 | Paul D. Williams, "After Westgate: Opportunities and Challenges in the War against Al-Shabaab," *International Affairs* 90, no. 4 (2014): 908.
102 | Ibid., 911.
103 | Ken Menkhaus, "Al-Shabab's Capabilities Post-Westgate," *CTC Sentinel* 7, no. 2 (February 24, 2014), Special Issue, https://www.ctc.usma.edu/posts/al-shababs-capabilities-post-westgate; and Williams, "After Westgate," 911.
104 | Jeremy Prestholdt, *Domesticating the World: African Consumerism and the Genealogies of Globalization* (Berkeley, CA: University of California Press, 2008), 2.
105 | Atwan, *Islamic State*, 15.
106 | Raphael Satter and Isil Sariyuce, "Turkey's Largest City is Rattled by Growing Signs of ISIS Support," October 14, 2014, http://www.businessinsider.com/turkeys-capital-is-rattled-by-growing-signs-of-isis-support-2014-10.
107 | Frances Woodhams, "Mall attack: will Kenya's shopping centre culture endure?" *The Telegraph*, September 30, 2013, http://www.telegraph.co.uk/expat/10340179/Mall-attack-will-Kenyas-shopping-centre-culture-endure.html.
108 | J.-A. Mbembé and Sarah Nuttall, "Writing the World from an African Metropolis," *Public Culture* 16, no. 3 (Fall 2004): 358.
109 | Bruce Janz, "The Terror of the Place: Anxieties of Place and the Cultural Narrative of Terrorism," *Ethics, Place & Environment* 11, no. 2 (2008): 201.

3. Designing the Shopping Mall

1 | Harry Gordon Selfridge, *The Romance of Commerce* (London: John Lane, 1918), 1.
2 | Shashi Tharoor, "Globalization and the Human Imagination," *World Policy Journal* 21, no. 2 (Summer 2004): 87.
3 | Thomas Anning-Dorson, Adelaide Kastner, and Mohammed Abdulai Mahmoud, "Investigation into Mall Visitation Motivation and Demographic Idiosyncrasies in Ghana," *Management Science Letters* 3 (2013): 368.
4 | Jennifer Smith, "The Mall in Motion: A Narrative Stroll through the Obstacle Course," *Speed: Technology, Media, Society* 1, no. 3 (June 1996): 6.
5 | Steadman, "The Changing Department Store Building, 1850 to 1940," 154.
6 | For more detailed discussions on changing patterns of consumption, see Mark Gottdiener, ed., *New Forms of Consumption: Consumers, Culture, and Commodification* (Lanham, MD: Rowman & Littlefield, 2000) and George Ritzer, *Enchanting a Disenchanted World: Revolutionizing the Means of Consumption*, 2nd ed. (Thousand Oaks, CA: Pine Forge Press, 2010).
7 | Walter Benjamin, *The Arcades Project*, Howard Eiland and Kevin McLaughlin, trans. (Cambridge, MA: Harvard University Press, 1999).
8 | Steadman, "The Changing Department Store Building, 1850 to 1940," 154.
9 | Royal Commonwealth Society, *Catalogue of the Library of the Royal Colonial Institute* (Spottiswoode & Co.: London, 1886), 86.
10 | Benjamin, *The Arcades Project*, 7.
11 | Jonathan Nitzan, "Human Security, Consumer Confidence and the Future of Neoliberalism," The Collaboratory for Digital Discourse and Culture (November 5, 2001): 1, http://www.cddc.vt.edu/digitalfordism/fordism_materials/Nitzan.pdf.
12 | Ibid.
13 | Rob Kroes, *If You've Seen One, You've Seen the Mall: Europeans and American Mass Culture* (Chicago: University of Illinois Press, 1996), 93.
14 | Ibid., 104.
15 | Guy Debord, *The Society of the Spectacle*, trans. Donald Nicholson-Smith (New York, NY: Zone Books, [1967] 1994).
16 | Benjamin, *The Arcades Project*, 7.
17 | "Mall," Merriam Webster, http://www.merriam-webster.com/dictionary/mall.

18 | Benjamin, *The Arcades Project*.
19 | Ibid., 31.
20 | Ibid., 42.
21 | Ibid., 37.
22 | Mark Gottdiener, ed., "Approaches to Consumption: Classical and Contemporary Perspectives," in *New Forms of Consumption: Consumers, Culture, and Commodification* (Lanham, MD: Rowman & Littlefield, 2000), 13.
23 | Benjamin, *The Arcades Project*, 37.
24 | Jerry Jacobs, *The Mall: An Attempted Escape from Everyday Life* (Prospect Heights, IL: Waveland Press, 1984), 1.
25 | Mica Nava, "Modernity's Disavowal: Women, the City and the Department Store," in *Modern Times: Reflections on a Century of English Modernity*, eds. Mica Nava and Alan O'Shea (London and New York: Routledge, 1997), 1.
26 | Alexandre B. Hedjazi and Hatem Fekkak, "Towards Militaristic Urban Planning: the Genealogy of the Post-Colonial European Approach to Social and Urban Insecurity," *Critical Planning* 19 (Fall 2010): 87. These newly designed urban forms of territorial control were further transposed to colonial cities.
27 | Trevor Boddy, "Underground and Overhead: Building the Analogous City," in *Variations on a Theme Park: The New American City and the End of Public Space*, ed., Michael Sorkin (New York,: NY: Hill and Wang, 1992), 130.
28 | Benjamin, *The Arcades Project*, 47.
29 | Ibid.
30 | Steadman, "The Changing Department Store Building, 1850 to 1940," 158.
31 | Ibid., 157.
32 | Ibid., 155.
33 | Decker, "Corporate Legitimacy and Advertising," 64; Owuor and Mbatia, "Nairobi," 122.
34 | Murillo, "'The Modern Shopping Experience,'" 375.
35 | Ibid., 373.
36 | Benjamin, *The Arcades Project*, 43.
37 | Steadman, "The Changing Department Store Building, 1850 to 1940," 159.
38 | Ibid., 378.
39 | Murillo, "'The Modern Shopping Experience,'" 378.
40 | Steadman, "The Changing Department Store Building, 1850 to 1940," 164.

41 | Harvie Ferguson, "Watching the World go Round: Atrium Culture and the Psychology of Shopping," in *Lifestyle Shopping: The Subject of Consumption*, ed. Rob Shields (London and New York: Routledge, 1992), 3.
42 | Ritzer, *Enchanting a Disenchanted World*, 66.
43 | Steadman, "The Changing Department Store Building, 1850 to 1940," 156.
44 | Crawford, "The World in a Shopping Mall," 18.
45 | Murillo, "'The Modern Shopping Experience,'" 381.
46 | Ibid., 377.
47 | Crawford, "The World in a Shopping Mall," 17-18.
48 | Debord, *The Society of the Spectacle* (Point 174).
49 | William S. Kowinski, "Mall-aise: American Society Might Literally Shop Till It Drops," *Chicago Tribune*, May 21, 1987, http://articles.chicagotribune.com/1987-05-21/features/8702070556_1_shopping-mall-suburban-downtown-citicorp-center.
50 | Cohen, "A Consumers' Republic," 238.
51 | J.C. Nichols, "Mistakes We Have Made in Developing Shopping Centers," *Technical Bulletin* no. 4 (August 1945), Urban Land Institute, Planning for Permanence: the Speeches of J.C. Nichols Western Historical Manuscript Collection-Kansas City, http://shs.umsystem.edu/kansascity/manuscripts/nichols/JCN078.pdf.
52 | Ibid.
53 | Steadman, "The Changing Department Store Building, 1850 to 1940," 165.
54 | Jackson, "All the World's a Mall," 1113.
55 | Darlene Miller, Etienne Nel, and Godfrey Hampwaye, "Malls in Zambia: Racialised retail expansion and South African foreign investors in Zambia," *African Sociological Review* 12, no. 1 (2008): 45.
56 | Ibid., 43.
57 | Ibid., 45.
58 | Ibid., 42.
59 | Bayat, "Politics in the City-Inside-Out," 111.
60 | Joel Stillerman and Rodrigo Salcedo, "Transposing the Urban to the Mall: Routes, Relationships, and Resistance in Two Santiago, Chile, Shopping Centers," *Journal of Contemporary Ethnography* 4, no. 3 (2012): 310.
61 | Murillo, "'The Modern Shopping Experience,'" 378.

62 | Brett Walton, "The Westgate Shopping Centre Siege – an Attack on Freedom, Society and the Future," http://www.fortitudemagazine.co.uk/industry/politics/westgate-shopping-centre-siege-attack-freedom-society-future/12447/.
63 | Owuor and Mbatia, "Nairobi," 122.
64 | Stillerman and Salcedo, "Transposing the Urban to the Mall," 328.
65 | Cohen, "A Consumers' Republic," 236.
66 | Maymanah Farhat, "New Media and the Spectacle of the War on Terror," in *Uncommon Grounds: New Media and Critical Practices in North Africa and the Middle East*, ed. Anthony Downey (London: I.B.Tauris, 2014), 185.
67 | Crawford, "The World in a Shopping Mall," 20.
68 | Kowinski, "Mall-aise."
69 | Marni Epstein, "How the Cold War Shaped the Design of American Malls," *Curbed*, June 11, 2014, http://curbed.com/archives/2014/06/11/how-the-cold-war-shaped-the-design-of-american-malls.php.
70 | Ibid.
71 | Ibid.
72 | Benjamin, *The Arcades Project*, 31.
73 | Decker, "Corporate Legitimacy and Advertising," 75.
74 | Underhill, *Call of the Mall*, 19.
75 | Gruen and Smith, *Shopping Town USA: The Planning of Shopping Centers* (New York, NY: Van Nostrand Reinhold, 1960), 14.
76 | Crawford, "The World in a Shopping Mall," 8.
77 | Jackson, "All the World's a Mall," 1116.
78 | Frank Bures, "The Life and Death of Malls," July 25, 2014, http://www.minnpost.com/thirty-two-magazine/2014/07/life-and-death-malls.
79 | The International Council of Shopping Centers (ICSC), "2014 Economic Impact of Shopping Centers."
80 | Phaidon, 2010, http://www.phaidon.com/store/architecture/jerde-partnership-you-are-here-9780714838304/.
81 | Jerde, "What We Do," 2015, http://www.jerde.com/Jerde-Philosophy.html.
82 | Murillo, "'The Modern Shopping Experience:'" 374.
83 | Miller, Nel, and Hampwaye, "Malls in Zambia," 36.
84 | Kearney, "The 2015 African Retail Development Index."
85 | Eve Fairbanks, "Africa's Obsession with Shopping Malls," September 23, 2013, *New Republic*, http://www.newrepublic.com/article/114826/westgate-mall-attack-al-shabab-assaults-symbol-african-urban-life.

86 | Rob Shields, "Spaces for the Subject of Consumption," in *Lifestyle Shopping: The Subject of Consumption*, ed. Rob Shields (London and New York, Routledge, 2005), 4.
87 | Nichols, "Mistakes We Have Made in Developing Shopping Centers."
88 | Smith, "The Mall in Motion," 2.
89 | Malcolm Gladwell, "The Terrazzo Jungle," *The New Yorker*, March 15, 2004, http://www.newyorker.com/magazine/2004/03/15/the-terrazzo-jungle.
90 | "Patents: Shopping Mall US 3992824 A," March 22, 1973, https://www.google.com/patents/US3992824.
91 | Underhill, *Call of the Mall*, 86.
92 | McConnell, "'Close Your Eyes and Pretend to Be Dead.'"
93 | Gladwell, "The Terrazzo Jungle."
94 | Neil Cohen, Jay Gattuso, Ken MacLennan-Brown, "CCTV Operational Requirements Manual," Home Office Scientific Development Branch, 2007, http://www.globalmsc.net/pdfs/operational-requirements.pdf.
95 | Smith, "The Mall in Motion," 4.
96 | Ibid., 3.
97 | Ibid., 5.
98 | Rohit Varman and Russell W. Belk, "Consuming Postcolonial Shopping Malls," *Journal of Marketing Management* 28, nos. 1-2 (February 2012): 64.
99 | National Counter Terrorism Security Office, "Counter Terrorism Protective Security Advice for Shopping Centres" (London, 2014), 17.
100 | Ibid., 46.
101 | Jonathan Sterne, "Sounds Like the Mall of America: Programmed Music and the Architectonics of Commercial Space," in *Music and Technoculture*, Rene T. A. Lysloff and Jr. Leslie C. Gay, eds (Middletown CT: Wesleyan University Press, 2003), 317.
102 | Sterne, "Sounds Like the Mall of America: Programmed Music and the Architectonics of Commercial Space," *Ethnomusicology* 41, no. 1 (Winter 1997): 38.
103 | Shields, "Spaces for the Subject of Consumption," 9.
104 | Sterne, "Sounds Like the Mall of America," 324.
105 | Sterne, "Sounds Like the Mall of America: Programmed Music and the Architectonics of Commercial Space," *Ethnomusicology* 41, no. 1 (Winter 1997): 25.
106 | Sterne, "Sounds Like the Mall of America," 324.

107 | Sterne, "Sounds Like the Mall of America: Programmed Music and the Architectonics of Commercial Space," *Ethnomusicology* 41, no. 1 (Winter 1997): 25.
108 | McConnell, "'Close Your Eyes and Pretend to Be Dead.'"
109 | Ibid.
110 | Sterne, "Sounds Like the Mall of America," 317.
111 | McConnell, "'Close Your Eyes and Pretend to Be Dead.'"
112 | Smith, "The Mall in Motion," 2.
113 | Ibid., 7.
114 | Ritzer, *Enchanting a Disenchanted World*, 8.
115 | Ibid., 7. See also Geoffrey Crossick and Serge Jaumain, eds., *Cathedrals of Consumption: The European Department Store, 1850-1939* (Aldershot: Ashgate, 1999).
116 | Clifford D. Shearing and Phillip C. Stenning, "From the Panopticon to Disney World: the Development of Discipline," in Anthony N. Doob and Edward L. Greenspan, Q.C., eds, *Perspectives in Criminal Law: Essays in Honour of John LL.J. Edwards* (Canada Law Book Inc., 1984), 304.
117 | "History," 2015, http://www.westgateoxford.co.uk/history.
118 | "Eat, pray, shop: Philippines embraces mall worshipping," January 17, 2015, Inquirer.net, http://lifestyle.inquirer.net/182411/eat-pray-shop-philippines-embraces-mall-worshipping.
119 | Ibid.
120 | Jacobs, *The Mall*, 38.
121 | Nichols, "Mistakes We Have Made in Developing Shopping Centers."
122 | Stan Feingold and David McIlvride, *It's a Mall World* (New York: NY, Films Media Group, 2006), Running time 47 minutes.
123 | "History," Mall of America, 2015, http://www.mallofamerica.com/about/moa/history.
124 | "Mall of America," Mall of America, 2015, http://www.mallofamerica.com/.
125 | Crawford, "The World in a Shopping Mall," 15.
126 | Ibid.
127 | Ibid., 15-16.
128 | "Pall-Mall," Oxford English Dictionary, 2015, http://www.oxforddictionaries.com/definition/english/pall-mall. "Mall," Merriam Webster.
129 | "Mall," Oxford English Dictionary, 2015, http://www.oxforddictionaries.com/definition/english/mall.
130 | Shields, "Spaces for the Subject of Consumption," 6.

131 | Feingold and David McIlvride, *It's a Mall World*.
132 | "The Dubai Mall," The Dubai Mall, 2015, http://www.thedubaimall.com/en/Index.aspx; "History," Mall of America.
133 | Mark Gottdiener, ed., "Introduction," in *New Forms of Consumption: Consumers, Culture, and Commodification* (Lanham, MD: Rowman & Littlefield, 2000), xvii.
134 | Gottdiener, "Approaches to Consumption," 24; Mark Gottdiener, ed. "The Consumption of Space and Spaces of Consumption," in *New Forms of Consumption: Consumers, Culture, and Commodification* (Lanham, MD: Rowman & Littlefield, 2000), 269; For a discussion on commodification of education, see Arthur G Powell, Eleanor Farrar, and David k. Cohen, *The Shopping Mall High School: Winners and Losers in the Education Marketplace* (Boston, MA: Houghton Mifflin, 1985); and George Ritzer, "McUniversity in the Postmodern Consumer Culture," *Quality in Higher Education* 2 (1996): 185-199.
135 | Crawford, "The World in a Shopping Mall," 15.
136 | Kroes, *If You've Seen One, You've Seen the Mall*, 128.
137 | Government of the Republic of Kenya, "Nairobi Metro 2030: A World Class African Metropolis," 2008, https://fonnap.files.wordpress.com/2011/09/metro2030-strategy.pdf.
138 | Debord, *The Society of the Spectacle*.
139 | "Welcome to Gateway Theatre of Shopping," Gateway Theatre of Shopping, 2015, http://gatewayworld.co.za/.
140 | Myriam Houssay-Holzschuch and Annika Teppo, "A Mall for All? Race and Public Space in Post-Apartheid Cape Town," *Cultural Geographies* 16, no. 3 (2009): 372.
141 | Salcedo, "When the Global Meets the Local at the Mall," 1098-1099.
142 | Ibid.
143 | Nitzan, "Human Security, Consumer Confidence and the Future of Neoliberalism," 2.
144 | Darlene Miller, "Changing African Cityscapes – Regional Claims of African Labor at South-African Owned Shopping Malls" Conference Paper no. 24 (Instituto de Estudos Sociais e Económicos, September 19, 2007, Mozambique), 18.
145 | Decker, "Corporate Legitimacy and Advertising."
146 | Ibid., 72.
147 | Crawford, "The World in a Shopping Mall," 13.
148 | Ibid.

149 | Gottdiener, "Approaches to Consumption," 23.
150 | Ibid.
151 | Tharoor "Globalization and the Human Imagination," 88-89.
152 | Stillerman and Salcedo, "Transposing the Urban to the Mall," 311.
153 | Varman and Belk, "Consuming Postcolonial Shopping Malls," 64.
154 | Ibid.
155 | Sarlo, *Scenes from Postmodern Life*, 16.
156 | Shelja Jose Kuruvilla and Nishank Joshi, "Influence of demographics, psychographics, shopping orientation, mall shopping attitude and purchase patterns on mall patronage in India," *Journal of Retailing and Consumer Services* 17 (2010): 259.
157 | Walton, "The Westgate Shopping Centre Siege."
158 | Westgate Mall, "About," http://westgate.co.ke/about.
159 | Ferguson, "Watching the World go Round," 23-24.
160 | Varman and Belk, "Consuming Postcolonial Shopping Malls," 66.

4. Securing the Shopping Mall

1 | The Institute for Economics and Peace records that, in 2014, terrorism-related deaths increased by 80 percent since the previous year. See, "2015 Global Terrorism Index," http://www.visionofhumanity.org/sites/default/files/English%20Media%20Release%20GTI%202015.pdf.
2 | Stephen Graham, *Cities under Siege: The New Military Urbanism* (London: Verso, 2010), xiii-xiv.
3 | Ibid.
4 | LaTourrette, Howell, Mosher, and MacDonald, "Reducing Terrorism Risk at Shopping Centers," 30.
5 | United States Army, "Case Study."
6 | Laville and Burke, "Why has the AK-47 become the jihadi terrorist weapon of choice?"
7 | Cerwyn Moore, "The Threat from Swarm Attacks: Case Studies from the North Caucasus," *CTC Sentinel* 5, no. 5 (May 22, 2012), https://www.ctc.usma.edu/posts/the-threat-from-swarm-attacks-case-studies-from-the-north-caucasus.
8 | LaTourrette, Howell, Mosher, and MacDonald, "Reducing Terrorism Risk at Shopping Centers;" National Counter Terrorism Security Office, "Counter Terrorism Protective Security Advice for Shopping Centres," 46.

9 | Faith Karimi, Ashley Fantz, and Catherine E. Shoichet, "Al-Shabaab threatens malls, including some in U.S.; FBI downplays threat," CNN, February 21, 2015, http://www.cnn.com/2015/02/21/us/al-shabaab-calls-for-mall-attacks/.
10 | Andrew Pulver, "Cannes terror attack simulation unnerves film festival attendees," *The Guardian*, April 27, 2016, http://www.theguardian.com/film/2016/apr/27/cannes-terror-attack-simulation-unnerves-film-festival-attendees.
11 | Adam Rodnitzky, "Best Practices for Implementing In-Store Analytics in Bricks and Mortar Retail," ShopperTrak, http://shoppertrak.com/wp-content/uploads/2014/05/Best-Practices-for-Implementing-In-Store-Analytics-in-Bricks-and-Mortar-Retail.pdf?mkt_tok=3RkMMJWWfF9wsR0nu6%2FPZKXonjHpfsX56egsWaW%2BlMI%2F0ER3fOvrPUfGjI4ATMZnI%2BSLDwEYGJlv6SgFT7PDMbR0oLgMWhM%3D.
12 | William G. Staples, *Everyday Surveillance: Vigilance and Visibility in Postmodern Life* (Lanham, MD: Rowman & Littlefield, 2014), 5.
13 | United States Department of State, "Country Reports on Terrorism 2013."
14 | The National Center for Biomedical Research and Training, "Shopping Center Security Terrorism Awareness Training Program," n.d. https://www.ncbrt.lsu.edu/pdf/Shopping%20Center%20Security%20Awareness%202014213.pdf.
15 | Harvey, "Neoliberalism as Creative Destruction," 23.
16 | Daniel Zwerdling, G. W. Schulz, Andrew Becker, and Margot Williams, "Under Suspicion at the Mall of America," National Public Radio, September 7, 2011, http://www.npr.org/2011/09/07/140234451/under-suspicion-at-the-mall-of-america.
17 | National Counter Terrorism Security Office, "Counter Terrorism Protective Security Advice for Shopping Centres," 49.
18 | The Joint Committee on Administration and National Security, and Defence and Foreign Relations, "Report of the Joint Committee on Administration and National Security; and Defence and Foreign Relations."
19 | Murithi Mutiga, "How al-Shabaab gave Kenyan businesses a boost," *The Guardian*, September 9, 2015, http://www.theguardian.com/commentisfree/2015/sep/09/kenya-security-industry-al-shabaab.
20 | Brian M. Jenkins, "International Terrorism: A New Kind of Warfare," The Rand Paper Series (1974).
21 | Burns Security Institute, "National Survey on Shopping Center Security" (Briarcliff Manor, NY, May 1978).

22 | Burns Security Institute, "National Survey on Shopping Center Security," 1.
23 | Ibid., 9.
24 | Ibid., 5.
25 | Nichols, "Mistakes We Have Made in Developing Shopping Centers."
26 | International CPTED Association, http://www.cpted.net/.
27 | National Crime Prevention Council, "Crime Prevention through Environmental Design Training Program," 2015, http://www.ncpc.org/training/training-topics/crime-prevention-through-environmental-design-cpted-.
28 | Ronda Kaysen, "Malls Work on their Security, but Keep it in the Background," *New York Times*, November 26, 2013, http://www.nytimes.com/2013/11/27/realestate/commercial/malls-work-on-their-security-but-keep-it-in-the-background.html?_r=0.
29 | Nichols, "Mistakes We Have Made in Developing Shopping Centers."
30 | Cohen, Gattuso, MacLennan-Brown, "CCTV Operational Requirements Manual."
31 | National Counter Terrorism Security Office, "Counter Terrorism Protective Security Advice for Shopping Centres," (London, 2014), 17.
32 | Willis Retail Practice, "Security and Terrorism Guidance for Retailers," March 24, 2015, http://www.willis.com/Documents/Publications/Services/Political_Risk/20150324_Retail_Risk_Insight_Security_and_Terrorism_Guidance_for_Retailers.pdf.
33 | National Counter Terrorism Security Office, "Counter Terrorism Protective Security Advice for Shopping Centres," 23.
34 | Ibid., 7.
35 | Ibid., 16.
36 | Willis Retail Practice, "Security and Terrorism Guidance for Retailers."
37 | Ibid.
38 | Tourrette, Howell, Mosher, and MacDonald, "Reducing Terrorism Risk at Shopping Centers," xii.
39 | Ibid., 38.
40 | Eric Grasser, "Protecting Malls from a Terrorist Threat," October 1, 2005, https://sm.asisonline.org/Pages/Protecting-Malls-from-a-Terrorist-Threat.aspx. Grasser is quoting Jade Hirt, national manager for staff development with IPC International Corporation.
41 | Davis, "Fortress Los Angeles," 154.
42 | Michel Foucault, *Discipline and Punish: The Birth of the Prison*, 2nd ed., Trans. Alan Sheridan (New York, NY: Vintage, 1995).

43 | Ibid., 200.
44 | "The Panopticon," UCL Bentham Project, University College London, 2016, https://www.ucl.ac.uk/Bentham-Project/who/panopticon.
45 | Ferguson, "Watching the World go Round," 31.
46 | Victoria Ruetalo, "From Penal Institution to Shopping Mecca: The Economics of Memory and the Case of Punta Carretas," *Cultural Critique* 68 (Winter 2008): 44.
47 | Shearing and Stenning, "From the Panopticon to Disney World," 303-304.
48 | Benjamin quoting Tony Moilin, Paris en l'an 2000 (Paris, 1869), pp. 26-29 ("Aspect des rues-galeries") in Benjamin, *The Arcades Project*, 55.
49 | Alison Wakefield, "The Public Surveillance Functions of Private Security," *Surveillance & Society* 2, no. 4 (2005): 530.
50 | Smith, "The Mall in Motion," 6.
51 | Michael Fickes, "ICSC's Terrorist Awareness Training Program," January 7, 2014, http://www.chainstoreage.com/article/icsc%E2%80%99s-terrorist-awareness-training-program; The National Center for Biomedical Research and Training, "Shopping Center Security Terrorism Awareness Training Program."
52 | Fickes, "ICSC's Terrorist Awareness Training Program."
53 | Underhill, *Call of the Mall*, 41.
54 | Ibid., 34.
55 | Shearing and Stenning, "From the Panopticon to Disney World," 301.
56 | Ibid., 302.
57 | Sarlo, *Scenes from Postmodern Life*, 13.
58 | Sterne, "Sounds Like the Mall of America," 337.
59 | "Security Information," Mall of America, 2015, http://www.mallofamerica.com/guests/security.
60 | Shearing and Stenning, "From the Panopticon to Disney World."
61 | National Counter Terrorism Security Office, "Counter Terrorism Protective Security Advice for Shopping Centres," 23.
62 | Staples, *Everyday Surveillance*, 11.
63 | National Counter Terrorism Security Office, "Counter Terrorism Protective Security Advice for Shopping Centres," 49-50. Italics are my emphasis.
64 | Ibid., Italics are my emphasis.
65 | "Your Westgate Oxford," 2015, http://www.westgateoxford.co.uk/
66 | Staples, *Everyday* Surveillance, 1.

67 | LaTourrette, Howell, Mosher, and MacDonald, "Reducing Terrorism Risk at Shopping Centers," 1.
68 | Karimi, Fantz, and Shoichet, "Al-Shabaab threatens malls."
69 | Willis Retail Practice, "Security and Terrorism Guidance for Retailers;" The Willis Retail Practice add a disclaimer towards the end of the report that notes: "If you intend to take any action or make any decision on the basis of the content of this publication you should first seek specific advice from an appropriate professional. Some of the information in this publication may be compiled from third party sources we consider to be reliable, however we do not guarantee and are not responsible for the accuracy of such."
70 | Ibid.
71 | National Counter Terrorism Security Office, "Counter Terrorism Protective Security Advice for Shopping Centres," 23.
72 | Staples, *Everyday Surveillance*, 4.
73 | Ibid.
74 | Kaysen, "Malls Work on their Security, but Keep it in the Background."
75 | "Mall of America Unveils Enhanced Service Portal," *Retailing Today*, November 13, 2013, http://www.retailingtoday.com/article/mall-america-unveils-enhanced-service-portal.
76 | Kaysen, "Malls Work on their Security, but Keep it in the Background."
77 | United States Department of Homeland Security, Transportation Security Administration, "Security Fees," https://www.tsa.gov/for-industry/security-fees.
78 | See, for example, Kotaro Okamoto et al., "Classification of Pedestrian Behavior in a Shopping Mall Based on LRF and Camera Observations," MVA2011 IAPR Conference on Machine Vision Applications, June 13-15, 2011, Nara, Japan; Rosemary R. Seva, Henry Been Lirn Duh, Martin G. Helander, "Structural Analysis of Affect in the Pre-purchase Context," *DLSU Business and Economics Review* 19, no. 2 (2010): 43-52.
79 | Rodnitzky, "Best Practices for Implementing In-Store Analytics in Bricks and Mortar Retail."
80 | Catherine Dupree, "Designed to Shop," *Harvard Magazine*, July-August 2002 http://harvardmagazine.com/2002/07/designed-to-shop.html.
81 | Giroux, "Selfie Culture at the Intersection of the Corporate and the Surveillance States," *Counter Punch*, February 6, 2015, http://www.counterpunch.org/2015/02/06/selfie-culture-at-the-intersection-of-the-corporate-and-the-surveillance-states/.

82 | Cohen, Gattuso, MacLennan-Brown, "CCTV Operational Requirements Manual;" Rodnitzky, "Best Practices for Implementing In-Store Analytics in Bricks and Mortar Retail."

83 | Dirk A. Prinsloo, "Cannibalisation amongst Same Retailers & Shopping Centres in South Africa," South African Council of Shopping Centres, 2009, http://urbanstudies.co.za/wp-content/uploads/2014/07/SACSC-CANIBALISATION-PAPER.pdf.

84 | Ibid.

85 | Nichols, "Mistakes We Have Made in Developing Shopping Centers."

86 | Peter Dreier, "Massacres and Movements: Challenging the Gun Industrial Complex," *New Labor Forum* 22, no. 2 (2013): 94.

87 | Phil Wahba, "Black Friday Was the Biggest Day Ever for Gun Sales," *Fortune*, December 1, 2015, http://fortune.com/2015/12/01/gun-sales-black-friday/; Sam Ro, "Here's why we call it 'Black Friday,'" Business Insider, November 25, 2015, http://www.businessinsider.com/meaning-of-black-friday-retail-accounting-2015-11.

88 | "Black Friday: online spending surge in UK and US," BBC, November 27, 2015, http://www.bbc.com/news/business-34931837.

89 | Bud Bradley, "Shopping Mall Security: Keeping Pace with a Changing Venue," April 29, 2014, AlliedBarton Security Services, http://www.alliedbarton.com/About-Us/Blog/Article/94/Shopping-Mall-Security-Keeping-Pace-with-a-Changing-Venue.

90 | Further muddling the distinction between terrorism and legitimate corporate practice, an internet company called Oraxy staged a fake terrorist attack on Cannes' five-star Hôtel du Cap, in which a group of masked men "in matching helmets and military-style utility vests approached the hotel's dock via boat, before one of them began marching up the steps towards frightened guests." The publicity stunt was launched during the 2016 Cannes Film Festival in order to garner as much publicity as possible during one of the busiest times of year for the area. See, Henry Barnes, "Publicity stunt 'terror attack' frightens guests at Cannes'Hôtel du Cap," *The Guardian*, May 14, 2016, http://www.theguardian.com/film/2016/may/14/publicity-stunt-terror-attack-cannes-hotel-du-cap.

91 | Melissa Hausmann, "Two Fundamental Rules for Integrating People Counting into Your Culture Using Traffic Data to Deliver Incremental Revenues," ShopperTrak, 2012, http://shoppertrak.com/wp-content/uploads/2014/05/Two-Fundamental-Rules-for-Integrating-People-Counting-into-Your-Culture.pdf?mkt_tok=3RkMMJWWfF9wsRonu6%2FNZKXonjHpfsX

56egsWaW%2BlMI%2F0ER3fOvrPUfGjI4ATMZkI%2BSLDwEYGJlv6Sg
FT7PDMbRooLgMWhM%3D.
92 | Peter Eachus, Alex Stedmon, and Les Baillie, "Hostile Intent in Public Crowded Spaces: A field Study," *Applied Ergonomics* 44 (2013): 703.
93 | Reed, *Terror at the Mall.*
94 | Czinkota, Knight, Liesch and, Steen, "Terrorism and International Business," 839.
95 | Ibid.
96 | Alexander, *Business Confronts Terrorism*, 54.
97 | Ibid., 54.
98 | Andria Simmons, "Flight training restrictions tightened after 9/11," September 9, 2011, http://www.ajc.com/news/news/local/flight-training-restrictions-tightened-after-911/nQLfM/.
99 | New York City Police Department, "Analysis of Al-Shabaab's Attack at the Westgate Mall in Nairobi, Kenya."
100 | Reed, *Terror at the Mall.*
101 | Foucault, *Discipline and Punish.*
102 | Staples, *Everyday Surveillance*, 30.
103 | LaTourrette, Howell, Mosher, and MacDonald, "Reducing Terrorism Risk at Shopping Centers," 32.
104 | Miller, "Changing African Cityscapes," 17.
105 | Darlene Miller, "New Regional Imaginaries in Post-Apartheid Southern Africa – Retail Workers at a Shopping Mall in Zambia," *Journal of Southern African Studies* 31, no. 1 (2005):132.
106 | Christopher Dickey, "Inside the NYPD's Report on the Kenya Shopping Mall Massacre," *The Daily Beast*, October 12, 2013, http://www.thedailybeast.com/articles/2013/12/10/inside-the-nypd-s-report-on-the-kenya-shopping-mall-massacre.html.
107 | Reed, *Terror at the Mall.*
108 | New York City Police Department, "Analysis of Al-Shabaab's Attack at the Westgate Mall in Nairobi."
109 | McConnell, "'Close Your Eyes and Pretend to Be Dead.'"
110 | Tansy Hoskins, "Westgate: Kenyan guards on the frontline," *Al Jazeera*, September 21, 2014, http://www.aljazeera.com/news/africa/2014/09/westgate-kenyan-guards-frontline-201492154142406265.html.
111 | Miller, "New Regional Imaginaries in Post-Apartheid Southern Africa," 132.
112 | Miller, "Changing African Cityscapes,"17.

113 | An image that emerged from the catastrophe crystalizes the tension between the modernity sold by the mall and the hostility enacted by the terrorists: in the Urban Gourmet Burgers restaurant, a couple lies in a bloody embrace under a large sign that reads "Urban." See, McConnell notes that "Australian architect Ross Langdon, 32, and his pregnant partner Elif Yavuz, a 33-year-old Dutch malaria specialist who was due to give birth two weeks later, were both hit multiple times and died," "'Close Your Eyes and Pretend to Be Dead.'"

114 | Jeffrey Gettleman, "Ominous Signs, Then a Cruel Attack," *New York Times*, September 27, 2013, http://www.nytimes.com/2013/09/29/sunday-review/making-sense-of-kenyas-westgate-mall-massacre.html?pagewanted=all&_r =1&.

115 | Reed, *Terror at the Mall*.

116 | The Joint Committee on Administration and National Security, and Defence and Foreign Relations, "Report of the Joint Committee on Administration and National Security; and Defence and Foreign Relations." See also Catrina Stewart, "Nairobi Westgate mall attack: Shopping centre re-opens two years after terror siege where al-Shabaab killed 67 people," *The Independent*, July 14, 2015, http://www.independent.co.uk/news/world/africa/nairobi-westgate-attack-shopping-mall-re-opens-two-years-after-terror-siege-where-al-shabaab-killed-10389082.html.

117 | Mbembé and Nuttall, "Writing the World from an African Metropolis," 353.

118 | Mike Pflanz, "Kenyan army admits that soldiers looted Westgate mall during siege," The Telegraph, October 29, 2013, http://www.telegraph.co.uk/news/worldnews/africaandindianocean/kenya/10411403/Kenyan-army-admits-that-soldiers-looted-Westgate-mall-during-siege.html.

119 | Cohen, Gattuso, MacLennan-Brown, "CCTV Operational Requirements Manual."

120 | Staples, *Everyday Surveillance*, 9.

121 | Henry A. Giroux, "Beyond the Spectacle of Terrorism: Rethinking Politics in the Society of the Image," *Situations: Project of the Radical Imagination* 2, no. 1 (2007): 28.

5. SPECTACLES OF THE SHOPPING MALL

1 | Harriet Alexander, "Tweeting Terrorism: How al Shabaab Live Blogged the Nairobi Attacks," *The Telegraph*, September 22, 2103, http://www.telegraph.co.uk/news/worldnews/africaandindianocean/kenya/10326863/Tweeting-terrorism-How-al-Shabaab-live-blogged-the-Nairobi-attacks.html.
2 | Jerry Abuga, "Media Council Tables Findings on Westgate Coverage," February 10, 2014, Media Council of Kenya, http://www.mediacouncil.or.ke/en/mck/index.php/news/101-media-council-tables-findings-on-westgate-coverage.
3 | Brian M. Jenkins, "International Terrorism: A New Kind of Warfare," The Rand Paper Series (1974): 4.
4 | Gabriel Weimann, "Cyber-Fatwas and Terrorism," *Studies in Conflict & Terrorism* 34, no. 10 (2011): 768.
5 | Cristina Archetti, *Understanding Terrorism in the Age of Global Media: A Communication Approach* (Palgrave Macmillan, 2013), 2.
6 | Aggrey Mutambo, "Bodies of Westgate terrorists 'are with the FBI', says KDF Chief Julius Karangi," *Daily Nation*, February 7, 2014, http://mobile.nation.co.ke/news/Julius-Karangi-Kenya-Defence-Forces-Westgate-Attack/-/1950946/2196566/-/format/xhtml/-/r60qhdz/-/index.html.
7 | Archetti, *Understanding Terrorism in the Age of Global Media*, 38.
8 | Aaron M. Hoffman, Dwaine H. A. Jengelley, Natasha T. Duncan, Melissa Buehler, and Meredith L. Rees, "How Does the Business of News Influence Terrorism Coverage? Evidence From *The Washington Post* and *USA Today*," *Terrorism and Political Violence* 22 (2010): 576.
9 | Ibid.
10 | For a list of some of the largest media conglomerates, see: "Media Data Base – International Media Corporations 2015," Institute of Media and Communications Policy, http://www.mediadb.eu/en.html; The intensification of "the role of privatized commercial culture in the militarization of the social field" has resulted in an ultimate synthetization of the discourses of news, entertainment, and security within the private space of the home. See Takacs, "Real War News, Real War Games," 181; Media conglomerates now specialize in combining media services with digital home security packages offering "professional 24/7 monitoring, home and energy management, video surveillance, [and] control from anywhere." Time Warner Cable Enterprises, "More than home security," 2016, http://www.timewarnercable.com/en/intelligenthome/overview.html.

11 | Dwayne Winseck, "The Political Economies of Media: The Transformation of the Global Media," in *The Political Economies of Media: The Transformation of the Global Media*, eds. Dal Yong Jin and Dwayne Winseck (London: Bloomsbury, 2011), 16.

12 | Ignacio Ramonet, "The Power of Television Pictures," February 20, 2002, UNESCO, http://www.unesco.org/webworld/points_of_views/200 202_ramonet.shtml.

13 | James M. Shultz et al., "Multiple Vantage Points on the Mental Health Effects of Mass Shootings," *Current Psychiatry Reports* 16, no. 9 (2014): 4, DOI 10.1007/s11920-014-0469-5.

14 | David L. Altheide, "Terrorism and the Politics of Fear," in *Cultures of Fear: A Critical Reader*, eds. Danielle Taana Smith and Uli Linke (London: Pluto Press, 2009), 12.57.

15 | Henry A. Giroux, "ISIS and the Spectacle of Terrorism: Resisting Mainstream Workstations of Fear," September 30, 2014, http://www.truth-out.org/news/item/26519-isis-and-the-spectacle-of-terrorism-resisting-mainstream-workstations-of-fear#a2.

16 | Ibid.

17 | "Paris Supermarket Siege Survivors Sue Media over 'Dangerous' Coverage," *The Guardian*, April 3, 2015, http://www.theguardian.com/world/2015/apr/03/paris-supermarket-siege-survivors-sue-media.

18 | Mutambo, "Bodies of Westgate terrorists 'are with the FBI.'"

19 | Abuga, "Media Council Tables Findings on Westgate Coverage." In the aftermath of the attacks, Linus Gitahi, the Chief Executive Officer of the Nation Media Group and a representative of the Media Owners Association said: "Overall, we are delighted with the coverage. We are delighted that we were as close as possible to the issues. It was not all gloom. There were many things that were done well," Mutambo, "Bodies of Westgate terrorists 'are with the FBI'."

20 | Catrina Stewart, "Nairobi Westgate mall attack: Shopping centre reopens two years after terror siege where al-Shabaab killed 67 people," *The Independent*, July 14, 2015, http://www.independent.co.uk/news/world/africa/nairobi-westgate-attack-shopping-mall-re-opens-two-years-after-terror-siege-where-al-shabaab-killed-10389082.html.

21 | Gabriel Weimann, "Terror on Facebook, Twitter, and Youtube," *Brown Journal of World Affairs* 16, no. 2 (2010): 45.

22 | Carl Boggs and Tom Pollard, "Hollywood and the Spectacle of Terrorism," *New Political Science* 28, no. 3 (2006): 351.

23 | Jason Straziuso, "'Send Me a Cruise Missile,' New Rap Song from Omar Hammami, American Militant in Somalia, Released," *Huffington Post*, April 12, 2011, http://www.huffingtonpost.com/2011/04/12/send-me-a-cruise-missile-omar-hammami_n_848167.html.
24 | Nel Hodge, "How Somalia's al-Shabab militants hone their image," *BBC News*, June 5, 2014, http://www.bbc.com/news/world-africa-27633367.
25 | Simon et al, "Twitter in the Cross Fire," 6.
26 | Ibid.
27 | "Nairobi Westgate shoot-out kills 11 in Kenya," *BBC News*, September 21, 2013, http://www.bbc.com/news/world-africa-24186780#TWEET897232.
28 | Bergen, "Are mass murderers using Twitter as a tool?"
29 | Weimann, "Cyber-Fatwas and Terrorism," 768. Weimann writes that one of the *fatwas* was titled, "Declaration of War against the Americans Occupying the Land of the Two Holy Places."
30 | Tal Samuel-Azran, *Al-Jazeera and US War Coverage* (New York, NY: Peter Lang, 2010), 53.
31 | Jytte Klausen, "Tweeting the *Jihad*: Social Media Networks of Western Foreign Fighters in Syria and Iraq," *Studies in Conflict & Terrorism* 38 (2015): 4.
32 | Bruneau Nordeste and David Carment, "A Framework for Understanding Terrorist Use of the Internet," Canadian Centre for Intelligence and Security Studies, The Norman Paterson School of International Affairs, Carleton University, ITAC CIEM Trends in Terrorism Series, 2006, http://www4.carleton.ca/cifp/app/serve.php/1121.pdf.
33 | Stacy Takacs, "Real War News, Real War Games: The Hekmati Case and the Problems of Soft Power," *American Quarterly* 65, no. 1 (2013): 180.
34 | "The Westgate Attack: A New Trend in al-Qaeda Communication Strategies," SITE Intelligence Group, January 15, 2014, https://news.siteintelgroup.com/Articles-Analysis/the-westgate-attack-a-new-trend-in-al-qaeda-communication-strategies.html.
35 | Archetti, *Understanding Terrorism in the Age of Global Media: A Communication Approach*, 41.
36 | Weimann, "Terror on Facebook, Twitter, and Youtube," 45.
37 | Weimann, "Cyber-Fatwas and Terrorism," 769.
38 | Klausen, "Tweeting the *Jihad*," 1.
39 | The Islamic State terrorist group is also known as the Islamic State in Iraq and Syria (ISIS) and the Islamic State in Iraq and the Levant (ISIL); J. M. Berger, "How ISIS Games Twitter," *The Atlantic*, June 16, 2014, http://

www.theatlantic.com/international/archive/2014/06/isis-iraq-twitter-social-media-strategy/372856/.
40 | Berger, "How ISIS Games Twitter."
41 | Ibid.
42 | "Google Removes Isis App from Play Store," July 18, 2014, *ITV News*, http://www.itv.com/news/story/2014-06-18/google-play-store-isis-app/.
43 | John Curtis Amble, "Combating Terrorism in the New Media Environment," *Studies in Conflict & Terrorism* 35 (2012): 341.
44 | Klausen, "Tweeting the *Jihad*," 1.
45 | Alexander, "Tweeting Terrorism;" Bergen, "Are Mass Murderers Using Twitter as a Tool?"
46 | Alexander, "Tweeting Terrorism."
47 | Alex Altman, "Why Terrorists Love Twitter," September 11, 2014, *Time*, http://time.com/3319278/isis-isil-twitter/.
48 | Bergen, "Are Mass Murderers using Twitter as a Tool?"
49 | US Department of State, "Center for Strategic Counterterrorism Communications (CSCC)," http://www.state.gov/r/cscc/.
50 | Steve Rose, "The ISIS Propaganda War: A Hi-Tech Media Jihad," *The Guardian*, October 7, 2014, http://www.theguardian.com/world/2014/oct/07/isis-media-machine-propaganda-war.
51 | Amble, "Combating Terrorism in the New Media Environment," 343; Vincent Bernatis, "The Taliban and Twitter: Tactical Reporting and Strategic Messaging," *Perspectives on Terrorism* 8, no. 6 (2014): 25.
52 | Jastinder Khera, "Authorities and militants take Nairobi battle to Twitter," September 24, 2013, *BBC News*, http://www.bbc.com/news/world-africa-24218276.
53 | Alexander, "Tweeting Terrorism."
54 | Ibid.
55 | Martha Crenshaw, "The Debate over 'New' vs. 'Old' Terrorism," in *Values and Violence: Intangible Aspects of Terrorism*, eds. Ibrahim A. Karawan, Wayne McCormack, and Stephen E. Reynolds (Springer, 2008).
56 | Simon et al, "Twitter in the Cross Fire," 4.
57 | Nanjira Sambuli, "How Useful is a Tweet? A review of the first tweets from the Westgate Mall Attack," Ihub Research, October 3, 2013, http://www.ihub.co.ke/blogs/16012; Daniel Howden, "Terror in Westgate mall: the full story of the attacks that devastated Kenya," *The Guardian*, October 4, 2013, http://www.theguardian.com/world/interactive/2013/oct/04/westgate-mall-attacks-kenya-terror#undefined.

58 | Sambuli, "How Useful is a Tweet?"
59 | Simon et al, "Twitter in the Cross Fire," 5.
60 | Kenyan Ministry of Interior, Twitter, https://twitter.com/InteriorKE/status/381960772420923392; Ministry of Interior and Coordination of National Government in The Office of the President, Government of Kenya, September 22, 2013, https://twitter.com/InteriorKE/status/381960772420923392; Simon et al, "Twitter in the Cross Fire," 8.
61 | Sambuli, "How Useful is a Tweet?"
62 | Ibid.
63 | Simon et al, "Twitter in the Cross Fire," 2.
64 | Ibid., 8
65 | Ibid.
66 | Ibid., 9.
67 | Dennis Okari, "Kenya's Westgate attack: Unanswered questions one year on," September 21, 2014, *BBC News*, http://www.bbc.com/news/world-africa-29282045.
68 | The Joint Committee on Administration and National Security, and Defence and Foreign Relations, "Report of the Joint Committee on Administration and National Security; and Defence and Foreign Relations."
69 | Warner, "Outside Westgate."
70 | Heidi Vogt and Patrick Mcgroarty, "Before Kenya Attack, a Warning on Terrorism," *The Wall Street Journal*, September 30, 2013, http://www.wsj.com/articles/SB10001424052702303643304579105222268968650.
71 | Lough and Sheikh, "UPDATE 3-Kenya launches probe as Shabaab leader confirms mall attack."
72 | "The Westgate Attack: A New Trend in al-Qaeda Communication Strategies," SITE Intelligence Group, January 15, 2014, https://news.siteintelgroup.com/Articles-Analysis/the-westgate-attack-a-new-trend-in-al-qaeda-communication-strategies.html.
73 | Laura Petrecca, "39 die in Kenya mall siege; hostages still held," *USA Today*, September 21, 2013, http://www.usatoday.com/story/news/world/2013/09/21/witness-kenya-mall-attackers-target-non-muslims/2846319/.
74 | Alexander, "Tweeting Terrorism."
75 | Vogt and Mcgroarty, "Before Kenya Attack, a Warning on Terrorism."
76 | Jenkins, "International Terrorism," 4.
77 | Vogt and Mcgroarty, "Before Kenya Attack, a Warning on Terrorism."
78 | Weimann, "Terror on Facebook, Twitter, and Youtube," 46.

79 | Anne Penketh, "Brussels Jewish Museum shooting: suspect with Islamist links arrested," *The Guardian*, June 1, 2014, http://www.theguardian.com/world/2014/jun/01/suspect-arrest-brussels-jewish-museum-shooting.
80 | Jason Burke, "Paris shootings: investigation launched into where gunmen got GoPro cameras," *The Guardian*, January 12, 2015, http://www.theguardian.com/world/2015/jan/12/paris-shootings-cameras-kouachi-brothers-amedy-coulibaly.
81 | Marcus Schulzke, "Simulating Terrorism and Insurgency: Video Games in the War of Ideas," *Cambridge Review of International Affairs* 27, no. 4 (2014): 632.
82 | Amble, "Combating Terrorism in the New Media Environment," 343.
83 | John Plunkett, "BBC Radio 1 criticised for airing 'Call of Duty' interview with Isis Briton," *The Guardian*, November 10, 2014, http://www.theguardian.com/media/2014/nov/10/bbc-radio-1-criticised-british-isis-militant-interview.
84 | Takacs, "Real War News, Real War Games," 177-178.
85 | Graham, *Cities under* Siege, xxv.
86 | Ibid., xxv-xxvi.
87 | Ibid.
88 | Giroux, "Beyond the Spectacle of Terrorism," 28.
89 | Ibid.
90 | Takacs, "Real War News, Real War Games," 177.
91 | Rose, "The Isis Propaganda War."
92 | Raf Sanchez, "Tweeting at Terrorists: Inside America's Social Media Battle with Online Jihad," *The Telegraph*, May 21, 2014, http://www.telegraph.co.uk/news/worldnews/al-qaeda/10829355/Tweeting-at-terrorists-inside-Americas-social-media-battle-with-online-jihad.html.
93 | Rose, "The Isis Propaganda War."
94 | Giroux, "ISIS and the Spectacle of Terrorism."
95 | Farhat, "New Media and the Spectacle of the War on Terror."
96 | Mona Moufahim and Michael Humphreys, "Marketing an Extremist Ideology: The Vlaams Belang's Nationalist Discourse," in *The Routledge Companion to Ethics, Politics and Organizations*, eds. Alison Pullen and Carl Rhodes (Oxon: Routledge, 2015), 85.
97 | Giroux, "ISIS and the Spectacle of Terrorism."
98 | Claudia Springer, "Military Propaganda: Defense Department Films from World War II and Vietnam," *Cultural Critique* 3 (Spring 1986): 151.
99 | Matt Delmont, "Visual Culture and the War on Terror," *American Quarterly* 65, no. 1 (March 2013): 157.

100 | Archetti, *Understanding Terrorism in the Age of Global Media*, 141.
101 | United States Army, "Antiterrorism Theme—Antiterrorism Strategic Plan," April 1, 2013, http://www.army.mil/standto/archive_2013-04-01/.
102 | Giroux, "Beyond the Spectacle of Terrorism," 20.
103 | Douglas Kellner, "September 11, Spectacles of Terror, and Media Manipulation: A Critique of Jihadist and Bush Media Politics," *Logos* 2, no. 1 (Winter 2003): 87.
104 | Nicholas Kulish, "In this Horror Film, Blood is all too Real: 'Terror at the Mall' on HBO Documents an Attack in Kenya," *New York Times*, September 14, 2014, http://www.nytimes.com/2014/09/15/arts/television/terror-at-the-mall-on-hbo-documents-an-attack-in-kenya.html?_r=0.
105 | Jeffory A. Clymer, *America's Culture of Terrorism: Violence, Capitalism, and the Written Word* (Chapel Hill: University of North Carolina Press, 2003), 215.
106 | Kulish, "In this Horror Film, Blood is all too Real."
107 | "'Terror at the Mall,' Documentary on Siege of Westgate Mall in Nairobi, Kenya, Coming to HBO," Press Release, September 2, 2014, http://blogs.indiewire.com/shadowandact/terror-at-the-mall-an-inside-look-at-the-siege-of-westgate-mall-in-nairobi-kenya-debuts-sept-15-on-hbo-20140902.
108 | Mutambo, "Bodies of Westgate terrorists 'are with the FBI.'"
109 | Reed, *Terror at the Mall*.
110 | "Westgate Mall Photographer Goran Tomasevic: 'If I Get Shot, I Get Shot'," September 28, 2013, http://www.buzzfeed.com/rachelzarrell/interview-with-westgate-mall-photographer-goran-tomasevic#.nsDaOrNN2.
111 | Jon Goss, "The 'Magic of the Mall': An Analysis of Form, Function, and Meaning in the Contemporary Retail Built Environment," *Annals of the Association of American Geographers* 83, no. 1. (1993), 20.
112 | Similarly, footage from the 2015 Tunisian Sousse terrorist attack has the same effect, where images of the perpetrator casually strolling a sunny beach armed with an assault weapon and surrounded by dead bodies is not easy to comprehend. See images in Chris Stephen, "Tourists desert Tunisia after June terror attack," BBC, September 25, 2015, http://www.theguardian.com/world/2015/sep/25/tourists-tunisia-june-terror-attack-economy-beach-hotel-sousse.
113 | *Elysium* is directed by South African Neill Blomkamp, and is "a science-fiction take on the haves and have-nots and the separation of wealth," a "parable that drew from the apartheid era in his native South Africa." Kyle Buchanan, "Matt Damon's Elysium is an Action Movie for the 99 Percent,"

Vulture, September 4, 2013, http://www.vulture.com/2013/04/elysium-matt-damons-action-movie-for-the-99.html.
114 | Quoted in Kroes, *If You've Seen One, You've Seen the Mall*, 104.
115 | McConnell, "'Close Your Eyes and Pretend to Be Dead.'"
116 | Radiolab, "Outside Westgate," November 29, 2014, http://www.radiolab.org/story/outside-westgate/.
117 | Warner, "Outside Westgate;" Nina Strochlic, "Westgate's Chilling Security Video Reveals Shopping Mall Bloodbath," *The Daily Beast*, September 15, 2014, http://www.thedailybeast.com/articles/2014/09/15/westgate-s-chilling-security-video-reveals-shopping-mall-bloodbath.html.
118 | Strochlic, "Westgate's Chilling Security Video Reveals Shopping Mall Bloodbath." In this quote, Strochlic paraphrases Margie Brand, one of the survivors of the Westgate Mall.
119 | "Shabaab Releases Video on Westgate Mall Raid, Names Western Malls as Targets for Lone Wolf Attacks," SITE Intelligence Group, February 21, 2015, http://news.siteintelgroup.com/blog/index.php/categories/jihad/entry/363-shabaab-releases-video-on-westgate-mall-raid,-names-western-malls-as-targets-for-lone-wolf-attacks.
120 | Benjamin R. Nadler, "Hawkers cash in on terror attack video," *Daily Nation*, October 1, 2013, http://www.nation.co.ke/news/Hawkers-cash-in-on-terror-attack-video/-/1056/2015270/-/4arkwsz/-/index.html.
121 | Ibid.

6. Conclusion: Specters of the Shopping Mall

1 | Ariel Zirulnick, "Kenyan consumers win this round against Al Shabaab as Westgate Mall reopens," Quartz Africa, July 18, 2015, http://qz.com/457808/kenyan-consumers-win-this-round-against-al-shabaab-as-westgate-mall-reopens/.
2 | Janz, "The Terror of the Place," 192.
3 | Ibid., 202.
4 | Terrorist groups often release a variety of threats using social media. See Karimi, Fantz, and Shoichet, "Al-Shabaab threatens malls, including some in U.S;" and many countries now have a terrorism risk alert hierarchy system, which they raise or lower depending on the scenario. See United States Department of Homeland Security, "National Terrorism Advisory System," 2016, http://www.dhs.gov/national-terrorism-advisory-system.

5 | Manji, "Bulldozers, Homes and Highways," 220.
6 | "Kenya's Westgate Shopping Mall Reopens," Aljazeera, July 18, 2015, http://www.aljazeera.com/news/2015/07/kenya-westgate-shopping-mall-reopen-150718012221949.html.
7 | Chrispin Mwakideu and James Shimanyula, "Kenya's Westgate Mall Re-opens amid Security Concerns," *Deutsche Welle*, July 17, 2015, http://www.dw.com/en/kenyas-westgate-mall-re-opens-amid-security-concerns/a-18591953.
8 | Zirulnick, "Kenyan consumers win this round against Al Shabaab as Westgate Mall reopens."
9 | Mbembé and Nuttall, "Writing the World from an African Metropolis," 365.
10 | Kristin Hoganson, "Bernath Lecture - Stuff It: Domestic Consumption and the Americanization of the World Paradigm," *Diplomatic History* 30, no. 4 (2006): 586.
11 | Tansy Hoskins, "Westgate: Kenyan guards on the frontline," *Al Jazeera*, September 21, 2014, http://www.aljazeera.com/news/africa/2014/09/westgate-kenyan-guards-frontline-201492154142406265.html.
12 | Murithi Mutiga, "How al-Shabaab gave Kenyan businesses a boost," *The Guardian*, September 9, 2015, http://www.theguardian.com/commentisfree/2015/sep/09/kenya-security-industry-al-shabaab.
13 | Giroux, "Beyond the Spectacle of Terrorism," 28.
14 | Leo Johnson, "Petropolis now: Are cities getting too big?" November 14, 2013, *New Statesman*, http://www.newstatesman.com/2013/11/petropolis-now.
15 | International Council of Shopping Centers, "Nairobi retail bouncing back from terrorist attack," August 19, 2015, http://www.icsc.org/press/nairobi-mall-scene-back-to-normal-a-year-after-terrorist-attack.
16 | "About Two Rivers Development," 2015, http://www.tworivers.co.ke/index.php/2015-04-13-03-25-27/about-two-rivers-development.
17 | Dinfin Mulupi, "East Africa's largest shopping mall to have strong international flavor," April 22, 2015, http://www.howwemadeitinafrica.com/east-africas-largest-shopping-mall-to-have-strong-international-flavour/48405/.
18 | Wakefield, "The Public Surveillance Functions of Private Security," 531-532.
19 | Marks and Bezzoli, "Palaces of Desire," 38-39.

20 | Coral Springs, "City Hall in the Mall," 2015, http://www.coralsprings.org/government/other-departments-and-services/city-hall-in-the-mall.
21 | Steven P. Aggergaard, "When 'Public Space' Isn't Public," June 9, 2015, *Bench & Bar of Minnesota*, http://mnbenchbar.com/2015/06/when-public-space-isnt-public/.
22 | John Reinan, "Black Lives Matter protesters question 'intertwined' relationship between Mall of America and Bloomington," *Star Tribune*, July 4, 2015, http://www.startribune.com/black-lives-matter-protesters-question-intertwined-relationship-between-mall-of-america-and-bloomington/311587741/;" Aggergaard, "When 'Public Space' Isn't Public."
23 | "Protesters Mass at Mall of America on Busy Shopping Day," *NBC News*, December 20, 2014, http://www.nbcnews.com/news/us-news/protesters-mass-mall-america-busy-shopping-day-n272326; Reinan, "Black Lives Matter protesters question 'intertwined' relationship between Mall of America and Bloomington."
24 | Crawford, "The World in a Shopping Mall," 22.
25 | Manji, "Bulldozers, Homes and Highways," 206; Amnesty International, "We are like rubbish in this country": Forced evictions in Nairobi, Kenya," 2013, https://www.amnesty.org/en/documents/afr32/005/2013/en/.
26 | Amnesty International, "We are like Rubbish in this Country."
27 | Harvey, "Neoliberalism as Creative Destruction," 39; Government of the Republic of Kenya, "Kenya Vision 2030: The Popular Version," Such "creative destruction" to modernize the city of Nairobi follows a similar pattern of renovating the Parisian city center in the nineteenth century by Georges-Eugène Haussmann, known as the "demolition artist," Benjamin, *The Arcades Project*, 11-12.
28 | Davis, "Fortress Los Angeles," 159.
29 | John Beardsley, "Kiss Nature Goodbye," *Harvard Design Magazine* 10 (2000), http://www.harvarddesignmagazine.org/issues/10/kiss-nature-goodbye.
30 | Rafael Marks and Marco Bezzoli, "Palaces of Desire: Century City, Cape Town and the Ambiguities of Development," *Urban Forum* 12, no. 1 (January 2001): 27.
31 | Hobden, "A Man, a Plan, a Mall."
32 | Staples, *Everyday Surveillance*, 205.
33 | Ritzer, *Enchanting a Disenchanted World*, 200.
34 | Joel Garreau, *Edge City - Life on the New Frontier* (Double Day, 1988), 199.

35 | Bayat, "Politics in the City-Inside-Out," 111.
36 | Claire Provost, "British Aid Money Invested in Gated Communities and Shopping Centres," *The Guardian*, May 2, 2014, http://www.theguardian.com/global-development/2014/may/02/british-aid-money-gated-communities-shopping-centres-cdc-poverty.
37 | Provost, "British Aid Money Invested in Gated Communities and Shopping Centres."
38 | Broll Property Group, "The Broll Report 2014/2015."
39 | Davis, "Fortress Los Angeles," 166.
40 | Williams, "After Westgate," 911.
41 | Keatinge, "The Role of Finance in Defeating Al-Shabaab."
42 | Kennedy Odedejan, "Terrorism's Fertile Ground," *New York Times*, January 8, 2014, http://www.nytimes.com/2014/01/09/opinion/terrorisms-fertile-ground.html?_r=0.
43 | Wakefield, "The Public Surveillance Functions of Private Security," 530-531.
44 | Marks and Bezzoli, "Palaces of Desire," 37.
45 | Davis, "Fortress Los Angeles," 170-171.
46 | María Bird Picó, "Captive Consumers: An Unsuccessful Prison has Proved to be a Great Mall," *Shopping Centers Today* 33, no. 3 (2012), http://sct.epubxp.com/i/55396-mar-2012/3; Ruetalo, "From Penal Institution to Shopping Mecca," 38.
47 | Nielson, "2014 State of the Shopping Center," 2014, http://www.nielsen.com/content/dam/corporate/us/en/reports-downloads/2014%20Reports/state-of-the-shopping-center-report-may-2014.pdf.
48 | The Headquarters, "Headquarters History," 2015, http://theheadquarters.com/history.
49 | Ibid.
50 | Ibid.
51 | Ruetalo, "From Penal Institution to Shopping Mecca," 48.
52 | Picó, "Captive Consumers."
53 | Ibid; José María López Mazz, "An Archeological View of Political Repression in Uruguay (1971-1985)," in *Memories from Darkness: Archaeology of Repression and Resistance in Latin America (Contributions to Global Historical Archaeology)*, eds. Pedro Funari, Andres Zarankin, and Melissa Salerno (New York, NY: Springer, 2010), 38.
54 | Mari Haymanon, "Burying the Past? Former Uruguayan Prison Becomes Shopping Mall," *Latin American News Dispatch*, December 21, 2009,

http://latindispatch.com/2009/12/21/feature-burying-the-past-former-uruguayan-prison-becomes-shopping-mall/.
55 | "An 'arresting' mall at former prison in Uruguay," http://blog2.icsc.org/?p=1319.
56 | Picó, "Captive Consumers."
57 | Haymanon, "Burying the Past?"
58 | Ibid.
59 | Stewart, "Nairobi Westgate Mall Attack."
60 | Abidin Kusno, "Remembering/Forgetting the May Riots: Architecture, Violence, and the Making of 'Chinese Cultures' in Post-1998 Jakarta," *Public Culture* 15, no. 1 (Winter 2003): 153-154.
61 | Sarlo, *Scenes from Postmodern Life*, 14.
62 | "About," Westgate Shopping Mall, 2015, http://westgate.co.ke/about.
63 | Zirulnick, "Kenyan Consumers Win this Round against Al Shabaab as Westgate Mall Reopens."
64 | Ibid; Italics were added to the titles of these books.
65 | Gruen, "Dynamic Planning for Retail Areas."
66 | Fabian Faurholt Csaba and S°ren Askegaard, "Malls and the Orchestration of the Shopping Experience in a Historical Perspective," *Advances in Consumer Research* 26, no. 1 (1999), http://www.acrwebsite.org/search/view-conference-proceedings.aspx?Id=8221.
67 | M. Jeffrey Hardwick, *Mall Maker: Victor Gruen, Architect of an American Dream* (Philadelphia, PA: University of Pennsylvania Press, 2004), 15.
68 | Frank Bures, "The Life and Death of Malls," *Minnesota Post, Thirty Two Magazine*, July 25, 2014, https://www.minnpost.com/thirty-two-magazine/2014/07/life-and-death-malls.
69 | George Ritzer, "New Cathedral of Consumption," September 30, 2012, https://georgeritzer.wordpress.com/2012/09/30/new-cathedral-of-consumption/.
70 | Zygmunt Bauman, "Desert Spectacular," in *The Flâneur*, trans., Keith Tester (New York, NY: Routledge, 2015), 155.
71 | Ritzer, "New Cathedral of Consumption."
72 | Hoganson, "Bernath Lecture – Stuff It," 587.
73 | Czinkota, Knight, Liesch, and Steen, "Terrorism and International Business," 834.
74 | Gottdiener, "Introduction," x.
75 | Prestholdt, *Domesticating the World*, 59.
76 | Giroux, "ISIS and the Spectacle of Terrorism."

77 | "About Us," Gateway Theatre of Shopping, 2015, http://gatewayworld.co.za/.
78 | Gladwell, "The Terrazzo Jungle."
79 | Salcedo, "When the Global Meets the Local at the Mall," 1091.

Bibliography

Abaza, Mona. "Shopping Malls, Consumer Culture and the Reshaping of Public Space in Egypt," *Theory, Culture & Society* 18, no. 5 (2001): 97-122.

Abdulsamed, Farah. "Somali Investment in Kenya," Africa Programme Briefing Paper, Chatham House (March 2011), 1. http://somalithinktank.org/wp-content/uploads/2011/03/Somali-Investmen-In-Kenya1.pdf.

"About Two Rivers Development." 2015, http://www.tworivers.co.ke/index.php/2015-04-13-03-25-27/about-two-rivers-development.

Abuga, Jerry. "Media Council Tables Findings on Westgate Coverage," February 10, 2014, Media Council of Kenya, http://www.mediacouncil.or.ke/en/mck/index.php/news/101-media-council-tables-findings-on-westgate-coverage.

Agamben, Giorgio. *The State of Exception*, trans. Kevin Attell (Chicago, IL: Chicago University Press, 2005).

Aggergaard, Steven P. "When 'Public Space' Isn't Public," June 9, 2015, *Bench & Bar of Minnesota*, http://mnbenchbar.com/2015/06/when-public-space-isnt-public/.

Aggrey Mutambo, "Bodies of Westgate terrorists 'are with the FBI', says KDF Chief Julius Karangi," *Daily Nation*, February 7, 2014, http://mobile.nation.co.ke/news/Julius-Karangi-Kenya-Defence-Forces-Westgate-Attack/-/1950946/2196566/-/format/xhtml/-/r60qhdz/-/index.html.

Al-Bulushi, Samar. "'Peacekeeping' as Occupation: Managing the Market for Violent Labor in Somalia," *Transforming Anthropology* 22, no. 1 (May 2014): 31-37.

Alexander, Guy. "Kenyan mall shooting: 'They threw grenades like maize to chickens'." September 22, 2013, http://www.theguardian.com/world/2013/sep/21/nairobi-shopping-centre-terror-attack.

Alexander, Harriet. "Tweeting Terrorism: How al Shabaab Live Blogged the Nairobi Attacks," *The Telegraph*, September 22, 2103, http://www.telegraph.co.uk/news/worldnews/africaandindianocean/kenya/10326863/Tweeting-terrorism-How-al-Shabaab-live-blogged-the-Nairobi-attacks.html.

AlliedBarton Security Services, "Partnering with Military Assistance Groups to Hire Our Heroes," n.d., http://www.alliedbarton.com/Security-Resource-Center/Case-Studies/View-Case-Study/ArticleId/239/Partnering-with-Military-Assistance-Groups-to-Hire-Our-Heroes.

Amnesty International. "We are like rubbish in this country": Forced evictions in Nairobi, Kenya," 2013, https://www.amnesty.org/en/documents/afr32/005/2013/en/.

Anning-Dorson, Thomas, Adelaide Kastner, and Mohammed Abdulai Mahmoud. "Investigation into Mall Visitation Motivation and Demographic Idiosyncrasies in Ghana," *Management Science Letters* 3: 367-384 (2013).

Archetti, Cristina. *Understanding Terrorism in the Age of Global Media: A Communication Approach* (Palgrave Macmillan, 2013).

Archive.is. "HSM Press Office," September 21, 2013, https://archive.is/CAJCc.

_____"EX HMS_PRESS2," September 22, 2013, https://archive.is/pVEkm.

_____"HSM Press Office," September 26, 2013, https://archive.is/XVBeU#selection-1609.0-1609.16.

Associated Press. "Deadly blast hits shopping mall in Nigerian capital Abuja," *The Guardian*, June 25, 2014, http://www.theguardian.com/world/2014/jun/25/deadly-blast-nigerian-shopping-mall-abuja.

Atwan, Abdel Bari. *Islamic State: The Digital Caliphate* (Berkeley, CA: University of California Press, 2015).

Barber, Benjamin R. "Jihad vs. McWorld," *The Atlantic*, March 1992 http://www.theatlantic.com/magazine/archive/1992/03/jihad-vs-mcworld/303882/.

Bauman, Zygmunt. "Desert Spectacular," in *The Flâneur*, trans., Keith Tester (New York, NY: Routledge, 2015).

Bayat, Asef. "Politics in the City-Inside-Out," *City & Society* 24, no. 2 (2012): 110-128.

Beardsley, John. "Kiss Nature Goodbye." *Harvard Design Magazine* 10 (2000), http://www.harvarddesignmagazine.org/issues/10/kiss-nature-good bye.
Beasley-Murray, Jon. "Translator's Introduction" of Beatriz Sarlo, Scenes from Postmodern Life, trans. Jon Beasley-Murray (Minneapolis, MN: University of Minnesota Press, 2001).
Beekarry, Navin, ed. *Combating Money Laundering And Terrorism Finance: Past And Current Challenges* (Edward Elgar Publishing, 2013).
Benjamin, Walter. *The Arcades Project*, Howard Eiland and Kevin McLaughlin, trans. (Cambridge, MA: Harvard University Press, 1999).
Bergen, Peter. "Al-Shabaab's American allies," CNN, September 24, 2013, http://edition.cnn.com/2013/09/23/opinion/bergen-al-shabaab-american-ties/.
Berthet, Elie. HRue et Passage du Caire," Paris chez soi (Paris {1854}).
Blank: Architecture, Apartheid and After, ed. Hilton Judin and Ivan Vladislavic´ (Rotterdam: NAi, 1998).
Boddy, Trevor. "Underground and Overhead: Building the Analogous City," in *Variations on a Theme Park: The New American City and the End of Public Space*, ed., Michael Sorkin (New York, NY: Hill and Wang, 1992), 123-153.
Boggs, Carl, and Tom Pollard. "Hollywood and the Spectacle of Terrorism," *New Political Science* 28, no. 3 (2006): 335-351.
Borg, Chris, and Earl Nurse. "Mall the Merrier: Africa's Growing Appetite for Shopping," CNN, October 2, 2015, http://www.cnn.com/2015/10/02/africa/shopping-malls-africa/.
Bourdieu, Pierre. *Firing Back: Against the Tyranny of the Market 2* (New York, NY: The New Press, 2003).
Bradley, Bud. "Shopping Mall Security: Keeping Pace with a Changing Venue." April 29, 2014, AlliedBarton Security Services, http://www.alliedbarton.com/About-Us/Blog/Article/94/Shopping-Mall-Security-Keeping-Pace-with-a-Changing-Venue.
Broll Property Group. "The Broll Report 2014/2015," 2015, http://www.broll.com/assets/uploads/documents/2015/04/The_Broll_Report_2014-2015.pdf.
Bures, Frank. "The Life and Death of Malls," July 25, 2014, http://www.minnpost.com/thirty-two-magazine/2014/07/life-and-death-malls.
Burke, Jason. "Paris shootings: investigation launched into where gunmen got GoPro cameras," *The Guardian*, January 12, 2015, http://www.the

guardian.com/world/2015/jan/12/paris-shootings-cameras-kouachi-brothers-amedy-coulibaly.

Burke, Timothy. *Lifebuoy Men, Lux Women: Commodification, Consumption, and Cleanliness in Modern Zimbabwe* (Durham, NC: Duke University Press, 2003).

Burns Security Institute. "National Survey on Shopping Center Security" (Briarcliff Manor, NY, May 1978).

Bush, George W. "At O'Hare, President Says 'Get On Board:' Remarks by the President to Airline Employees O'Hare International Airport Chicago, Illinois." September 27, 2001, http://georgewbush-whitehouse.archives.gov/news/releases/2001/09/20010927-1.html.

———"President Holds Prime Time News Conference," The White House, Press Release, October 11, 2001, http://georgewbush-whitehouse.archives.gov/news/releases/2001/10/20011011-7.html.

Chakravorti, Bhaskar, Jianwei Dong, and Kate Fedosova. "Colonialism's Enduring Dividends: Why European Companies Have an Advantage in Emerging Markets," *Foreign Affairs*, February 13, 2014, https://www.foreignaffairs.com/articles/africa/2014-02-13/colonialisms-enduring-dividends.

"Charlie Hebdo attack: Three days of terror." *BBC News*, January 14, 2015, http://www.bbc.com/news/world-europe-30708237.

Chege, Miriam Mukami. "Competitive Strategies Adopted by Nakumatt Holdings Limited to Gain Competitive Advantage," MA Thesis, University of Nairobi, October 2014, p. 27.

Chomsky, Noam. *Profit Over People: Neoliberalism and Global Order* (New York, NY: 2011).

Clapper, James R. "Statement for the Record: Worldwide Threat Assessment of the US Intelligence Community," Senate Select Committee on Intelligence, 2014.

Clymer, Jeffory A. *America's Culture of Terrorism: Violence, Capitalism, and the Written Word* (Chapel Hill: University of North Carolina Press, 2003).

Cohen, Lizabeth. "A Consumers' Republic: The Politics of Mass Consumption in Postwar America," *Journal of Consumer Research* 31, no. 1 (June 2004): 236-239.

Cohen, Neil, Jay Gattuso, Ken MacLennan-Brown. "CCTV Operational Requirements Manual," Home Office Scientific Development Branch, 2007, http://www.globalmsc.net/pdfs/operational-requirements.pdf.

Coquery-Vidrovitch, Catherine. "From Residential Segregation to African Urban Centres: City Planning and the Modalities of Change in Africa South of the Sahara," *Journal of Contemporary African Studies* 32, no. 1 (2014): 1-12.

Cowell, Alan. "Subway and Bus Blasts in London Kill at Least 37," *The New York Times*, July 8, 2005, http://www.nytimes.com/2005/07/08/world/europe/subway-and-bus-blasts-in-london-kill-at-least-37.html.

Crawford, Margaret. "The World in a Shopping Mall," in *Variations on a Theme Park: The New American City and the End of Public Space*, ed., Michael Sorkin, (New York, NY: Hill and Wang, 1992): 3-30.

Crossick, Geoffrey, and Serge Jaumain, eds. *Cathedrals of Consumption: The European Department Store, 1850-1939* (Aldershot: Ashgate, 1999).

Csaba, Fabian Faurholt, and S°ren Askegaard. "Malls and the Orchestration of the Shopping Experience in a Historical Perspective," *Advances in Consumer Research* 26, no. 1 (1999), http://www.acrwebsite.org/search/view-conference-proceedings.aspx?Id=8221.

Czinkota, Michael R, Gary Knight, Peter W Liesch, and John Steen. "Terrorism and International Business: A Research Agenda," *Journal of International Business Studies* 41 (2010): 826-843.

David, Herbling. "Westgate aftershock cuts Nakumatt sales by Sh4bn," *Business Daily*, August 5, 2014, http://www.businessdailyafrica.com/Corporate-News/Westgate-aftershock-cuts-Nakumatt--sales-by-Sh4-billion-/-/539550/2410022/-/10ab1lkz/-/index.html.

Davidson, Helen, Peter Walker and Michael Safi. "Sydney siege ends as police storm Lindt Cafe and hostages run out," *The Guardian*, December 15, 2014, http://www.theguardian.com/australia-news/2014/dec/15/sydney-siege-ends-police-storm-lindt-cafe-hostages-run-out.

Davis, Mike. "Fortress Los Angeles: The Militarization of Urban Space," in Michael Sorkin, ed., *Variations on a Theme Park: The New American City and the End of Public Space* (New York, NY: Hill and Wang, 1992).

_____*Planet of Slums* (London: Verso, 2006): 154-180.

De Boef Suzanna, and Paul M. Kellstedt. "The Political (and Economic) Origins of Consumer Confidence," *American Journal of Political Science* 48, no. 4 (October 2004): 633-649.

Debord, Guy. *The Society of the Spectacle*, trans. Donald Nicholson-Smith (New York, NY: Zone Books, [1967] 1994).

Decker, Stephanie. "Corporate Legitimacy and Advertising: British Companies and the Rhetoric of Development in West Africa, 1950-1970," *The Business History Review* 81, no. 1 (Spring 2007): 59-86.

Deleuze, Gilles, and Felix Guattari. *Anti-Oedipus: Capitalism and Schizophrenia*, 10th ed., Trans. Robert Hurley, Mark Seem, and Helen R. Lane (Minneapolis: University of Minnesota Press, 2000).

Derrida, Jacques. *Of Grammatology*, Gayatri Chakravorty Spivak, Trans. (Johns Hopkins Press, 2013).

Dickey, Christopher. "Inside the NYPD's Report on the Kenya Shopping Mall Massacre," *The Daily Beast*, October 12, 2013, http://www.thedailybeast.com/articles/2013/12/10/inside-the-nypd-s-report-on-the-kenya-shopping-mall-massacre.html.

Dijck, José van. "Datafication, Dataism and Dataveillance: Big Data between Scientific Paradigm and Ideology." *Surveillance & Society* 12, no. 2 (2014): 197-208.

Dupree, Catherine. "Designed to Shop." *Harvard Magazine*, July-August 2002 http://harvardmagazine.com/2002/07/designed-to-shop.html.

Eachus, Peter, Alex Stedmon, and Les Baillie. "Hostile Intent in Public Crowded Spaces: A field Study." *Applied Ergonomics* 44 (2013): 669-670.

"Eat, pray, shop: Philippines embraces mall worshipping." January 17, 2015, Inquirer.net, http://lifestyle.inquirer.net/182411/eat-pray-shop-philippines-embraces-mall-worshipping.

Embassy of the United States, "State, Defense Officials Work with African Partners for Stability," October 24, 2013, http://london.usembassy.gov/africa181.html.

Epstein, Marni. "How the Cold War Shaped the Design of American Malls." *Curbed*, June 11, 2014, http://curbed.com/archives/2014/06/11/how-the-cold-war-shaped-the-design-of-american-malls.php.

Fairbanks, Eve. "Africa's Obsession with Shopping Malls," September 23, 2013, http://www.newrepublic.com/article/114826/westgate-mall-attack-al-shabab-assaults-symbol-african-urban-life.

Farhat, Maymanah. "New Media and the Spectacle of the War on Terror." in *Uncommon Grounds: New Media and Critical Practices in North Africa and the Middle East*, ed. Anthony Downey (London: I.B. Tauris, 2014): 184-200.

Federal Bureau of Investigation. "A Conversation with Our Legal Attaché in Nairobi, Part 1." January 2014, http://www.fbi.gov/news/stories/2014/january/a-conversation-with-our-legal-attache-in-nairobi-part-1.

Feingold, Stan, and David McIlvride, *It's a Mall World* (New York: NY, Films Media Group, 2006), Running time 47 minutes.

Ferguson, Harvie. "Watching the World go Round: Atrium Culture and the Psychology of Shopping," in *Lifestyle Shopping: The Subject of Consumption*, ed. Rob Shields (London and New York: Routledge, 1992): 21-39.

Fickes, Michael. "ICSC's Terrorist Awareness Training Program." January 7, 2014, http://www.chainstoreage.com/article/icsc%E2%80%99s-terrorist-awareness-training-program.

Foster, Hal. "Bigness," *London Review of Books* 23, no. 23 (November 29, 2001): 13-16, http://www.lrb.co.uk/v23/n23/hal-foster/bigness.

Francis, David. "Al-Shabab Threat against Mall of America Could Be a Call to Action." *Foreign Policy*, February 23, 2015, http://foreignpolicy.com/2015/02/23/al-shabab-threat-against-mall-of-america-could-be-a-call-to-action/.

Friedman, Vanessa. "After a Tragedy, the Memorabilia," New York Times, January 21, 2015, http://www.nytimes.com/2015/01/22/fashion/after-a-tragedy-like-the-charlie-hebdo-shooting-come-the-products.html.

Gachino, Geoffrey. "Industrial Policy, Institutions and Foreign Direct Investment: The Kenyan Context," *African Journal of Marketing Management* 1, no. 6 (September 2009): 140-160.

Garreau, Joel. *Edge City - Life on the New Frontier* (Double Day, 1988).

Gateway Theatre of Shopping. "Welcome to Gateway Theatre of Shopping." 2015, http://gatewayworld.co.za/.

_____"About Us." http://gatewayworld.co.za/home/about.

Gettleman, Jeffrey. "Ominous Signs, Then a Cruel Attack," *New York Times*, September 27, 2013, http://www.nytimes.com/2013/09/29/sunday-review/making-sense-of-kenyas-westgate-mall-massacre.html?pagewanted=all&_r=1&.

Gettleman, Jeffrey, and Nicholas Kulish. "Gunmen Kill Dozens in Terror Attack at Kenyan Mall," *The New York Times*, September 21, 2013, http://www.nytimes.com/2013/09/22/world/africa/nairobi-mall-shooting.html?pagewanted=all&_r=0.

Giroux, Henry A. "Beyond the Spectacle of Terrorism: Rethinking Politics in the Society of the Image," *Situations: Project of the Radical Imagination* 2, no. 1 (2007): 17-51.

———. "ISIS and the Spectacle of Terrorism: Resisting Mainstream Workstations of Fear," September 30, 2014, http://www.truth-out.org/news/item/26519-isis-and-the-spectacle-of-terrorism-resisting-mainstream-workstations-of-fear#a2

———. "Neoliberalism's War against the Radical Imagination," *Tikkun* 29, no. 3 (2014), https://muse.jhu.edu/journals/tikkun/v029/29.3.giroux.pdf.

———. "Selfie Culture at the Intersection of the Corporate and the Surveillance States," Counter Punch, February 6, 2015, http://www.counterpunch.org/2015/02/06/selfie-culture-at-the-intersection-of-the-corporate-and-the-surveillance-states/.

Gladwell, Malcolm. "The Terrazzo Jungle." *The New Yorker*, March 15, 2004, http://www.newyorker.com/magazine/2004/03/15/the-terrazzo-jungle.

Glanz, James, Sebastian Rotella, and David E. Sanger. "In 2008 Mumbai Attacks, Piles of Spy Data, but an Uncompleted Puzzle," *The New York Times*, December 21, 2014, http://www.nytimes.com/2014/12/22/world/asia/in-2008-mumbai-attacks-piles-of-spy-data-but-an-uncompleted-puzzle.html.

Global Impact Investing Network. "The Landscape for Impact Investing in East Africa: Kenya," August 2015, http://www.thegiin.org/assets/documents/pub/East%20Africa%20Landscape%20Study/05Kenya_GIIN_eastafrica_DIGITAL.pdf.

Goss, Jon. "The 'Magic of the Mall': An Analysis of Form, Function, and Meaning in the Contemporary Retail Built Environment," *Annals of the Association of American Geographers* 83, no. 1. (1993): 18-47.

———. "Once-upon-a-Time in the Commodity World: An Unofficial Guide to Mall of America," *Annals of the Association of American Geographers* 89, no. 1 (1999): 45-75.

Gottdiener, Mark, ed. "Approaches to Consumption: Classical and Contemporary Perspectives," in *New Forms of Consumption: Consumers, Culture, and Commodification* (Lanham, MD: Rowman & Littlefield, 2000): 3-31.

———. "Introduction," in *New Forms of Consumption: Consumers, Culture, and Commodification* (Lanham, MD: Rowman & Littlefield, 2000).

_____"The Consumption of Space and Spaces of Consumption," in *New Forms of Consumption: Consumers, Culture, and Commodification* (Lanham, MD: Rowman & Littlefield, 2000): 265-284.

Government of the Republic of Kenya. "Kenya Vision 2030: The Popular Version," 2007, http://www.vision2030.go.ke/wp-content/uploads/2015/06/Popular_Version1.pdf.

_____"Nairobi Metro 2030: A World Class African Metropolis." 2008, https://fonnap.files.wordpress.com/2011/09/metro2030-strategy.pdf.

Government of Namibia. Namibia's Vision 2030. http://www.npc.gov.na/?page_id=210.

Government of the State of Qatar. Qatar's Vision 2030. http://www.gsdp.gov.qa/portal/page/portal/gsdp_en/qatar_national_vision.

Graham, Stephen. *Cities under Siege: The New Military Urbanism* (London: Verso, 2010).

Grossberg, Lawrence, Cary Nelson, and Paula Treichler, eds. *Cultural Studies* (New York, NY: Routledge, 1992).

Gruen, Victor. "Dynamic Planning for Retail Areas." *Harvard Business Review* 22 (November - December 1954), mall.lampnet.org/filemanager/download/1474/Gruen_HBR_54.pdf.

Gruen, Victor, and Larry Smith. *Shopping Towns USA: The Planning of Shopping Centers* (New York, NY: Reinhold Publishing Corporation, 1967).

Gundan, Farai. "Kenya Joins Africa's Top 10 Economies after Rebasing of its Gross Domestic Product (GDP)," Forbes, October 1, 2014, http://www.forbes.com/sites/faraigundan/2014/10/01/kenya-joins-africas-top-10-economies-after-rebasing-of-its-gross-domestic-product/.

Harding, Luke, and Kim Willsher. "'Something from Dante's hell': harrowing details of Bataclan siege," *The Guardian*, November 17, 2015, http://www.theguardian.com/world/2015/nov/17/something-from-dantes-hell-harrowing-details-of-bataclan-siege.

Harvey, David. "Neoliberalism as Creative Destruction," *The Annals of the American Academy of Political and Social Science* 610, no. 1 (2007): 21-44.

Hausmann, Melissa. "Two Fundamental Rules for Integrating People Counting into Your Culture Using Traffic Data to Deliver Incremental Revenues," ShopperTrak, 2012, http://shoppertrak.com/wp-content/uploads/2014/05/Two-Fundamental-Rules-for-Integrating-People-Counting-into-Your-Culture.pdf?mkt_tok=3RkMMJWWfF9wsRonu6%2FNZKX onjHpfsX56egsWaW%2BlMI%2F0ER3f0vrPUfGjI4ATMZkI%2BSLD wEYGJlv6SgFT7PDMbR00LgMWhM%3D.

"Hawkers." News 24 Kenya. 2015, http://www.news24.co.ke/Tags/Topics/hawkers.

Hayward, Keith J. *City Limits: Crime, Consumer Culture and the Urban Experience* (London: Glasshouse Press, 2004).

Hirsch, Afua. "Kenyan authorities had been warned about threat to buildings 'day before attacks'," *The Guardian*, September 28, 2013, http://www.theguardian.com/world/2013/sep/28/kenya-authorities-warned-of-attack.

"History." 2015, http://www.westgateoxford.co.uk/history.

Hobden, Deborah. "A Man, A Plan, A Mall: The Role of Globalizing Elites in the Development of Accra, Ghana," *Global-e*, http://global-ejournal.org/2014/09/08/vol8iss7/.

_____ "'Your Mall with it All:' Luxury Development in a Globalizing African City," *Perspectives on Global Development and Technology* 13 (2014): 129-147.

Hodge, Nel. "How Somalia's al-Shabab militants hone their image," *BBC News*, June 5, 2014, http://www.bbc.com/news/world-africa-27633367.

Hoganson, Kristin. "Bernath Lecture - Stuff It: Domestic Consumption and the Americanization of the World Paradigm," *Diplomatic History* 30, no. 4 (2006): 571-594.

Holston, James. "Insurgent Citizenship in an Era of Global Urban Peripheries." *City & Society* 21, no. 2 (2009): 245-267.

Hoskins, Tansy. "Westgate: Kenyan guards on the frontline," *Al Jazeera*, September 21, 2014, http://www.aljazeera.com/news/africa/2014/09/westgate-kenyan-guards-frontline-201492154142406265.html.

Houssay-Holzschuch, Myriam, and Annika Teppo. "A Mall for All? Race and Public Space in Post-Apartheid Cape Town," *Cultural Geographies* 16, no. 3 (2009): 309-379.

Howden, Daniel. "Terror in Westgate mall: the full story of the attacks that devastated Kenya," *The Guardian*, October 4, 2013, http://www.theguardian.com/world/interactive/2013/oct/04/westgate-mall-attacks-kenya-terror.

HSM Press Office. "TRANSCRIPT: Speech of HSM Leader, Shaykh Mukhtar Abu Zubayr, regarding the #Westgate Operation," Twitlonger, September 25, 2013, http://www.twitlonger.com/show/n_1rp1qpv.

Human Rights Watch. "Somalia: Stop War Crimes in Mogadishu," February 14, 2011, http://www.hrw.org/news/2011/02/14/somalia-stop-war-crimes-mogadishu.
Insurance Information Institute. "Does My Business Need Terrorism Insurance?" 2015, http://www.iii.org/article/does-my-business-need-terrorism-insurance.
International Council of Shopping Centers. "Nairobi retail bouncing back from terrorist attack," August 19, 2015, http://www.icsc.org/press/nairobi-mall-scene-back-to-normal-a-year-after-terrorist-attack.
"International CPTED Association." http://www.cpted.net/.
Islamic State Report no. 1 (May-June 2014). https://azelin.files.wordpress.com/2014/06/islamic-state-of-iraq-and-al-shc48im-22islamic-state-report-122.pdf.
Jacobs, Jerry. *The Mall: An Attempted Escape from Everyday Life* (Prospect Heights, IL: Waveland Press, 1984).
Jackson, Kenneth T. "All the World's a Mall: Reflections on the Social and Economic Consequences of the American Shopping Center," *The American Historical Review* 101, no. 4 (October 1996): 1111-1121.
Jamaica's Vision 2030. http://www.vision2030.gov.jm/.
Janz, Bruce. "The Terror of the Place: Anxieties of Place and the Cultural Narrative of Terrorism," *Ethics, Place & Environment*, 11, no. 2 (2008): 191-203.
Jerde. "What We Do." 2015, http://www.jerde.com/Jerde-Philosophy.html.
Jogee, Rubina. "A K-Means Cluster Analysis of Mall Shopping Motivations in a Developing Context," Proceedings of 9th Annual London Business Research Conference, August 4-5, 2014, Imperial College, London, http://www.wbiworldconpro.com/uploads/london-conference-2014-august/marketing/1418271332_513-Rubina.pdf.
Johnson, Leo. "Petropolis now: Are cities getting too big?" November 14, 2013, *New Statesman*, http://www.newstatesman.com/2013/11/petropolis-now.
Joseph, Jonathan. "Terrorism as a social relation within capitalism: theoretical and emancipatory implications," *Critical Studies on Terrorism* 4, no. 1 (2011): 23-37.
Judin, Hilton, and Ivan Vladislavic.' *Blank: Architecture, Apartheid and After* (Rotterdam: NAi, 1998).
Karimi, Faith, Ashley Fantz and Catherine E. Shoichet. "Al-Shabaab Threatens Malls, Including Some in U.S.; FBI Downplays Threat." *CNN*,

February 21, 2015, http://www.cnn.com/2015/02/21/us/al-shabaab-calls-for-mall-attacks/index.html.

Kaysen, Ronda. "Malls Work on their Security, but Keep it in the Background." *New York Times*, November 26, 2013, http://www.nytimes.com/2013/11/27/realestate/commercial/malls-work-on-their-security-but-keep-it-in-the-background.html?_r=0.

Kearney, A. T. "The 2015 African Retail Development Index – Retail in Africa: Still the Next Big Thing," 2015, https://www.atkearney.com/documents/10192/6437503/Retail+in+Africa.pdf/b038891c-0e81-4379-89bb-b69fb9077425.

"Kenya: A Different Country." *The Economist*, September 28, 2013, http://www.economist.com/news/middle-east-and-africa/21586851-national-politics-has-shifted-response-attack-somali-terrorists/print.

"Kenya: New Mall Set to Change How Kisumu Shops." *The Nation*, July 2, 2015, http://allafrica.com/stories/201507020248.html.

"Kenya's Westgate Shopping Mall Reopens." Aljazeera, July18, 2015, http://www.aljazeera.com/news/2015/07/kenya-westgate-shopping-mall-reopen-150718012221949.html.

Khera, Jastinder. "Authorities and militants take Nairobi battle to Twitter," September 24, 2013, *BBC News*, http://www.bbc.com/news/world-africa-24218276.

Kilcullen, David. "Westgate mall attacks: urban areas are the battleground of the 21st century," *The Guardian*, September 27, 2013, http://www.theguardian.com/world/2013/sep/27/westgate-mall-attacks-al-qaida.

Klein, Naomi. *The Shock Doctrine: The Rise of Disaster Capitalism* (New York, NY: Metropolitan Books, 2008).

Kleinman, Arthur, and Joan Kleinman, "Cultural Appropriations of Suffering," in *Cultures of Fear: A Critical Reader*, Danielle Taana Smith and Uli Linke, eds. (London: Pluto Press, 2009), 288-303.

Klopp, Jacqueline M. "Pilfering the Public: The Problem of Land Grabbing in Contemporary Kenya," *Africa Today* 47, no. 1 (Winter 2000): 7-26.

Kowinski, William S. "Mall-aise: American Society Might Literally Shop Till It Drops." *Chicago Tribune*, May 21, 1987, http://articles.chicagotribune.com/1987-05-21/features/8702070556_1_shopping-mall-suburban-downtown-citicorp-center.

Krieger, Tim, and Daniel Meierrieks. "The Rise of Capitalism and the Roots of Anti-American Terrorism," CESifo Working Paper no. 4887 (July 2014).

Kriel, Robyn. "Kenya's Westgate Mall Reopens, Nearly Two Years after Bloody Terror Attack," July 19, 2015, CNN, http://www.cnn.com/2015/07/18/africa/kenya-westgate-mall-reopens/.

Kroes, Rob. *If You've Seen One, You've Seen the Mall: Europeans and American Mass Culture* (Chicago: University of Illinois Press, 1996).

Kulish, Nicholas. "In This Horror Film, Blood Is All Too Real: 'Terror at the Mall' on HBO Documents an Attack in Kenya," *New York Times*, September 14, 2014, http://www.nytimes.com/2014/09/15/arts/television/terror-at-the-mall-on-hbo-documents-an-attack-in-kenya.html?_r=0.

Kuruvilla, Shelja Jose, and Nishank Joshi. "Influence of demographics, psychographics, shopping orientation, mall shopping attitude and purchase patterns on mall patronage in India," *Journal of Retailing and Consumer Services* 17 (2010): 259-269.

Kusno, Abidin. "Remembering/Forgetting the May Riots: Architecture, Violence, and the Making of 'Chinese Cultures' in Post-1998 Jakarta," *Public Culture* 15, no. 1 (Winter 2003): 153-154.

Lakhani, Sadaf. "What Does Social Exclusion Have to Do with the Attacks at Westgate, Nairobi? Asking the Right Questions," December 11, 2013, http://blogs.worldbank.org/publicsphere/what-does-social-exclusion-have-do-attacks-westgate-nairobi-asking-right-questions.

Larobina, Michael D., and Richard L. Pate. "The Impact of Terrorism on Business," *Journal of Global Business Issues* 3, no. 1 (Spring 2009): 147-156.

LaTourrette, Tom, David R. Howell, David E. Mosher, and John MacDonald. "Reducing Terrorism Risk at Shopping Centers: An Analysis of Potential Security Options" (Santa Monica, CA: RAND Technical Report, 2006), http://www.rand.org/content/dam/rand/pubs/technical_reports/2006/RAND_TR401.pdf.

Linehan, Denis. "Re-ordering the Urban Archipelago: Kenya Vision 2030, Street Trade and the Battle for Nairobi City Centre," *Aurora Geography Journal* 1 (2007): 21-37.

Linke, Uli, and Danielle Taana Smith. "Cultures of Fear: Introduction," in *Cultures of Fear: A Critical Reader* (London: Pluto Press, 2009): 19-23.

Loewenstein, Antony. *Disaster Capitalism: Making a Killing Out of Catastrophe* (London: Verso, 2015).

Lough, Richard, and Abdi Sheikh. "UPDATE 3-Kenya launches probe as Shabaab leader confirms mall attack," Reuters, September 25, 2013, http://www.reuters.com/article/2013/09/25/kenya-attack-idUSL5N-0HL0MS20130925.

Makoha, Timothy. "Eastleigh deserves Government tour," *Standard*, November 3, 2009, http://www.standardmedia.co.ke/article/1144027579/eastleigh-deserves-government-tour.

Makori, Ben. "Kenya's Westgate shopping mall reopens after massacre," Reuters, July 18, 2015, http://www.reuters.com/article/us-kenya-attacks-westgate-idUSKCN0PS0HZ20150718.

"Mall." Merriam Webster. http://www.merriam-webster.com/dictionary/mall

Mall of America. "Facts." 2015, http://www.mallofamerica.com/about/moa/facts.

_____"History." 2015, http://www.mallofamerica.com/about/moa/history.

_____"Mall of America." 2015, http://www.mallofamerica.com/.

Mamdani, Mahmood. "Senseless [and sensible] violence: Mourning the dead at Westgate Mall," *Aljazeera*, September 26, 2013, http://www.aljazeera.com/indepth/opinion/2013/09/senseless-sensible-violence-mourning-dead-at-westgate-mall-201392563253438882.html.

Manji, Ambreena. "Bulldozers, Homes and Highways: Nairobi and the Right to the City," Review of African Political Economy 42, no. 144 (2015): 206-224.

Marks, Rafael, and Marco Bezzoli. "Palaces of Desire: Century City, Cape Town and the Ambiguities of Development," *Urban Forum* 12, no. 1 (January 2001): 27-48.

Masters, Jonathan. "Al-Shabab," September 5, 2014, Council on Foreign Relations, http://www.cfr.org/somalia/al-shabab/p18650.

Mbembé, J.-A., and Sarah Nuttall. "Writing the World from an African Metropolis," *Public Culture* 16, no. 3 (Fall 2004): 347-372.

Mbote, Kamau. "East Africa's Growing Middle Class Demands for More Shopping Malls," April 29, 2014, http://afkinsider.com/53224/east-africas-growing-middle-class-demands-shopping-malls/.

McConnell, Tristan. "'Close Your Eyes and Pretend to Be Dead': What really happened two years ago in the bloody attack on Nairobi's Westgate Mall," *Foreign Policy*, September 20, 2015, http://foreignpolicy.com/2015/09/20/nairobi-kenya-westgate-mall-attack-al-shabab/.

Menkhaus, Ken. "Al-Shabab's Capabilities Post-Westgate," *CTC Sentinel* 7, no. 2 (February 24, 2014), Special Issue, https://www.ctc.usma.edu/posts/al-shababs-capabilities-post-westgate.
Michona, Richard, Jean-Charles Chebat, L.W. Turley. "Mall Atmospherics: The Interaction Effects of the Mall Environment on Shopping Behavior," *Journal of Business Research* 58 (2005): 576-583.
Miller, Darlene. "Changing African Cityscapes – Regional Claims of African Labor at South-African Owned Shopping Malls" Conference Paper no. 24 (Instituto de Estudos Sociais e Económicos, September 19, 2007, Mozambique).
_____"New Regional Imaginaries in Post-Apartheid Southern Africa – Retail Workers at a Shopping Mall in Zambia." *Journal of Southern African Studies* 31, no. 1 (2005): 117-145.
Miller, Darlene, Etienne Nel, and Godfrey Hampwaye. "Malls in Zambia: Racialised retail expansion and South African foreign investors in Zambia," *African Sociological Review* 12, no. 1 (2008): 35-54.
Morell, Michael, and Bill Harlow. *The Great War of Our Time: The CIA's Fight Against Terrorism—From al Qa'ida to ISIS* (New York, NY: Twelve Hachette Book Group, 2015).
Mousseau, Michael. "Urban Poverty and Support for Islamist Terror: Survey Results of Muslims in Fourteen Countries," *Journal of Peace Research* 48, no. 1 (2011): 35-47.
Mugera, Solomon, and Moses Rono. "Could Westgate deal a fatal blow to the ICC?" *BBC News*, October 17, 2013, http://www.bbc.com/news/world-africa-24562337.
Mukoya, Thomas. "Man allegedly attempts to enter Kenyan shopping mall with bomb." CBS News, September 8, 2015, http://www.cbsnews.com/news/suspect-attempts-to-enter-kenyan-shopping-mall-with-bomb/.
Mulupi, Dinfin. "East Africa's largest shopping mall to have strong international flavor," April 22, 2015, http://www.howwemadeitinafrica.com/east-africas-largest-shopping-mall-to-have-strong-international-flavour/48405/.
Murillo, Bianca. "'The Modern Shopping Experience': Kingsway Department Store and Consumer Politics in Ghana," *Africa* 82, no. 3 (2012): 368-392.
Murphy, Jarrett. "Feds Allege Ohio Mall Terror Plot." *CBS News*, June 15, 2004, http://www.cbsnews.com/news/feds-allege-ohio-mall-terror-plot/.

Mutambo, Aggrey. "Bodies of Westgate terrorists 'are with the FBI', says KDF Chief Julius Karangi," *The Nation*, February 7, 2014, http://mobile.nation.co.ke/news/Julius-Karangi-Kenya-Defence-Forces-Westgate-Attack/-/1950946/2196566/-/format/xhtml/-/r60qhdz/-/index.html.

Mwakideu, Chrispin, and James Shimanyula, "Kenya's Westgate Mall Reopens amid Security Concerns," *Deutsche Welle*, July 17, 2015, http://www.dw.com/en/kenyas-westgate-mall-re-opens-amid-security-concerns/a-18591953.

"Nairobi anti-Hawking squad to be unveiled." News 24 Kenya, September 20, 2013, http://www.news24.co.ke/National/News/Nairobi-anti-Hawking-squad-to-be-unveiled-20130920.

Nance, Malcolm W. *Terrorist Recognition Handbook: A Practitioner's Manual for Predicting and Identifying Terrorist Activities*, 3rd ed. (Boca Raton, FL: CRS Press, 2014).

Nath, Anjali. "Seeing Guantánamo, Blown Up: Banksy's Installation in Disneyland." *American Quarterly* 65, no. 1 (2013): 185-192.

National Counter Terrorism Security Office. "Counter Terrorism Protective Security Advice for Shopping Centres," (London, 2014).

National Crime Prevention Council. "Crime Prevention through Environmental Design Training Program." 2015, http://www.ncpc.org/training/training-topics/crime-prevention-through-environmental-design-cpted-.

Nava, Mica. "Cosmopolitan Modernity: Everyday Imaginaries and the Register of Difference," *Theory, Culture & Society*, Special Issue on Cosmopolis 19, no. 1-2 (2002): 81-99.

_____ "Modernity's Disavowal: Women, the City and the Department Store," in *Modern Times: Reflections on a Century of English Modernity*, Mica Nava and Alan O'Shea, eds. (1997): 38-76.

New York City Police Department. "Analysis of Al-Shabaab's Attack at the Westgate Mall in Nairobi, Kenya." November 1, 2013, http://www.scribd.com/doc/190795929/NYPD-Westgate-Report.

Nichols, J.C. "Mistakes We Have Made in Developing Shopping Centers," *Technical Bulletin* no. 4 (August 1945), Urban Land Institute, Planning for Permanence: the Speeches of J.C. Nichols Western Historical Manuscript Collection-Kansas City, http://shs.umsystem.edu/kansascity/manuscripts/nichols/JCN078.pdf.

Nielson. "2014 State of the Shopping Center." 2014, http://www.nielsen.com/content/dam/corporate/us/en/reports-downloads/2014%20Reports/state-of-the-shopping-center-report-may-2014.pdf.

Nitzan, Jonathan. "Human Security, Consumer Confidence and the Future of Neoliberalism." The Collaboratory for Digital Discourse and Culture (November 5, 2001): 1, http://www.cddc.vt.edu/digitalfordism/fordism_materials/Nitzan.pdf.

Nitzan, Jonathan, and Shimshon Bichler. "Economy of the Occupation: Cheap Wars." *Socioeconomic Bulletin* 10 (September 2006).

Njogu, Kimani, Kabiri Ngeta, and Mary Wanjau, eds. *Ethnic Diversity in Eastern Africa: Opportunities and Challenges* (Nairobi: Twaweza Communications, 2010).

Obonyo, Raphael. "Nairobi's Emerging Cities Dilemma." March 24, 2014, http://www.worldpolicy.org/blog/2014/03/24/kenyas-emerging-cities-dilemma.

Odedejan, Kennedy. "Terrorism's Fertile Ground," *New York Times*, January 8, 2014, http://www.nytimes.com/2014/01/09/opinion/terrorisms-fertile-ground.html?_r=0.

Okamoto, Kotaro, et al. "Classification of Pedestrian Behavior in a Shopping Mall Based on LRF and Camera Observations," MVA2011 IAPR Conference on Machine Vision Applications, June 13-15, 2011, Nara, Japan.

Okari, Dennis. "Kenya's Westgate attack: Unanswered questions one year on," September 21, 2014, BBC News, http://www.bbc.com/news/world-africa-29282045.

Örtenwalla, Per, Ola Almgrenb, and Edward Deverell. "The Bomb Explosion in Myyrmanni, Finland 2002," *International Journal of Disaster Medicine* 1, no.2 (2003): 120-126.

Otiso, Kefa M., and George Owusu. "Comparative Urbanization in Ghana and Kenya in Time and Space," *Geojournal* 71 (2008): 143-157.

"Outside Westgate." Radiolab, November 29, 2014, http://www.radiolab.org/story/outside-westgate/.

Owuor, Samuel, and Teresa Mbatia. "Nairobi." In *Capital Cities in Africa: Power and Powerlessness*, eds. Simon Bekker and Göran Therborn (Dakar and Cape Town: CODESRIA and Human Sciences Research Council, 2011): 119-140.

"Paris Supermarket Siege Survivors Sue Media over 'Dangerous' Coverage." *The Guardian*, April 3, 2015, http://www.theguardian.com/world/2015/apr/03/paris-supermarket-siege-survivors-sue-media.

"Patents: Shopping Mall US 3992824 A." March 22, 1973, https://www.google.com/patents/US3992824.

Percy, Sarah, and Anja Shortland. "The Business of Piracy in Somalia," *Journal of Strategic Studies* 36, no. 4 (2013): 541-578.

Petrecca, Laura. "39 Die in Kenya Mall Siege; Hostages Still Held," *USA Today*, September 21, 2013, http://www.usatoday.com/story/news/world/2013/09/21/witness-kenya-mall-attackers-target-non-muslims/2846319/.

Pflanz, Mike. "Kenyan army admits that soldiers looted Westgate mall during siege," The Telegraph, October 29, 2013, http://www.telegraph.co.uk/news/worldnews/africaandindianocean/kenya/10411403/Kenyan-army-admits-that-soldiers-looted-Westgate-mall-during-siege.html.

"Police Probe Blasts at Bangkok Shopping Centre." *BBC News*, February 2, 2015, http://www.bbc.com/news/world-asia-31087786.

Powell, Arthur G, Eleanor Farrar, and David k. Cohen. *The Shopping Mall High School: Winners and Losers in the Education Marketplace* (Boston, MA: Houghton Mifflin, 1985).

Prestholdt, Jeremy. *Domesticating the World: African Consumerism and the Genealogies of Globalization* (Berkeley: CA, University of California Press, 2008).

———"On the Global Repercussions of East African Consumerism," *The American Historical Review* 109, no. 3 (June 2004): 755-781.

Prinsloo, Dirk A. "Cannibalisation amongst Same Retailers & Shopping Centres in South Africa." South African Council of Shopping Centres, 2009, http://urbanstudies.co.za/wp-content/uploads/2014/07/SACSC-CANIBALISATION-PAPER.pdf.

———"Past and Future Changes in Shopping Patterns, Behaviour and Centre Development," Urban Studies, http://www.urbanstudies.co.za/past-and-future-changes-in-shopping-patterns-behaviour-and-centre-development/.

"Protesters Mass at Mall of America on Busy Shopping Day." *NBC News*, December 20, 2014, http://www.nbcnews.com/news/us-news/protesters-mass-mall-america-busy-shopping-day-n272326.

Provost, Claire. "British Aid Money Invested in Gated Communities and Shopping Centres," *The Guardian*, May 2, 2014, http://www.theguardian.com/global-development/2014/may/02/british-aid-money-gated-communities-shopping-centres-cdc-poverty.

Purdum, Todd S. "After the Attacks: The White House; Bush Warns of a Wrathful, Shadowy and Inventive War," *New York Times*, September 17, 2001, http://www.nytimes.com/2001/09/17/us/after-attacks-white-house-bush-warns-wrathful-shadowy-inventive-war.html?pagewanted=all.

Purkiss, Jessica. "The Westgate mall attack highlights Kenya-Israel ties." September 27, 2013," *Middle East Monitor*, https://www.middleeastmonitor.com/articles/africa/7551-the-westgate-mall-attack-highlights-kenya-israel-ties.

Rajagopal, Arvind. "The Violence of Commodity Aesthetics: Hawkers, Demolition Raids, and a New Regime of Consumption," *Social Text* 68, 19, no. 3 (Fall 2001): 91-113.

Reed, Dan. *Terror at the Mall*, 2014, Home Box Office.

Reinan, John. "Black Lives Matter protesters question 'intertwined' relationship between Mall of America and Bloomington." *Star Tribune*, July 4, 2015, http://www.startribune.com/black-lives-matter-protesters-question-intertwined-relationship-between-mall-of-america-and-bloomington/311587741/.

Research ICT Africa, "Kenya Vision 2030." http://www.researchictafrica.net/countries/kenya/Kenya_Vision_2030_-_2007.pdf.

Ritzer, George. "McUniversity in the Postmodern Consumer Culture." *Quality in Higher Education* 2 (1996): 185-199.

_____ *Enchanting a Disenchanted World: Revolutionizing the Means of Consumption*, 2nd ed. (Thousand Oaks, CA: Pine Forge Press, 2010).

_____ "New Cathedral of Consumption." September 30, 2012, https://georgeritzer.wordpress.com/2012/09/30/new-cathedral-of-consumption/.

Rodnitzky, Adam. "Best Practices for Implementing In-Store Analytics in Bricks and Mortar Retail." ShopperTrak, http://shoppertrak.com/wp-content/uploads/2014/05/Best-Practices-for-Implementing-In-Store-Analytics-in-Bricks-and-Mortar-Retail.pdf?mkt_tok=3RkMMJWWfF9wsRonu6%2FPZKXonjHpfsX56egsWaW%2BlMI%2FoER3fOvrPUfGjI4ATMZnI%2BSLDwEYGJlv6SgFT7PDMbRooLgMWhM%3D.

Rogers, Simon. "England Riots: Which Shops were Looted?" *The Guardian*, December 6, 2011, http://www.theguardian.com/uk/datablog/2011/dec/06/england-riots-shops-raided.

Ruetalo, Victoria. "From Penal Institution to Shopping Mecca: The Economics of Memory and the Case Of Punta Carretas," *Cultural Critique* 68 (Winter 2008): 38-65.

Salcedo, Rodrigo. "When the Global Meets the Local at the Mall," *American Behavioral Scientist* 46, no. 8 (April 2003): 1084-1103.

Sarlo, Beatriz. *Scenes from Postmodern Life*, trans. Jon Beasley-Murray (Minneapolis, MN: University of Minnesota Press, 2001).

Schulzke, Marcus. "Simulating Terrorism and Insurgency: Video Games in the War of Ideas," *Cambridge Review of International Affairs* 27, no. 4 (2014): 627-643.

"Security Information." Mall of America, 2015, http://www.mallofamerica.com/guests/security.

Sedlmaier, Alexander. "From Department Store to Shopping Mall: New Research in the Transnational History of Largescale Retail," *Jahrbuch fur Wirtschaftsgeschichte* [Economic History Yearbook] 46, no. 2 (December 2005): 9-16.

Seierstad, Åsne. *One of Us: The Story of Anders Breivik and the Massacre in Norway*, trans. Sarah Death (New York, NY: Farrar, Straus and Giroux, 2015).

Selfridge, Harry Gordon. *The Romance of Commerce* (London: John Lane, 1918).

Seva, Rosemary R., Henry Been Lirn Duh, Martin G. Helander. "Structural Analysis of Affect in the Pre-purchase Context," *DLSU Business and Economics Review* 19, no. 2 (2010): 43-52.

Shearing, Clifford D., and Phillip C. Stenning. "From the Panopticon to Disney World: the Development of Discipline." in Anthony N. Doob and Edward L. Greenspan, Q.C., eds, *Perspectives in Criminal Law: Essays in Honour of John LL.J. Edwards* (Canada Law Book Inc 1984): 335-349.

Shields, Rob, ed. "Spaces for the Subject of Consumption," in *Lifestyle Shopping: The Subject of Consumption* (London and New York: Routledge, 1992): 1-19.

Shiner, Cindy. "Rioters Torch Aspirations of Upper Class," *The Washington Post*, May 17, 1998, http://www.washingtonpost.com/wp-srv/inatl/longterm/indonesia/stories/rioters051798.htm.

Shultz, James M. et al., "Multiple Vantage Points on the Mental Health Effects of Mass Shootings," *Current Psychiatry Reports* 16, no. 9 (2014): 4, DOI 10.1007/s11920-014-0469-5.

Smith, Danielle Taana, and Uli Linke, eds. "Fear: A Conceptual Framework," in *Cultures of Fear: A Critical Reader* (London: Pluto Press, 2009): 1-18.

Smith, David, Abdalle Ahmed, and Tom McCarthy. "Al-Shabaab leader Ahmed Abdi Godane killed by US air strike in Somalia," *The Guardian*, September 5, 2014, http://www.theguardian.com/world/2014/sep/05/al-shabaab-leader-godane-killed-us-airstrike-somalia.

Smith, Jennifer. "The Mall in Motion: A Narrative Stroll through the Obstacle Course," *Speed: Technology, Media, Society* 1, no. 3 (June 1996).

"Somali al Shabaab rebels ban use of the Internet," *Reuters*, January 9, 2104, http://www.reuters.com/article/2014/01/09/us-somalia-rebels-internet-idUSBREA080M920140109.

Sorkin, Michael, ed. "Introduction," in *Variations on a Theme Park: The New American City and the End of Public Space* (New York,: NY: Hill and Wang, 1992): xi-xv.

Soto, Hernando De. "The Capitalist Cure for Terrorism," *The Wall Street Journal*, http://www.wsj.com/articles/the-capitalist-cure-for-terrorism-1412973796.

"Southdale Center: The First Indoor Shopping Mall." Minnesota History Center, 2015, http://libguides.mnhs.org/southdale.

Springs, Coral. "City Hall in the Mall," 2015, http://www.coralsprings.org/government/other-departments-and-services/city-hall-in-the-mall.

Staples, William G. *Everyday Surveillance: Vigilance and Visibility in Postmodern Life* (Lanham, MD: Rowman & Littlefield, 2014).

Steadman, Philip. "The Changing Department Store Building, 1850 to 1940," *The Journal of Space Syntax* 5, no. 2 (2014): 151-167.

Sterne, Jonathan. "Sounds Like the Mall of America: Programmed Music and the Architectonics of Commercial Space," *Ethnomusicology* 41, no. 1 (Winter 1997): 22-50.

_____"Sounds Like the Mall of America: Programmed Music and the Architectonics of Commercial Space," in *Music and Technoculture*, Rene T. A. Lysloff and Jr. Leslie C. Gay, eds (Middletown CT: Wesleyan University Press, 2003).

Stewart, Catrina. "Nairobi Westgate Mall Attack: Shopping Centre Reopens Two years after Terror Siege where al-Shabaab Killed 67 People,"

The Independent, July 14, 2015, http://www.independent.co.uk/news/world/africa/nairobi-westgate-attack-shopping-mall-re-opens-two-years-after-terror-siege-where-al-shabaab-killed-10389082.html.

Stillerman, Joel, and Rodrigo Salcedo. "Transposing the Urban to the Mall: Routes, Relationships, and Resistance in Two Santiago, Chile, Shopping Centers," *Journal of Contemporary Ethnography* 4, no. 3 (2012).

Straziuso, Jason. "NYPD report on Kenya attack isn't US gov't view," Associated Press, December 13, 2013, http://bigstory.ap.org/article/nypd-report-kenya-attack-isnt-us-govt-view.

Swaine, Jon, Ben Jacobs, and Paul Lewis. "Baltimore Protests Turn into Riots as Mayor Declares State of Emergency," *The Guardian,* April 28, 2015, http://www.theguardian.com/us-news/2015/apr/27/baltimore-police-protesters-violence-freddie-gray.

Takacs, Stacy. "Real War News, Real War Games: The Hekmati Case and the Problems of Soft Power," *American Quarterly* 65, no. 1 (2013): 177-184.

Tanguay, Liane. *Hijacking History: American Culture and the War on Terror* (Montreal: McGill-Queen's University Press, 2013).

"'Terror at the Mall,' Documentary on Siege of Westgate Mall in Nairobi, Kenya, Coming to HBO," Press Release, September 2, 2014, http://blogs.indiewire.com/shadowandact/terror-at-the-mall-an-inside-look-at-the-siege-of-westgate-mall-in-nairobi-kenya-debuts-sept-15-on-hbo-20140902.

Tharoor, Shashi. "Globalization and the Human Imagination," *World Policy Journal* 21, no. 2 (Summer 2004): 85-91.

The Dubai Mall. "The Dubai Mall." 2015, http://www.thedubaimall.com/en/Index.aspx.

"The Great Sixth-Avenue Bazaar.; Opening Day at Macy & Co.'s--A Place Where Almost Anything May be Bought," *New York Times,* April 4, 1878, http://query.nytimes.com/gst/abstract.html?res=9F0CE5DB143EE73BBC4C53DFB2668383669FDE.

The Headquarters. "Headquarters History." 2015, http://theheadquarters.com/history.

The International Council of Shopping Centers (ICSC). "2014 Economic Impact of Shopping Centers," 2015, http://www.icsc.org/uploads/default/2014-Economic-Impact-Kit.pdf.

_____"About," 2015, http://www.icsc.org/.

The Joint Committee on Administration and National Security, and Defence and Foreign Relations. "Report of the Joint Committee on Administration and National Security; and Defence and Foreign Relations on the Inquiry into the Westgate Terrorist Attack, and Other Terror Attacks in Mandera in North-Eastern and Kilifi in the Coastal Region," December 2013, http://info.mzalendo.com/media_root/file_archive/REPORT_OF_THE_COMMITTEE_ON_WESTGATE_ATTACK_-_4.pdf.

"The 'Magic of the Mall': An Analysis of Form, Function, and Meaning in the Contemporary Retail Built Environment." *Annals of the Association of American Geographers* 83, no. 1. (1993): 18-47.

The National Center for Biomedical Research and Training. "Shopping Center Security Terrorism Awareness Training Program," n.d. https://www.ncbrt.lsu.edu/pdf/Shopping%20Center%20Security%20Awareness%202014213.pdf.

Topping, Alexandra. "France sieges: After Charlie Hebdo attack, how terror unfolded," *The Guardian*, January 10, 2015, http://www.theguardian.com/world/2015/jan/10/france-sieges-charlie-hebdo-gunmen-killed-printworks-kosher-supermarket.

UN Habitat. "The State of African Cities 2010: Governance, Inequality and Urban Land Markets," 2010, https://www.citiesalliance.org/sites/citiesalliance.org/files/UNH_StateofAfricanCities_2010.pdf.

Underhill, Paco. *Call of the Mall: The Geography of Shopping* (New York, NY: Simon & Schuster, 2005).

United Nations. "International Day of Peace," http://www.un.org/en/events/peaceday/.

United States Department of State. "Country Reports on Terrorism 2013," 2014, http://www.state.gov/documents/organization/225886.pdf.

Varman, Rohit, and Russell W. Belk. "Consuming Postcolonial Shopping Malls," *Journal of Marketing Management* 28, nos. 1-2 (February 2012): 62-84.

Vogt, Heidi, and Patrick Mcgroarty. "Before Kenya Attack, a Warning on Terrorism," *Wall Street Journal*, September 30, 2013, http://www.wsj.com/articles/SB10001424052702303643304579105222268968650.

Walton, Brett. "The Westgate Shopping Centre Siege – an Attack on Freedom, Society and the Future," http://www.fortitudemagazine.co.uk/industry/politics/westgate-shopping-centre-siege-attack-freedom-society-future/12447/.

Wakefield, Alison. "The Public Surveillance Functions of Private Security," *Surveillance & Society* 2, no. 4 (2005): 529-545.
Walton, Brett. "The Westgate Shopping Centre Siege – an Attack on Freedom, Society and the Future," http://www.fortitudemagazine.co.uk/industry/politics/westgate-shopping-centre-siege-attack-freedom-society-future/12447/.
Weimann, Gabriel. "Terror on Facebook, Twitter, and Youtube," *Brown Journal of World Affairs* 16, no. 2 (2010): 45-56.
_____"Cyber-Fatwas and Terrorism," *Studies in Conflict & Terrorism* 34, no. 10 (2011): 765-781.
"Westgate." http://westgate.com.sg/en/.
"Westgate." 2015, http://westgateohio.com/.
"Westgate Center." 2015, http://shopwestgatecenter.com/.
"Westgate Mall." 2015, http://www.thewestgatemall.com/.
"Westgate Mall." 2015, http://www.shopatwestgatemall.com/.
"Westgate Mall." 2015, http://www.westgatemall.com/.
"Westgate Mall." 2015, http://www.westgatemall.com.cn/#.
"Westgate Mall." 2015, http://www.westgatemalltx.com/.
"Westgate Mall Photographer Goran Tomasevic: 'If I Get Shot, I Get Shot'," September 28, 2013, http://www.buzzfeed.com/rachelzarrell/interview-with-westgate-mall-photographer-goran-tomasevic#.nsDaOrNN2.
"Westgate Shopping City." 2015, http://westgate-shopping.com/.
"Westgate Shopping Centre." 2015, http://www.westgateshoppingcentre.ca/.
Westgate Shopping Mall Facebook page. December 8, 2015, https://www.facebook.com/westgateshoppingmall/.
Williams, Paul D. "After Westgate: Opportunities and Challenges in the War against Al-Shabaab," *International Affairs* 90, no. 4 (2014): 907-923.
Willis Retail Practice. "Security and Terrorism Guidance for Retailers." March 24, 2015, http://www.willis.com/Documents/Publications/Services/Political_Risk/20150324_Retail_Risk_Insight_Security_and_Terrorism_Guidance_for_Retailers.pdf.
Winseck, Dwayne. "The Political Economies of Media: The Transformation of the Global Media." In *The Political Economies of Media: The Transformation of the Global Media*, eds. Dal Yong Jin and Dwayne Winseck (London: Bloomsbury, 2011): 3-48.

Woodhams, Frances. "Mall Attack: Will Kenya's Shopping Centre Culture Endure?" *The Telegraph*, September 30, 2013, http://www.telegraph.co.uk/expat/10340179/Mall-attack-will-Kenyas-shopping-centre-culture-endure.html.
World Travel and Tourism Council. "Economic Impact Analysis," 2015, http://www.wttc.org/research/economic-research/economic-impact-analysis/.
Yardley, Jim. "Report on Deadly Factory Collapse in Bangladesh Finds Widespread Blame," *New York Times*, March 22, 2013, http://www.nytimes.com/2013/05/23/world/asia/report-on-bangladesh-building-collapse-finds-widespread-blame.html?_r=0.
"Your Westgate Oxford." 2015, http://www.westgateoxford.co.uk/.
Zeleza, Tiyambe. *A Modern Economic History of Africa: The Nineteenth Century* (Nairobi: East African Educational Publishers, 1997).
Zimmerman, Andrew. "Africa in Imperial and Transnational History: Multi-Sited Historiography and the Necessity of Theory." *Journal of African History* 54, no. 3 (November 2013): 331-340.
Zirulnick, Ariel. "Kenyan consumers win this round against Al Shabaab as Westgate Mall reopens." Quartz Africa, July 18, 2015, http://qz.com/457808/kenyan-consumers-win-this-round-against-al-shabaab-as-westgate-mall-reopens/.
Zwerdling, Daniel, G.W. Schulz, Andrew Becker, and Margot Williams. "Under Suspicion at the Mall of America." National Public Radio, September 7, 2011, http://www.npr.org/2011/09/07/140234451/under-suspicion-at-the-mall-of-america.

Zeitdiagnosen bei transcript

Ferdi De Ville,
Gabriel Siles-Brügge
TTIP
Wie das Handelsabkommen den Welthandel verändert und die Politik entmachtet
(übersetzt aus dem Englischen von Michael Schmidt)

Mai 2016, 192 Seiten, kart.,
19,99 €,
ISBN 978-3-8376-3412-9,
E-Book/E-PUB: 17,99 €

■ TTIP – das Ende von Politik und Demokratie? Die erste politikwissenschaftliche Analyse zum umstrittenen Handelsabkommen blickt hinter die Fassaden von Chlorhühnern und Hormonfleisch. Sie zeigt: TTIP radikalisiert einen längst eingeleiteten Prozess einer depolitisierenden »deep liberalization«. Sie zeigt aber auch: Der zivilgesellschaftliche Protest birgt die Chance, die Handelspolitik zu repolitisieren.

»Das Buch [ist] nicht nur eine genaue Analyse des geplanten Abkommens, sondern auch der Rolle und Funktion des EU-Binnenmarktes und damit eine implizite Kritik an so mancher Abstrusität des TTIP-Widerstandes, die man nur dringend zur Lektüre empfehlen kann.«
Werner Rätz/attac, www.werner-raetz.de, 10.08.2016

www.transcript-verlag.de